The Media Handbook

The Media Handbook provides a practical introduction to the complete media planning and buying process. Emphasizing basic media planning and buying calculations along with the practical realities of offering plan alternatives and evaluating the plan, this edition incorporates three new topics—consolidation, consumer control, and communication accountability—reflecting the critical changes in how media today are planned, bought, and sold.

Author Helen Katz looks at the larger marketing, advertising, and media objectives, and follows with an exploration of major media categories, including those emerging, such as branded entertainment and viral marketing. She provides a comprehensive analysis of planning and buying, with a continued focus on how those tactical elements tie back to the strategic aims of the brand and client.

The Media Handbook includes:

- numerous examples to provide a better sense of how media planning and buying work in the real world;
- examples of research studies to give readers additional references for more in-depth information;
- media terms defined when they are introduced, making readers more comfortable in subsequent discussions; and
- a selection of key resources offered as an appendix for individuals or companies wishing to find out more about a particular service or system.

This popular text is perfect for advanced students in advertising, media planning/ buying, communication, public relations, and marketing, and it will also serve as an informative reference volume for practitioners.

Helen Katz is Senior Vice President and Director of Research for Starcom Mediavest Group. She has an extensive professional background in media research and has taught advertising and media planning at Michigan State University, the University of Illinois, Northwestern University, and Bradley University.

Communication Series

Jennings Bryant/Dolf Zillman, General Editors

Selected titles in Media and Advertising include:

Alexander/Owens/Carveth/Hollifield/Greco
Media Economics: Theory and Research, Third Edition

Moore/Farrar/Collins
Advertising and Public Relations Law

Reichert/Lambiase
Sex in Advertising: Perspectives on Erotic Appeal

Sylvie/Wicks/Hollifield/Lacy/Sohn
Media Management: A Casebook Approach, Fourth Edition

The Media Handbook

A Complete Guide to Advertising
Media Selection, Planning,
Research, and Buying

4th Edition

Helen Katz

Routledge
Taylor & Francis Group

NEW YORK AND LONDON

First published 1995
by NTC Business Books,
an imprint of NTC/Contemporary Publishing Company

Second edition published 2003
Third edition published 2007
by Lawrence Erlbaum Associates, Inc.

This edition published 2010
by Routledge
270 Madison Avenue, New York, NY 10016

Simultaneously published in the UK
by Routledge
2 Park Square, Milton Park, Abingdon, Oxon OX14 4RN

*Routledge is an imprint of the Taylor & Francis Group,
an informa business*

© 1995 NTC/Contemporary Publishing Company
© 2003, 2007 Lawrence Erlbaum Associates, Inc.
© 2010 Taylor & Francis

Typeset in Sabon by RefineCatch Limited, Bungay, Suffolk
Printed and bound in the United States of America on acid-free
paper by IBT Global

Library of Congress Cataloging-in-Publication Data
Katz, Helen E.
  The media handbook / by Helen Katz.—4th ed.
    p. cm.
  1. Advertising media planning. 2. Mass media and business.
    3. Marketing channels. I. Title.
  HF5826.5.K38 2010
  659—dc22
  2009043449

ISBN13: 978–0–415–87353–6 (hbk)
ISBN13: 978–0–415–87354–3 (pbk)
ISBN13: 978–0–203–86455–5 (ebk)

To my daughters, Stephanie, Caroline, and Vanessa

Contents

Foreword   ix
Preface   xi
Acknowledgments   xiii
Introduction   xiv

1 What is Media?   1

2 Media in the Marketing Context   10

3 Developing Optimal Media Objectives   33

4 Exploring the Media, Part 1: Traditional   50

5 Exploring the Media, Part 2: Beyond Traditional   103

6 Terms, Calculations, and Considerations   120

7 Creating the Plan   143

8 Offering Alternatives   163

9 Making the Media Buys   174

10 Evaluating the Media Plan   187

Appendix A: Key Research Resources   193
Appendix B: Key Media Organizations   197
Notes   203
Index   210

Foreword

I was somewhat curious when Helen Katz first offered me the privilege of writing this introduction to her book, which updates a comprehensive yet practical approach to media planning, and well-worn copies of which I have found in nearly every media executive's personal library on Madison Avenue. My position as an admirer and strong supporter of her work cannot alone account for her having done so, since Helen has many friends more knowledgeable and experienced than I with regard to the art and science of planning, buying, and measuring media. Rather I suspect that the significance of her choice lies in my peculiar and sometimes controversial position in the television industry as resident blasphemist and occasional pariah.

As an advocate of the need for vast improvements in traditional audience measurement, particularly through analysis of the data collected in a TV's set-top box, in many ways I represent a very nontraditional point of view in the media world. Many years before it was fashionable to be interested in different approaches to measurement, Ms. Katz had an open mind. She raised many questions, voiced concerns and provided suggestions when prodded. Where others saw only obstacles with set-top box data, Helen recognized potential for improved insight into television audiences. Ten years removed from our first encounter, her approach to set-top box data, which she applies to all media measurement, has been adopted by Madison Avenue: experiment, measure, evaluate, retool—all while keeping an eye on the advertising objective.

The fourth edition of *The Media Handbook* helps take its readers down the path of new and emerging media. From a few short sections at the end of the chapter on media types, the new edition includes a whole chapter that is dedicated to helping media specialists understand a wide panoply of new communications opportunities, from mobile marketing to sponsorship to guerilla marketing activities. The latest edition also acknowledges the increasing demand by marketers to make the media plan ever more accountable, and does so by focusing more on how each media type can demonstrate return on investment for the advertiser (including through the use of set-top box data!).

Fundamentally, media must exist in an almost constant state of experimentation regardless of the platform, be it television, digital media, mobile communication, print, or out of home just to keep the attention of the fickle consumer. Competition for the hearts and minds of prospective customers is keen, and the media professional must be ever vigilant. Will mobile advertising become the predominant form of personalized marketing communication? Will search extension powered by links to offline data become the standard method for customer acquisition? Predicting the future is not the goal of a media plan, we leave that to others in the industry. What Ms. Katz understands better than most is that the object of the media plan is to uncover the right combination of media to deliver a specific advertising message to a particular audience. With her most recent work, Ms. Katz outlines a strategy to cope with the advances and retreats associated with the landscape and provides the key to overcoming these frequently significant advertising hurdles, to help readers understand and be able to execute strategic, creative, and rigorous media planning.

Frank S. Foster
Vice President of Media Insight
AT&T

Preface

Since the last edition of *The Media Handbook* came out in 2007, the worlds of media, advertising, and marketing have seen significant changes occur. We have witnessed the first sizable decline in adspend, due to the recession of 2008–2009; the emergence of powerful new forms of communication, such as social networks; and consumers today have taken even greater control of their media usage—and advertising exposure—than ever before, creating individual TV schedules with their DVRs, or selecting magazines and newspapers to read online instead of print.

Yet at the same time, the fundamentals of media planning and buying remain comfortingly similar. Advertisers still look to convey their messages to a selected group of consumers whom they believe are the most appropriate prospects for their products and services. Media still deliver those messages to the audience (in traditional, and increasingly beyond traditional ways). And consumers still respond to both ads and media content, though perhaps in more sophisticated or direct ways.

The goal of *The Media Handbook* has changed slightly to reflect the changing times. It remains a basic introduction to the media planning and buying process. It can help the college student gain a clearer understanding of what media is, and how it fits into the overall marketing process. Or it can be a useful reference book for people working in the advertising or media industries whose responsibilities sometimes overlap with the media function. What is different, however, is the recognition that those working in media require a broader perspective of what constitutes media and how consumers respond to both media and brands. That is, today's media specialist must increasingly work as a marketing specialist, looking beyond traditional media to all the means available for brands to communicate successfully with consumers.

This book begins with a look at those larger marketing, advertising, and media objectives, followed by an exploration of major media categories and then a new chapter dedicated to the emerging forms of communication that go "beyond traditional." The nuts and bolts of planning and buying take up much of the remainder of the text, with a continued focus on how those tactical elements tie back to the strategic aims of the brand and client.

Media terms are defined when they are introduced so that, in the jargon-filled worlds of media acronyms, the reader will start to feel more comfortable in subsequent discussion of GRPs, DMAs, or BDIs. This book also includes numerous examples, mostly of actual national brands in largely fictitious situations, in order to provide a better sense of how media planning and buying work in the real world. Examples of research studies, from both the industry and the academic world, are noted to give readers additional resources to go to for more in-depth information. At the end of the book, a selection of key resources is offered as an appendix for those individuals or companies that wish to find out more about a particular service or system.

Media planning and buying are not, and should not be thought of as, mystical or esoteric. The media function certainly involves a good deal of expertise and intelligent thinking, and also requires a judicious combination of art and science, creativity and mathematical applications, but it should be fairly easy to understand by anyone involved in the marketing of a product or service. Indeed, it should really be a prerequisite that all those who are trying to sell something, whether it is a widget or an image, should have the basic knowledge of how media planning operates. That is where the message ends up, and if it is placed incorrectly or not seen by the chosen target audience, even the most creative or inspiring ad will be unable to boost sales.

This latest edition of *The Media Handbook* is intended to give you sufficient details to make you feel comfortable about all elements of the media planning and buying process, while at the same time expanding your understanding of the importance of media in all its myriad forms in the broader marketing picture.

Acknowledgments

The longer I work in the advertising industry, the more I am indebted to all those who have helped in my on-the-job education. That started in 1989 at DDB Needham Worldwide, under the guidance of Kevin Killion, my first boss and ongoing friend and mentor. When I moved to Zenith Media New York in 1999, I was privileged to work under the guidance of Wendy Marquardt and Peggy Green, both of whom helped me learn much about how media planning and buying truly work together. I returned to Chicago in 2001, to GM Planworks, where my research skills were honed—thanks to the inspiring leadership of Jana O'Brien, and the richly challenging consumer-focused demands of my esteemed clients at General Motors, Michael Browner and Betsy Lazar. Starting in 2005, I moved to a global research role for Starcom Mediavest Group, where Kate Sirkin and Tracey Scheppach have demonstrated the passion, commitment, and focus on media that make coming to work each day rewarding and enjoyable.

I remain grateful to my former professors and supporters from the academic world: Kim Rotzoll, Steve Helle, Kent Lancaster, and Bruce Vanden Bergh all helped me become enamored of research. My editor at Routledge, Linda Bathgate, continues to give me all necessary support, making my writing job as easy as it could be.

This fourth edition demanded my time and attention that would otherwise have been spent with my family (husband Eric and daughters Stephanie, Caroline, and Vanessa). I am happy to dedicate this latest version to them for the never-ending joy and happiness they have given me.

Introduction

This book is deliberately designed as a media handbook. It will not tell you every last detail about each individual medium, nor will it go into great depth on non-media advertising elements, such as the creative message or the consumer research that goes on behind the scenes, though it will show you how the consumer must remain at the center of all you do in media. What you will get by the end of the book is a complete picture of how media planning, buying, and research work. You will see what each function entails, and how they fit together with each other and within the framework of the marketing mix. You will know enough by the end of this book to be able to create your own media plan, or undertake a print or broadcast buy. Even if you are not directly responsible for either of those tasks, a greater understanding of how media fit into the marketing picture will help you communicate with those who do such work. Each chapter builds on and works off the preceding ones, although once you have been through them all, it is designed to be very easy for you to refer to specific tasks or concepts at a later date. At the end of each chapter, you will see a checklist of questions that you should ask yourself if you actually have to fulfill the objective of that particular chapter (such as setting objectives, or evaluating the plan). At the end of the book, you will find a list of additional resources you can turn to for help in media planning, buying, and research.

Chapter 1

What is Media?

It's 7:30 a.m. You wake up and turn on your satellite radio, then click on the Web to catch the latest world news. During breakfast you turn on the television to catch a few minutes of the morning news shows. Before heading off to work you check your email on the Internet. On the subway to work you listen to your iPod (commercial-free), looking out of the window at a few outdoor billboards on the highway that you pass by.

In that brief time span, you have been immersed in the world of media. Very broadly, that world includes radio, Internet, television, newspapers, magazines, and outdoor billboards. Although you selected satellite radio to listen to music, or the Internet to see the latest news, or the television to watch a program, what you also did was receive information through a means of communication, or a *medium*. Given this broad definition, you can see that there are in fact hundreds of different media available, such as direct mail, skywriting, coupons, stadium signs, key rings, and food containers. All of these, and many other media, offer us ways of communicating information to an audience. As advertising media professionals, we are interested in looking at the media as a means of conveying a specific kind of information—an *advertising message*—about a product or service to consumers.

The media play a very important role in our lives. Media help fulfill two basic needs—they *inform* and they *entertain*. We turn to the media when we want to hear the latest world news or what happened in financial markets, for instance. We also look to the media to fill our evenings and weekends with escapist fare to get us out of our everyday, humdrum routine. So television entertains us with movies, dramas, comedies, reality shows, and sports. Radio offers us a wide variety of music, talk, and entertainment to listen to. We turn to magazines to find out more about our favorite hobbies and interests. Newspapers help us keep up with the world around us. And the Internet provides limitless information and a means of shared entertainment and communication.

The informational role of the media is perhaps best illustrated by considering what happens during a national or international crisis, such as the 2001 terrorist attack on the World Trade Center and the Pentagon or the global financial crisis in the fall of 2008. On each occasion, millions of people were glued to their television sets, clicking to favorite websites, tuned in to their radios, and reading newspapers and magazines for daily in-depth coverage and subsequent follow-up stories.

The media also affect our lives through their entertainment function. Television situation comedies such as *All in the Family* and *Mary Tyler Moore* not only reflected what was happening in U.S. society in the 1970s, but also helped to influence attitudes and behaviors concerning the issues of race and equality. Stories appearing in magazines such as *People* or *InStyle* let us know what is happening in other people's lives, both famous and ordinary. And we take our cell phones with us everywhere so that we can go online to get the latest sports scores or watch a video "soundbite" while we relax.

What Media are out There?

Historically, the world of media was broadly divided into two types—print and electronic. Print media included magazines and newspapers, while electronic media covered radio, television and the Internet. Other media types are not quite so easily categorized. Thus outdoor billboards are generally defined as a *print* medium, while out of home options such as transit ads, or stadium signage, are variously classified as non-traditional, alternative, or ambient media. Exhibit 1.1 provides a list of each type.

In today's ever-changing media world, however, these distinctions are fast becoming obsolete. Is a newspaper that is read online in the print or electronic columns? Where does one place cell phones or word of mouth or product placement? What is increasingly distinguishing one media type from another is how much consumer control there is in the medium's use. Magazines and newspapers have always been under their readers' control; after all, they choose what to read. Regular TV, on the other hand, is more passive; the networks decide what programs to air, and when. But now, with technologies such as digital video recorders (DVRs),

Exhibit 1.1 Major Print and Electronic Media

Print Media	Electronic Media
Magazines: Consumer, Farm, Business	Television: Broadcast, Cable, Syndication, Spot
Newspapers: National, Local	Radio: Network, Local
Outdoor billboards	Internet
Direct mail	Mobile
Yellow Pages	

it is the viewer who has become the program scheduler, controlling what he wants to see, and when. Exhibit 1.2 shows how a list of media types might look if divided into those two categories. This is a topic that will reverberate throughout this book, reflecting one of the major changes in how people use media and, therefore, how the advertising media business works.

The Role of Media in Business

It is important to emphasize here that the focus of this book is commercial media. That is, the communications media we will be talking about are not there simply to beautify the landscape or fill up the pages of a newspaper. They are designed to sell products to customers. Of course, there are also media that convey information but are not commercial in intent. *Consumer Reports* is a magazine that does not carry any advertising. Neither does public television (except for sponsorships, which we'll talk about later). The white pages of the telephone directory, web search engines, and airline safety instructions are all informative yet are not advertisements in and of themselves (even if they can carry advertisements within them). And books certainly communicate information to their readers. Here, however, we shall concentrate on those media that currently accept advertising messages. It is worth emphasizing the word *currently*. Twenty-five years ago, you did not find commercial messages at supermarkets, schools, doctors' offices or ski slopes. Today, advertisers can reach people in all of these places. Even novels are not immune. A popular British author wrote Bulgari Jewelers into her fictional story in 2000, for which the company paid her. Companies are routinely paying bloggers to write about their products, without the authors publicly acknowledging the payment. While these ventures were criticized by the public, that does not mean other similar attempts will not be tried again in the future. For what is true for today may very well change by tomorrow.

The generic term *media* (or *medium* in the singular) means different things to different people. To Joe Smith sitting at home on a Friday

Exhibit 1.2 Lean Forward vs. Lean Back

Lean Forward	Lean Back
Magazines	Television (other)
Newspapers	Radio
Direct Mail	Outdoor
Yellow Pages	
Television (via DVRs, Video On Demand)	
Internet	

evening, the "media" mean whatever TV shows he watches or magazines he leafs through. For the local Chevy car dealer, the media provide a way to advertise this week's deals on Malibus and Silverados. And the Podunk Electric Utility Company uses the media to remind its customers that they can get free replacement light bulbs.

Strictly speaking, a "medium" may be defined as a means by which something is accomplished, conveyed, or transferred. This deliberately broad definition means that consumer media would cover everything from handbills passed out in parking lots to "For Sale" signs taped to lamp posts to the ten-page advertising supplement that fell out of the last copy of *Business Week* you read, to electronic flashing signs in Times Square to the young hip folk who are "planted" in certain upscale bars to surreptitiously promote certain liquor brands.

How the Media Business has Changed

The media business can be thought of as an ocean. Each media type starts out as a few drops of water (individual newspapers or radio stations). They flourish and grow, and as more drops form, they start to combine together, creating ponds that turn into streams, and rivers, and oceans. That has a certain kind of predictability to it. It starts out small, then grows and flourishes as more and more companies enter the field. Over time, a handful of these companies start to grow by buying out their competitors and the industry consolidates, to the point where only a few extremely large players remain. This cycle has occurred in all but the newest media, from newspapers to radio to magazines to television. Even the Internet, one of the most diverse media forms in terms of its offerings, has seen those consolidate in recent years as popular websites get bought out by larger, better funded companies who are often rooted in traditional media. As an example, MySpace, one of the two biggest social networking sites, was purchased by News Corporation (owner of Fox TV Network and many newspapers worldwide) in 2005 for $580 million. In the outdoor industry, there used to be tens, if not hundreds of locally based companies, each of whom focused their efforts on selling ads in their city or region. Today, there are just two companies—Viacom and Clear Channel—that between them are responsible for more than half of all billboards in the U.S.

But what does media industry consolidation have to do with advertising? Why does it matter that the TV network NBC (itself owned by Comcast) also owns the Bravo, USA Network, and Sci-Fi cable networks and the Spanish-language network Telemundo? How is a media plan or buy affected by the fact that the Tribune Company owns WGN TV and radio stations and the *Chicago Tribune* newspaper? Well, what happens is that, while consumers are being offered more and more media choices (more radio stations on satellite radio, more online newspapers, more TV shows they want to watch via their TiVos), the advertisers trying to reach them find that they must negotiate with fewer and fewer companies selling advertising space or time. This paradox is something we shall return to throughout this book.

Media vs. Communications

In the business world, we think of a medium as a way to transfer and convey information about goods or services from the producer to the consumer, who is a potential buyer of that item. There are various ways to accomplish that in business besides using radio, television, or magazines. Product or company publicity, sales brochures, or exhibits can all be useful ways of conveying information to potential buyers. You should note that throughout this book, we will refer to all potential buyers as "consumers" but we should really think of them as *us*. One of the biggest dangers in media planning or buying is, as we shall learn in Chapter 3, to categorize viewers or listeners or readers into broad consumer groups (such as "Adults 18–49") that make it all too easy to forget that, in the infamous words of one of the founders of the advertising industry, David Ogilvy, "that person is your wife." And as we shall also learn in subsequent chapters, technology is enabling advertisers to use mass media in an individualized way, to reach their "true targets" (e.g., sending dog food company advertising just to dog owners), in ways that bring television full circle to a more personalized, one-to-one form of media.

Although this book is titled the MEDIA Handbook, it is increasingly important to think of media in the broadest terms, as communications. Advertising media used to be thought of solely as traditional, or mass. That is, planners and buyers worked with television, radio, magazines, newspapers, and outdoor. Anything beyond that was considered more specialized. Direct mail was handled by one group; event marketing by another; and promotions by a third. Today, most agencies look for integrated ways to make contact with consumers, whether that is paying to display their brand of soft drink in *American Idol*, sponsoring a blimp flying over a popular baseball field in the summer, or putting the brand's message on coffee cup holders in Starbucks. The goal of these disparate efforts is to surround the target audience with a holistic campaign that presents them with the same message about the brand in various creative ways.

The Role of Media in Consumers' Lives

As our lives grow increasingly busy and demanding, and as technology moves ahead with ever-more sophisticated ways to improve our lives, it seems that the media are playing a more and more important role in what we do, where we go, or how we behave. As the example at the opening of this chapter suggested, many of us wake up to the sound of the radio; we read the newspaper or check the Internet while watching morning television and eating breakfast; and we connect to our offices via email and a smartphone. We commute to work either in the car listening to music on regular or satellite radio, or on the bus or train surrounded by posters with advertising messages on them (or listening to an iPod during the commute). At work, we are likely to see a broad array of Internet advertising or email advertising messages, while many of us watch (or record) our favorite soap operas at lunchtime. When we get home in the evening, we'll probably turn on the TV to catch the local news, and after dinner we'll forget about our daily worries by watching a few episodes of prime-time TV that we saved on our DVRs, while catching up with the daily newspaper. Before we go to sleep for the night, we may check some information online, and then we'll probably glance through a couple of magazines while lying in bed.

When you sit down to watch TV and see a commercial that then appears in the magazine you are looking through and on the website you are browsing, and is mentioned again in that night's evening newscast because of the tie-in to a local charity event, you generally don't think about the effort that went into coordinating all of those elements. In fact, if the "seams" between them are too obvious, then something probably isn't working right! While you, as a member of the reading or listening or viewing audience, are interested primarily in the particular program or publication, the medium is interested in you as a potential buyer, offering you up to advertisers who wish to talk to you.

The role of media in conveying information through advertising messages is not something consumers generally consider. Indeed, when they do think about it, they are likely to complain about being inundated by commercial messages! Yet despite the fact that no one has yet proven "how advertising works," businesses continue to believe in its power, as evidenced by the $264 billion spent in the U.S. on advertising in 2008.

How Media Work with Advertising

Advertising in the media performs the dual role of informing and entertaining. It informs us of the goods and services that are available for us to purchase and use. And, along the way, it often entertains us with some humorous, witty, or clever use of words and pictures. For example, let's say you have created a new razor blade for young men that has a built-in counter to tell you how many times you've used it. You've shown it to some friends and neighbors, all of whom are convinced that it would be extremely useful to that target group. You have talked to several distributors and manufacturers of razors and have some interest in producing it. Now, however, the question arises of what to do next. How do you inform people you don't know personally about this wonderful new product?

This is where the media can help. You could place an advertisement on TV announcing this brand new razor type. Perhaps you'd take out magazine ads in men's magazines that show the product and explain what it does. You might create a long-form commercial message, or infomercial, that you pay cable networks targeted to men to air at night and on weekends. You'd want to have a website for your new product that allows people to purchase online directly from the site. Your message, that "*Razor Sharp is the Razor you can count on,*" would then be disseminated to an audience of hundreds, or possibly thousands, depending on your location. You might also generate additional publicity by persuading a national or local celebrity to endorse the product, and send out an electronic news release to TV stations and/or men's magazines. Or perhaps you would decide to solicit help from influential media bloggers, offering them a free sample in exchange for their online discussion of the product. Whatever form of communication you use, all involve sending a message through a medium of one kind or another.

Again, it is important to keep in mind that we are talking of media in the broadest sense. So in trying to promote your *Razor Sharp* blades, your TV and print ads or website can show people what the product looks like and demonstrate how it works. Then, you might sponsor a men's grooming night at the local department store as a public relations effort to heighten awareness of the product and how well it works. You could send out press releases in advance to notify the media of the event and thereby generate additional publicity both for the event and for your razor. You could offer retailers a special deal, such as contributing funds to the ads that they run (an advertising allowance), if they will promote the product in their weekly newspaper ads. You might also arrange for razors to be handed out on college campuses or in health clubs so that people can learn more about *Razor Sharp*. By advertising the product in a wide variety of media, each one fulfills a slightly different role, but your overall message—that "*Razor Sharp is the Razor you can count on*"—is conveyed clearly and consistently.

Media advertising also performs another vital function. It helps offset the cost of the media communication itself to consumers. If we did not have commercials on television or radio or the Web, the cost of the informational or educational content would have to come through sponsorships, taxes, or government monies. Public broadcasting in the U.S. derives most of its income through semi-annual pledge drives, during which viewers and listeners are asked to give money to pay for the services. Government funding provides additional revenues. But even here, more and more public broadcasting television stations are accepting restricted forms of paid commercials as long as they are image-oriented and not hard-sell. Indeed, there is even a network available, Public Broadcasting Marketing, to help advertisers place their spots on public TV stations across the country.

To give you a sense of how much companies spend to advertise, Exhibit 1.3 shows who the top global advertisers were in 2008.

Tasks in Media

The broad field of advertising media can be broken down into four primary tasks:

- Planning how best to use media to convey the advertising message to the target consumer (the *media planner*)
- Buying media space and time for the message (the *media buyer*)
- Selling that space or time to the advertiser (the *media seller*)
- Analyzing the relationship between consumers, media, and the brands that advertise to them in those media (the *media researcher*).

Most large companies handle the media planning and buying functions through an advertising agency. Smaller firms will usually handle this task themselves, through their marketing director, or public relations coordinator. The role of the planner is to decide where and when the message should be placed, how often, and at what cost. The plan is then implemented by the media buyer, who negotiates with the media providers themselves to agree on the space and time needed and to determine or confirm where the ad will appear. That buyer will, of course, be dealing

Exhibit 1.3 Top Global Advertisers in 2008

		Worldwide Measured Media Spending ($ million)	% of Total
1	Procter & Gamble	$9,358	25.8%
2	Unilever	$5,295	14.6%
3	L'Oreal	$3,426	9.4%
4	General Motors Corp.	$3,345	9.2%
5	Toyota Motors Corp.	$3,202	8.8%
6	Ford Motor Corp.	$2,902	8.0%
7	Johnson & Johnson	$2,361	6.5%
8	Nestle	$2,181	6.0%
9	Coca-Cola Co.	$2,177	6.0%
10	Honda Motor Co.	$2,047	5.6%
		$36,294	

Source: Advertising Age, 12.8.08, p. 10.

with the salesperson at the media company, whose job it is to sell as much advertising space or time as possible. Throughout this process, the researcher tries to offer insights into how and why the media impact the consumer's brand decisions.

Summary

The focus of *The Media Handbook* is the role of media in communicating and conveying information about products and services to potential consumers. It is designed to explore this media world in detail, looking at the changing structure of the industry itself, the various types of communication that are available (printed, aural, visual) and how to use these forms in day-to-day business. The aim here is to provide a better understanding of what the media are and how they work. Media can be classified in several ways—print versus electronic, or active versus passive. Within these categories, consumers choose from a wide array of media in their daily lives, turning to them for both information and entertainment. Advertising in the media also helps to offset the costs of production and distribution. Any company that advertises in the media must deal either directly or indirectly with the planning and buying of advertising space or airtime. This handbook will show you how to do this efficiently and successfully.

Chapter 2

Media in the Marketing Context

Although this book is designed to take the media specialist through the planning and buying of media, those functions do not occur in a vacuum. Both media and advertising are part of the bigger picture of the world of marketing. The primary goal of marketing is to increase sales and profits. To return to our earlier example, where we were wondering how to market our reusable razor blade, *Razor Sharp*, we had considered many elements beyond which media to use. To market any product effectively involves not simply advertising it, but also figuring out how much to charge for it, where to distribute it, and how to manufacture it. In marketing jargon, these four critical elements are known as the "Four Ps": Product, Price, Place (distribution), and Promotion. Although your job as a media specialist does not necessarily involve making the decisions on all of these criteria, it is critical that you have a clear understanding of how they work and, more importantly, how they can impact your media decisions and strategy. This chapter will guide you through these four marketing basics.

In order to sell anything, you must first have a *product* or service. You have to decide how much you need to charge for it (the *price*) so that you can make a profit. You must also figure out how and where the product will be made available to people (*place*, or distribution). And last, but not least, you must consider how you will let potential buyers know what you are offering (*promotion*). Within that last category, there are several key channels of communication: advertising, personal selling, sales promotion, direct marketing, event marketing, and publicity. All can be thought of as media, or ways of conveying information to potential buyers. You can see how these elements work in Exhibit 2.1.

One of the most important things to remember here is that the arrows move in many directions. Almost any decision you make concerning media will have an impact on something else in the marketing mix. For example, if you decided to advertise on network television, you would have to ensure that your product was in fact available throughout the country. Or if you chose to concentrate your advertising efforts during holiday periods (Memorial Day, Fourth of July, and so on), you might consider lowering your price at that time to boost sales even further.

The task of the media planner is to consider all of the marketing information available on the product and to use that information to determine how best to reach the target audience with the brand message through advertising media. In this way, the media plan can be thought of as the pivot point, or hub of the overall marketing plan (Exhibit 2.2).

Getting to Know the Consumer

There are two critical pieces of information that you as a media specialist need to know in order to successfully market a product. The first is an understanding of how your consumers view and use your product or service. The second is how they view and use different media types. While much of the former has been developed over many years and is considered fairly traditional market research, the latter is a relatively new phenomenon within the media world, applying market or consumer research principles and processes to enhance the understanding of how and why people use media. First, this chapter will delve into the consumer–brand relationship, and then we will begin to explore the consumer–media relationship.

Exhibit 2.1 The Marketing Mix

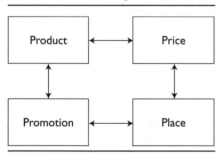

Exhibit 2.2 Moving Toward the Media Plan

Consumers and Brands

First, you must know more about the brand and the product category. A *brand* is the individual product or service that you are trying to sell. It can be thought of as the name on the label. So Campbell's Tomato soup is a brand, as is their Chicken Noodle soup, or their Clam Chowder variety. The *product category* could either be defined as all brands of tomato soup, or all kinds of soup. In the case of a service, such as insurance, the product category could be one type of insurance, such as life or home or auto, or all types. The brand would be one particular company such as Allstate Insurance, or State Farm or Geico.

One way to think about brands is to consider your own behavior. When you go to the grocery store, you are usually not thinking in terms of *product categories* or *brands*. More likely, you are thinking about buying a container of Minute Maid orange juice, three boxes of Kraft Macaroni and Cheese dinners, or a box of Kellogg's Frosted Flakes cereal. Similarly, when you have to decide which restaurant to go to, you will not categorize them the way marketers do, into quick-service, family-style, or steakhouses, but will instead think in terms of the types of food—Chinese, Mexican, Indian, etc. And within those groups, you will probably categorize them by geography, thinking of the specific restaurants by area.

What we need to know as marketers and media specialists, however, is how the consumer decides *which* brands and products to buy, as well as the process he or she goes through when purchasing an item. This will vary, depending on the type of product. While a consumer might pick up any brand of floor cleaner, the decision process she goes through to select the car she drives will take far longer because there are more elements to consider and often a higher price involved. Understanding these decision processes will help you decide which media might best be used both to reach your target and to convey the desired message at the right time. For selling your new razor blade with built-in counter, you could probably use a traditional medium such as magazines to increase awareness of your product. A company trying to sell a more complex product, however, such as a car or computer, will use a wide variety of communication forms to sell its product.

Here, we will take a general look at how consumers view and use brands. From there, we can establish some foundations for the media plan. We will start this by going back into the past and looking at what has happened in the marketplace both to the brand and to the product category in which we are interested.

In looking at how consumers use brands, we must answer several key questions: how much do consumers already know about the brand (brand and advertising awareness)? And when, where, and how often do they buy it (purchase dynamics)?

What do People Know About the Brand?

People have the opportunity to be exposed to at least 5,000 ads every week, so it isn't surprising that they don't remember many of them. In fact, a study conducted by the Newspaper Association of America in the 1990s showed that the percentage of people who can accurately remember the name of the brand they last saw advertised on television had fallen to an all-time low of 4 percent of those surveyed. Indeed, 86 percent of TV viewers claim not to attend to regular commercial breaks. And although we talk about "great" ads that we saw on television last night, or read in a newspaper or magazine, we are probably unlikely to remember the brand which was being advertised. Is Tiger Woods the spokesman for Nike or Adidas? Does Ashton Kutcher advertise Nikon or Canon cameras? In today's increasingly competitive marketing climate, consumers are also likely to be exposed to more than one brand name in an ad. This *comparison advertising* is extremely common in categories such as pain relievers, automobiles, and detergents. But while your brand, Brand A, emphasizes how much better it is than Brand B, will your target audience remember A or B?

How the Media Specialist Gets to Know
Consumers and Brands

Finding out how aware your consumers are of your brand and its advertising is quite straightforward, though not without pitfalls. The easiest way to do this is through a survey (mail, telephone, online or in person), in which you simply ask people what they remember about certain ads. You can do this in one of two ways—either *unaided*, where no prompts or assistance are provided, or *aided*, where you offer some kind of memory aid, such as mentioning something from the advertisement or giving an actual list of brand names and asking for further information on the advertising. The *unaided* method demands more on the part of consumers, asking them to tap deeper into their memories to *recall* the information you are seeking. With the *aided* method, you are basically asking people to recognize a brand and/or advertisement when it is placed before them, and then prompting them for additional information about it.[1]

There are other issues to keep in mind with brand-awareness research. The most important is that you cannot expect complete accuracy. That is, there is always the danger with any kind of memory check that you will not get full information from the people you survey. Obviously, the longer the time between when people see an ad and when they are questioned about it, the less they will remember about it. Human memory is highly fallible. They may attribute pieces of one ad to another ad, or recite a list of brand attributes from Brand A that really belong to Brand B.

So if you do test consumer awareness of your ads, be sure that you keep in mind the possibility of inaccuracies in the responses.

In addition, you must remember that all of these responses are what consumers *claim* to recognize or recall. Even if you give people a questionnaire to fill out on their own, they may not put down their real feelings or thoughts. They might not want to offend the interviewer or admit how they really feel, or for whatever reason do not want to tell the truth. For instance, they may have a vague recollection of your brand's name, but write down that they are very familiar with it.

Having said that, awareness checks do play a vital role in letting you know more about how your consumer interacts with the brand and its advertising. If no one can recall your brand name after it has been advertised on television every day for the past year, then you have a problem. It could be the message isn't convincing at all, or it could be you are advertising it in the wrong medium. Perhaps people can recall the brand name very easily but nothing about the advertising has stuck in their minds. Many companies conduct brand *tracking research* where they conduct consumer surveys on a regular (weekly, monthly, or quarterly) basis, to see how well people are aware of their brand and its advertising. This kind of data becomes very useful for monitoring not only the health of the brand over time, but also for building statistical models that show the relationship between the media dollars spent and the results obtained. We will cover this in more detail in Chapter 7.

The goal of increasing brand awareness should not be understated. It is commonly accepted that without consumer awareness of your brand, even the most spectacular media plan will be unlikely to generate many sales. People are far more likely to purchase a brand whose name they have heard before than one about which they have no information. There are many companies that conduct this kind of research. Some of the larger ones are listed in the Appendix.

If you want to probe further into people's responses, you can find out more through focus groups, which are groups of five to ten people who are interviewed together by a moderator. They are probed for their beliefs, attitudes, or feelings toward a given brand or product category and its advertising to help in development of the creative message as well as the marketing and media strategy.

A newer, more in-depth technique for understanding consumers, at least in the marketing world, is the use of ethnography. Developed in sociology and anthropology, the technique involves close observation of what consumers are doing. This may include visiting their homes to watch them prepare a meal (for a brand such as Kraft salad dressing) or spending a few hours with them in the gym (for a brand such as Nike). The idea is to see up close how the brand or product category really fits into people's lives.[2]

The Consumer Decision Process

Many research studies have been conducted over the years to demonstrate the decision process that a consumer typically goes through when buying a routine product. In its simplest form, this process has three steps:

1. Think.
2. Feel.
3. Do.

People must first *think* about the item (i.e., be aware of it and know it exists). They must then develop some kind of attitude or *feeling* toward it (i.e., like it and prefer it to others); and finally they must take some action with regard to it (decide on it, and actually buy it). This latter stage is the *do* part of the model.

The process is in fact far more involved than this. We can break these three stages down further, coming up with eight stages the consumer goes through in buying a product or service. These are:

1. Need.
2. Awareness.
3. Preference.
4. Search.
5. Selection.
6. Purchase.
7. Use.
8. Satisfaction.

To begin with, the consumer must first have a *need* to fulfill. He or she then becomes *aware* of the brands available to satisfy that need. After that, several brands are considered acceptable, and a *preference* developed for one or more of them. The consumer will then *search* for the brand(s) desired, and make a *selection* of one over the others. A specific brand is *purchased* and *used*. Finally, the level of *satisfaction* obtained with that purchase helps determine whether that brand is bought on a future occasion. This is discussed in detail in the next chapter.

Of course, in reality, life isn't always as simple. There are occasions (and products) where people think about a product, buy it, and only at that point do they develop attitudes toward it. This is especially true for new product launches, where consumers have not had a chance to develop emotional bearings for the brand or category. Another point to keep in mind is that the decision process can sometimes get stalled at a point before purchase. In our *Razor Sharp* example, your male target may be made aware of the brand, decide that they'd like to buy it, but be unable to find it in their grocery store or pharmacy, and give up. Or they could try it, and decide they actually prefer to stick with Gillette's product.

How the Consumer Buys Products

One of the main drawbacks to using surveys or holding discussions with consumers about how they buy is that they are telling you what they *think* they do which may be very different from what they actually do in real life. Moreover, measuring their brand awareness and advertising recall often ends up being a poor predictor of sales. So in addition to looking at awareness, or the top of the decision tree, you should also pay attention to what is happening at the bottom of the tree, with the purchase cycle. When are people buying your product? How much is bought? Is there some kind of seasonality to their purchases? All of this information will prove to be critical in planning and buying your media, and will have a major impact on how and when you schedule your ads.

When Do People Buy?

The answer to this question is more complex than it seems at first. You might say "Well, they buy my product all the time." But if you look more closely at purchase behavior, you will probably detect some kind of pattern. While people are buying houses "all the time," they are more likely to do so when interest rates are low and prices are depressed. People buy cars "all the time," but sales typically increase when the new models come into the showrooms in the fall. And more sales occur in the second half of the month than in the first. Even everyday kinds of items have a timing component to purchases. Sales of cheese are higher at the weekends and around paydays because that is when people have more money to go shopping. Moving companies are busiest between May and October because that is when most people change their residence. Greeting card sales go up before every holiday (whether traditional, such as Christmas, or "Hallmark holidays," such as Grandparents Day and Bosses Day).

If you know when consumers are most likely to buy your product, you can time your media advertising to take advantage of that purchase cycle. For major purchases in particular, you might also want to consider when people are *thinking about* buying. This might occur several weeks, or even months, before they make the actual purchase. So whereas Mr. and Mrs. Smith might buy a new Toro lawnmower in May, they will probably start to think about which one to get several months prior to that. This provides you with a valuable opportunity to get your brand's message to the Smiths early in their decision-making process.

How Much Do They Buy?

The size of consumer purchases is another important element of the purchase cycle for the media specialist to know. That is, what proportion of your brand's sales comes from each size of the product? For Coca-Cola, it offers numerous sizes of its soda, from 12oz cans, to 2 liter bottles, to six-packs. The company needs to know which one is most popular. Do most people buy their soda in plastic bottles, glass bottles, or cans? Does Coke sell three times as many cans as bottles, perhaps suggesting that this is where the majority of messages should focus? It turns out that nearly 50 percent of Coca-Cola volume consumed in a seven-day period is in plastic bottles, with around 6 percent from glass bottles and the remainder from cans (source: MRI, 2009). This kind of information is not only important for production and distribution purposes but it can also play a key role in your media planning, for the users of each size are likely to be different kinds of people, with different media habits. The casual drinker who picks up the individual can is more likely to be a working professional female who is married, college-educated, and living in the north central region of the country, while those who purchase the plastic bottles are fairly similar demographically, but more likely to be parents and to live in the south. A profile of the Coca-Cola glass buyer is shown in Exhibit 2.3. Young working women prefer to watch programs such as *The Simple Life* and *The Bachelorette*, and read *Cosmopolitan* and *Glamour;* older adults are more likely to choose *60 Minutes* and *Reader's Digest*. Based on these differences in media preference, you may well end up with two media plans, one for the occasional purchaser of the single can, and another for the frequent user who consumes several plastic bottles per week.

Looking at the Marketplace

Once you know about how consumers view and use your brand, the next step for the media specialist is to examine what has been happening to that brand in the marketplace in recent times. Given this information on

Exhibit 2.3 Profile of Coca-Cola Glass Buyer

Hispanic
Household income < $50,000
South/Southwest
Child < 6 years
A county
Lived at present address < 1 year
Male
Work part-time

Source: MRI 2007.

past efforts to sell your product, you can decide whether to continue along the same path or try something different in terms of your media planning and buying. Examining the marketplace involves doing an analysis of historical data on both the brand and the product category. As the famous philosopher George Santayana said, those who do not learn from the past are condemned to repeat it.

Some of the basic questions the media specialist might ask include the following:

- How long has this brand been available?
- How successful has it been throughout its history?
- How has it been positioned in the past?
- What do you know about the company that makes this brand?

You can think of this as genealogical work—trying to dig up as much "family background" on the brand as possible. You may find that the company has been in business for 150 years, suggesting possible leverage to be gained by emphasizing in the message the long heritage the brand possesses and even placing it in media vehicles that have also been around a long time. Or perhaps the company has been around forever, but is now moving in a different direction, starting to explore new opportunities, suggesting the use of new or different media. Altoids, for example, for many years just made mints. It then started expanding its product line; first, it created sour candy, then it began moving into the highly competitive chewing gum arena. Despite the fierce competition, the brand captured several market share points because it responded to the underlying consumer desire for a stronger-tasting food to eat between meals. But the new product may be targeted at different groups of consumers which, in turn, may result in a need for more diverse, and/or more selective media. While its traditional mint brand would continue to have a strong outdoor billboard and print presence, reaching a broad audience, the gum has more appeal to teens and young adults, who might not have seen the ads much before. The company could feature its gum in titles such as *Seventeen* or on Facebook, appealing to younger people who want to try the latest new products.

What are the Competitors Up To?

In doing an historical analysis of the brand, you must also deal with competitive issues. That is, you should not only explore and uncover as much marketing and media information as possible about your *own* brand, but you should also to do the same for *all* the brands against which you do or plan to compete. The marketing part of these issues may be divided into three main areas:

- Product category trends.
- Brand trends and share of market.
- Brand's share of requirements.

Product Category Trends

Whether your brand has been available for half a century, two years, or is about to be launched, one of the most important preplanning considerations for the media specialist is what is happening in your product category. If you are creating a media plan for the manufacturer of a Cannondale mountain bike, you would want to know whether sales of bicycles are increasing, decreasing, or flat. That will immediately influence your media budget, who you choose to target, and how you go about trying to reach them. In some instances, in order to determine how the category has fared, you will have to decide what your "category" really is. If you are selling an oatmeal cookie, then it might seem obvious that it belongs in the cookie category. But perhaps this is a low-calorie, low-cholesterol cookie that belongs more appropriately in the "diet and health food" classification. Does a yogurt drink fit better into yogurt products or milk drinks? And what about flash drives? Do they belong with software or in the office supplies section, along with pens and paper?

How you define your product category will determine not only your assessment of the strengths or weaknesses of that category, but also the direction and potential marketing and media strategies you employ for your particular brand. To take the yogurt drink example, if you decide it is part of the health foods category, you might want to advertise in health magazines and sponsor local running races where you can offer free samples. As a milk drink, however, you may prefer to advertise in parenting books such as *Child* magazine. You could also work with schools and children's activity centers to get the word out among those who work with kids. Or you might choose to advertise the product to both target groups using a combination of those media.

There are numerous stories in advertising lore of how the redefinition of a product category gave new life to a moribund product or service. Perhaps the most renowned case of redefinition is that of Arm and Hammer Baking Soda. By finding a new use for an established product (keeping refrigerators smelling fresh), the brand in effect positioned itself in two completely distinct categories—baking products and home fresheners. Today, it has a huge market share in the latter category, and has expanded into numerous other cleanser-related areas, from carpet freshener to toothpaste.

Once you have determined to which product category your brand rightfully belongs (or the category to which you wish it to belong), you are then in a position to examine trends in that category. You can do this in one of several ways. You may have access to product category sales from a trade association or manufacturers' group of some kind (such as the Juvenile Products Manufacturers Association if you are marketing children's toys, or the Electronics Industries Association if you are marketing electronics items). You can often find such data in trade journals in your particular field (such as *Supermarket News* for supermarket food sales or *Chemical Week* for sales of liquid nitrogen). One invaluable source for this type of information is the journal *Sales and Marketing Management*, which comes out several times a year with over- all category sales (see Exhibit 2.4). *Advertising Age* also produces an advertising-to-sales ratio in all major product categories annually that shows spending on advertising relative to sales. In many larger com- panies, these data are routinely collected, usually within the marketing department.

In looking at category trends, be careful to look back beyond the past year. In fact, if you can find five to ten years of data, you'll be in a much stronger position to see what the real trends are. Another important point to remember is that there will be many factors to explain the rise or fall of product sales. These trends do not occur in a vacuum. Sales for con- struction products fell in 2008 not because people had stopped building houses, but because the general economic recession meant that the rate of new home construction fell considerably as credit for home loans became much harder to get.

Exhibit 2.4 Example Ad : Sales Ratio

Industry	SIC Code	Advertising as % of sales
Transportation Services	4700	25.4
Motion Pictures, Videotape Production	7812	25.1
Perfume, Cosmetics, Toiletry Preparations	2844	20.3
Mailing, Reproduction, Commercial Art Services	7330	15.1
Distilled and Blended Liquor	2085	14.1
Food and Kindred Products	2000	13.3
Pottery and Related Products	3260	13.1
Educational Services	8200	12.2
Rubber and Plastics Footwear	3021	11.9
Ordnance and Accessories	3480	11.5
Dolls and Stuffed Toys	3942	11.0
Special Cleaners, Polishes, Preparations	2842	10.3
Games, Toys, Child Vehicles, excluding Dolls	3944	9.8
Soap, Detergent, Toiletry Preparations	2840	9.8
Auto Repair, Services, Parking	7500	9.2

Source: Schoenfeld & Associates. 2009.

Interpreting Sales Trends

Four factors that help explain sales trends are economic, social, political, and cultural trends. And each will, in turn, influence your media choices. For instance, if you are selling a new high-end plasma TV with lots of fancy features, the overall health of the economy is going to have a large impact on whether people feel they can afford to spend the money to purchase such a piece of entertainment equipment. If you decide that despite the economic downturn you want to emphasize a sophisticated image for your product, aiming it at innovators who always want to buy the latest equipment, then you might use magazines targeted to electronics aficionados, such as *Electronic House* or *Sound & Vision*. If, on the other hand, you choose to emphasize how the large screen returns TV to a family viewing experience, you might look to a broader audience and use more popular, broad-based vehicles such as *FamilyFun* or *Entertainment Weekly*.

Politics can play an important role in the marketing of goods and services. For satellite TV services trying to promote themselves to rival cable subscribers, what happens in Washington at the Federal Communication Commission, or in state or local politics will affect what they are allowed to sell and whether consumers are likely to buy the service. In 2009, the Supreme Court refused to hear an appeal in a case against the cable operators' desire to offer a "networked DVR," whereby cable subscribers could record programs for later viewing, with the storage held by the cable operator rather than on a device in the viewer's home. TV networks and movie studios tried to object to this as a copyright violation.

Cultural changes, while slower to occur, can also explain movements in product sales that have implications for media planning and buying. This is seen in the growth of ethnic foods, such as Mexican or Chinese dishes. The increasing popularity of different ethnic food products can be attributed in part to the enormous growth of the Hispanic and other immigrant populations in the U.S., leading to a greater diversity of cultures that are gradually intermingling and changing tastes and preferences. People living in the west are 16 percent more likely than the average to consume soy sauce, and 6 percent less likely than the norm to eat ketchup. The marketers of these foods try different ways of reaching their target audiences, through product sampling in stores or sponsorship of community events.

Finally, social changes, which also tend to happen slowly, can ultimately have a major impact on media activities. The cigarette companies of today have a much tougher job selling their product than they did 20 or 30 years ago, primarily because smoking is no longer considered socially acceptable due to the proven health risks it carries. The marketing task is made more difficult because since 1971 they have been forbidden, by law, from advertising on television at all, and since 1999, from being on any outdoor billboards.

So while you as a media specialist may not have to pinpoint all the reasons behind category trends, it is important for you to gain a broad understanding of what is really happening in the category and not simply limit yourself to whether sales are up or down. Having this additional background information will help you decide which media you can or should be using in your plan.

What Should You Measure?

Another important issue when looking at category trends is deciding which trends you should be measuring. Sales? Units? Volume? The answer to this may ultimately depend on the types of data you are able to obtain, but you need to keep in mind that what seems to be a trend when examining one number may disappear or be reversed if you turn to another. For example, while sales of your smart phones could be going up in dollar terms, you may actually be selling fewer units if sales are rising primarily due to price increases (i.e., you make more money on each unit sold, but sell fewer units as result). When looking at category trends in dollar terms, always remember to factor in the effects of inflation. What may seem to be a 7 percent annual growth rate could turn out to be a 2 to 3 percent rate once inflation has been accounted for. Perhaps the category trend line shows that the number of units of shampoo sold is declining, but volume is holding steady. This might occur if the unit size has been enlarged, so the same total volume is being sold but in larger bottles. Again, ideally, you want to look at several trend lines using diverse measurements so that you can get an overall picture of what is going on in the category.

Brand Trends

When you turn your attention to individual brands, you perform similar analyses to those done at the category level. This time, however, you focus your attention on specific brand names. The use of the plural here is critical: You are not just looking at how *your* brand has been doing over the past several years but, even more importantly, you need to track how your brand's *competitors* have been faring during that same period. This requires finding the answers to the following questions:

- How many competitors are there?
- How many of these are major, and how many minor? In some categories, where there are just a few players, such as the airline industry, you should probably consider all of them, but in larger categories, such as fast-food restaurants, where myriad companies have offerings, you will do better to pay attention to the ones you believe are your most serious threats. In certain instances, it is a good idea to

look at all of the competitors regardless of their size; you may find that the fourth-tier player of three years ago has gradually been gaining market share and is now a far bigger concern. HP computers were for several years largely ignored by the likes of IBM or Dell, seen primarily as a printer company (its heritage). Today, however, HP is the number-one seller of personal computers.

- How is the category characterized? Is it an oligopoly, where three or four brands define the category, or are there 20 or 30 brands each shouting to be heard?
- How aggressively do the brands in this category compete against one another? For example, is it advertising-driven, or promotion-driven, or does everyone rely heavily on the Internet or direct mail? You can answer this either from your own experience in the category, or by looking at any available syndicated data on competitive media expenditures.

For *each* competitor (ideally for all of them, but at least for the major ones), you must also find out the following:

- What is the company's financial position? This can be found by looking at stock market information or Standard & Poors reports, where available, or by obtaining a recent issue of the company's annual report.
- How does the competitor position its brand? To determine this, you will have to use your own judgment. Examine the advertising for the brand and see what is being emphasized. Is it similar to your own current efforts, or not? If it is dissimilar, is that because there is an actual difference between the two brands, or do consumers just perceive a distinction between them? And who has the more favorable position?
- How does the competitor promote its brand? Which media are used? How much does the competitor spend to promote its brand? Where and when does it spend its money? The answers to these questions may come from several sources. Many large companies, and/or their agencies, subscribe to syndicated competitive spending data from either Kantar Media or Nielsen Monitor Plus. Both show, on a weekly, monthly, quarterly, and annual basis, how much money was spent by a brand in each major media category (see Exhibit 2.5). Smaller businesses may simply try to keep track of where their competitors' ads are appearing. This is not too difficult if you are dealing with a local product, but gets more complicated the wider the area that you or your competitors try to cover. You can also subscribe to a clipping service which will do the tracking for you (see Appendix for more on this).

Exhibit 2.5 Example of Competitive Reporting Data

Selected Spending for Coca-Cola Company, October 2007–March 2008

SUBSIDIARY	BRAND	Total Dollars (000)	Network TV Dollars (000)	Spot TV Dollars (000)	Spanish Language TV Dollars (000)	Cable TV Dollars (000)	Syndication TV Dollars (000)	Magazines Dollars (000)	Sunday Magazines Dollars (000)	Local Magazines Dollars (000)	Hispanic Magazines Dollars (000)	Business-to-Business Magazines Dollars (000)	National Newspaper Dollars (000)	Local Newspaper Dollars (000)	Hispanic Newspaper Dollars (000)	Network Radio Dollars (000)	National Spot Radio Dollars (000)	Local Radio Dollars (000)	US Internet Dollars (000)	Outdoor Dollars (000)
Coca-Cola	Coca-Cola Zero Soft Drink	19,312.8	15,923.5	83.7		624.2		48.3							7.3	515.7	6.2		2,031.4	72.4
Coca-Cola	Mycokerewards.com Online	8,829.8																	8,829.8	
Coca-Cola USA	Coca-Cola Classic Soft Drink	49,029.6	37,202.6	1,337.7	4,859.6	1,676.7	1,959.5	1,154.5			33.6		178.7	97.2		322.3			1.7	205.4
Coca-Cola USA	Coca-Cola Company CP	3,927.4	1,756.0							11.7	3.5	484.7	1,243.0	320.8	103.3				4.4	
Coca-Cola USA	Coca-Cola Various Soft Drinks	24,870.2											357.4	203.6				8,932.2	5,339.3	10,037.7
Coca-Cola USA	Diet Coke Plus Soft Drink	10,772.0	4,531.0	0.1		77.0		5,733.0											282.6	148.3
Coca-Cola USA	Diet Coke Soft Drink	21,461.3	14,421.6			26.0		6,528.7					160.3						271.2	53.5

Source: Kantar Media Intelligence, 2008, October 2007–March 2008.

Share of Market

Once you have looked at the trends for your brand and its competitors, you must then put that information together and see how your brand is faring in the marketplace. The percentage of total category sales that your brand enjoys is known as the *market share*. You should try to examine how this figure has changed over time. Have you been gaining or losing market share in the past few years? Again, be careful to avoid over-simplifying the picture. It could be that you have been losing market share, but so have your major competitors, because of the entry of several new brands into the category. We can see this in the media arena in television. Whereas ten years ago the four broadcast networks commanded 90 percent of the prime-time audience, today fewer than half of all viewers tune in to ABC, CBS, FOX or NBC at that time, with the remainder watching cable networks.

Share of Requirements

One of the most useful pieces of information you can examine is the source of your brand's sales. This is known as the *share of requirements*. It is calculated by taking the percentage of total category volume accounted for by a particular brand's users. Quite simply, it tells you whether your brand is being bought primarily by your customers or by your various competitors' customers. And, conversely, how much of your competitors' sales are coming from your brand users. Looking at this figure, you will be able to determine what percentage of the volume that you sell is accounted for by your users, as opposed to people who usually buy another brand.

Let's say you are a manufacturer of a local brand of pretzels (Pioneer Pretzels), competing with other regional brands as well as a major national brand. As you can see in Table 2.1, Pioneer Pretzels buyers account for 27 percent of all the pretzels sold in the last 30 days. Of all the pretzels they purchase, 15 percent of their usage is to your brand (Pioneer), and 12 percent is to other brands. This means that 55 percent (15% / 27%) of their total category volume is given to your brand, which

Table 2.1 Example of Share of Requirements

	Total Category Volume	Brand Share of Volume	Brand Share of Requirements
National Pretzels	38%	25%	65%
Regional Pretzels	42%	29%	69%
Pioneer Pretzels	27%	15%	55%
Other Brands	9%	5%	65%

gives Pioneer a 55 percent share of requirements. This is the lowest figure among all pretzel types, suggesting that Pioneer's users are not especially brand loyal, which could harm sales and future market share.

Where is Your Brand Sold?

Once you have found out as much as possible about how your brand stacks up against the competition, you need to think about geographic and distribution considerations. Specifically, you must look at where your brand is selling well and where it is doing poorly in terms of markets, regions, or states, and in terms of type of retail outlet. This holds true whether your brand is available on a national, regional, or local basis. For unless your product is sold in just one store or location, there are likely to be some differences in sales according to geography and distribution outlet. What you discover by looking at the sales for your brand in these ways may lead you to develop a media plan with regional or local differences.

Indeed, more and more marketers have adopted a regional approach to selling, realizing that people in Boise have different tastes, customs, and buying habits than people in Boston or Baton Rouge. So marketers are customizing their marketing and media plans (and, in some cases, their products) to meet the needs of specific areas of the country. While some regional differences are obvious, such as higher snowblower sales in Maine than in Arizona, others might seem surprising (such as the fact that insecticides sell most heavily in the south). These types of differences occur not just at the product category level but also for individual brands. Dannon yogurt sells far better on the East coast than does Yoplait, which has traditionally been stronger out West.

To understand geographic skews, the media specialist can turn to two pieces of information:

- Development indices.
- Market share.

Development Indices

You could, in theory, obtain sales data from every region or store in the country and look through them to find out your brand's sales picture. But a more efficient method for analyzing geographic strengths and weaknesses is to look at how the product category is doing across the U.S. and, then, how the brand is developing over time. Both of these are calculated by using *development indices*.

Category Development Index

The category development index, or CDI, looks at product category sales in each potential region or market. A norm, or average, is calculated at 100, and then each area is assigned a value relative to that, expressed as a percent. Numbers below 100 indicate the category has lower than average sales in a given region, whereas those above 100 suggest sales of the category are greater than the national average in a certain part of the country. If, on average, 30,000 tractors are sold per month per region across the U.S., that might mean 25,000 units are sold in the East, 45,000 in the West, and 33,000 in the South. Eastern sales would index at 83 (25,000/30,000), meaning that sales in that area are 17 percent below the national norm, while sales in the West would have a CDI of 150 (45,000/30,000), indicating that that region's sales are 50 percent higher than average. Those in the South have a CDI of 110 (33,000/30,000), which shows that southern sales are 10 percent higher than the norm. Based on such information, a company might decide to concentrate its marketing and media efforts in those regions with higher CDIs, as that is where there is greater potential for all tractor sales.

Brand Development Index

You should not rely solely on the CDI in making geographic media decisions, however. You also need to look at how your brand stacks up against other brands in the category. One tool for this job is the brand development index, or BDI. The calculation is very similar to that of the CDI. You calculate a norm, or average for all brands (or chief competitors) in the category, which is again set at 100, and then see how your own brand is doing in comparison. The John Deere tractor company might find its BDI for tractor sales is 10 percent above average in the eastern region and 5 percent below the norm in the West, suggesting that it is doing better than other brands in the category in the East, but slightly less well in comparison in the West.

When you look at the BDI, you need to keep the CDI in mind too. Once you have these two sets of data, you should compare your BDI to your CDI. In that way you will be able to find those markets where your brand is doing better than the category overall and, conversely, where your brand appears to be underperforming the category (see Exhibit 2.6). For John Deere, its eastern BDI is greater than the CDI, so the brand is doing better than the category in that region. In the West, however, its BDI is below the CDI, so there is room for improvement here.

Armed with this information, you may choose to adopt one of three possible marketing and media strategies. You can focus your attention on those areas of the country where your brand is doing better than the

Exhibit 2.6 BDI versus CDI

		Category Index	
		High	Low
Brand Index	High	Both brand and category growing	Brand growing and category declining
	Low	Brand declining and category growing	Both brand and category declining

category, playing to your strengths. Or you might choose to give more attention (and money) to the weaker markets where the category is doing well but your brand isn't, to try and bolster your sales there. Alternatively, you might decide to play it safe and concentrate on markets where both category and brand are successful. The one strategy you should probably avoid is pouring money into areas where both brand and category are doing poorly, as that suggests there is something about all the brands that is not liked or does not meet the needs of those consumers. To try to rectify that situation single-handedly is probably going to be more trouble (and cost) than it is worth.

Market Share

When looking at the development indices, you can also find out how your competition is doing in each territory and calculate their BDIs. It is common to see that where your brand is doing well, your competitors are having a harder time, and vice versa. The exception here would be for a new or relaunched category where all brands are selling well, such as smartphones.

One way of investigating sales further in geographic terms is to look at your share of the market by region or locality. Is your brand number one in sales in the Central region but in third place in the South? Are you neck-and-neck in New York, but a distant second in Florida? Faced with these different scenarios you should explore some of the possible reasons behind the distinctions. And here you should go back to the other "Ps" of the marketing process. Perhaps you have *distribution* problems in Florida that are harming sales. Maybe your brand is being undercut in price in the South by a local manufacturer. Or it could be that your chief competitor is flooding the local airwaves with *promotional messages* in New York and drowning out yours. By putting together the information you gather from the development indices with your market share figures, you will start to create a picture of how your brand is doing across the country. That will help you decide what marketing and media tactics might be needed in each situation.

One last scenario to consider is a deliberate geographic restriction on product sales. This may be taken for several reasons. You might choose to test launch a new product in only one market, or one region of the country to see how it fares there first. This is what Comcast did with its rollout of a TiVo DVR interface, beginning solely in Boston, before expanding to New England and other markets. Or you might "create" demand by making your product hard to find, as was the case with children's Webkinz toys in 2005–2006, where parents would scramble to get the much-desired, but hard-to-come-by new creatures the minute they arrived in the select few stores who were authorized to sell them. In either scenario, the advertising required to support these tactics is going to be far smaller than for products available more broadly.

The media plan will not be the miracle solution to all of the problems you might encounter, and you should not expect it to turn a floundering brand into a superstar. But, as we shall see in subsequent chapters, the better your understanding of the marketing situation your brand is in, the more likely you are to come up with creative solutions to the problems. For example, if your problem is distribution, you might want to include extra trade promotions or incentives in your plan to encourage retailers or distributors to push your brand further. Pricing discrepancies might be alleviated by offering a coupon or on-pack premium to offset the lower-priced competitors. And if your consumers are being faced with a barrage of competitive messages in one medium, it might be wise to consider placing your own advertising in completely different media, or perhaps move to non-traditional media or special events to raise your own voice elsewhere.

Finally, if possible, you should try to look at your brand's geographic strengths and weaknesses over time to see where the trends are going. Have you always been weaker in the Southwest, or does this seem to have started only in the past year? Is the overall category development index flattening out across the country, or moving to different areas? This is especially likely to be true for new product categories when they are first introduced, as was the case when the low-carbohydrate craze started. As always, looking at several years of data will help you to avoid acting on "blips" in the numbers that might have disappeared without cause within a few months.

Consumers and Media

Although a successful marketing plan requires a thorough understanding of consumers' relationships with the brand, there is, increasingly, the realization that a similarly thorough knowledge is needed to learn how consumers interact with media. In subsequent chapters, we will explore in greater detail the characteristics of each major media form, but here we will introduce the notion of the value of media *context*, or environment.

As you start to learn more about the way consumers use and think about your brand, you can also begin to investigate how they use and think about media. Do your tractor owners, for example, rely on the early morning farming report on the radio? Are they going online to check on crop prices? With the Razor Sharp brand, are the men you want to reach with your message about its reusability interested in men's health and fitness magazines? If so, how do they read them and what do they think about them? And in both cases, how do they respond to ads placed in those key media contexts, compared to seeing the same message placed elsewhere?

The impact of context has long been explored by the academic community, primarily by looking at the effects of consumer involvement with the media in which ads appear.[3]

The advertising industry has begun exploring media context. Agencies such as Starcom Mediavest Group, with its Consumer Context Planning (CCP) function, or Media Kitchen with its Communication Planning approach are each recognizing that media should be thought of more from the consumers' viewpoint, and that it is no longer enough to know basic media usage figures (how often a program is watched or a magazine read). Rather, consumers' relationships with the media can be critical to the way they respond to the brand message. The highly positive reaction to General Motors' Hummer H2 vehicle when it was introduced in 2003 was attributed in part to the finding that the consumers being targeted had an extremely strong relationship with news-oriented media. The inclusion of more of that genre in the media plan, instead of the more traditional new vehicle launch of high-profile network television, helped H2 far surpass its first-year sales goals.

We shall return to the topic of context throughout the discussion of media in this book.

A Word About Budgets

One of the most important preplanning issues to look at is how much money you are likely to have to spend for media for the coming year. You may be given a specific amount upfront, or you may have a range within which to work. In many situations, the media specialist is likely to come up with two or three alternative media plans at different spending levels, showing what could be achieved with $500,000, versus $1,000,000, versus $2,000,000, for example. We will say more about this in Chapter 8. If possible, you should try to be flexible on the budget at this point, keeping in mind that if you lock yourself into a set figure from the very beginning you may limit your creativity later on when you put the plan together.

Timing and Other Issues

The last major area to explore in the preplanning phase is that of timing. This may include the month of the year, the week of the month, the day of the week, or the hour of the day. While some timing considerations can be rationalized and justified, others may be out of your control. Some companies skew their messages toward pay periods, such as the 15th and 30th of the month, knowing that people are more likely to spend money when they have just been paid. Packaged-goods marketers may choose an end-of-week schedule to reflect the increase in grocery store shopping from Wednesday through Friday. Other considerations may be out of your control. The CEO of the company that makes your brand of sports drink may demand that you purchase television time during the US Open Golf tournament. He not only likes golf but also wants to get tickets to the event. The marketing manager may refuse to have the brand advertised in any magazine that accepts liquor advertisements. Perhaps your candy company has been a sponsor of a local parade for the past fifty years and you cannot break with that tradition.

There might also be key timing opportunities that you should consider. If you are going into a Summer or Winter Olympics year, you might want to look for some way to tie your brand into that. While this sounds out of the league of any but the largest national advertisers, there may be an Olympic swim team member in your own town whom your brand of swim goggles could support in some way. Or if your city is celebrating its 200th anniversary and your pen factory has been around for almost as long, you could get involved in the preparations for related events. Or maybe next year has been designated the Year of the Child so you can look for opportunities to promote your diaper brand. Be alert and open to new ideas and opportunities such as these that might come along infrequently and sporadically but could greatly enhance your brand's profile and help sales locally, regionally, or even nationally.

Summary

Before getting down to this year's plan it is important to know as much as possible about what has happened in the past. Find out everything you can on how your company has operated in previous years, how your brand has performed, and what the competitors have done. Looking at trends in the product category is not only helpful, but might lead to new ways to define or position what you have to sell. Be aware of cultural, social, political, and economic forces that might impact your performance.

As you examine your brand, consider who its real competitors are and learn about their past and present marketing plans. Determine your brand's share of market and share of requirements too.

Preplanning should include an analysis of geographic variations in sales through category and brand development indices. Think about how consumers purchase and use your brand, how aware they are of it and its advertising, and when and how much they actually buy.

As you learn more about consumers' relationship with your brand and its competitors, also consider how they respond to the media that are important to their lives. Examining the context, or environment, of your brand's messages can provide you with critical information early on in the planning process that will be helpful as you develop your plans. Finally, keep in mind any budgeting or timing constraints that will affect your media plan.

Checklist—Media in the Marketing Context

1. Have you considered all elements of the marketing mix (price, place, product, and promotions)?
2. How much do consumers know about your brand?
3. Do you need to conduct research on your consumer, through focus groups, surveys, or analysis of syndicated data?
4. When do consumers buy your product? Which time of year, month, day of week or time of day?
5. How much do consumers buy? Is there a difference by product size or flavor?
6. Have you analyzed the history of your brand (how long it has been available, how successful it has been in the past, how it has been positioned in the past)? Include the company's history here, too.
7. What are your brand's chief competitors doing?
8. What are the product category trends?
9. How is your brand faring compared to competitors in terms of market share and share of requirements?
10. How does each major competitor position its brand and promote it?
11. Have you calculated the category and brand development indices for your brand?
12. Are there regional differences for your brand's sales and market share?
13. Do your consumers have any special relationships with particular media that might affect their response to brand messages?
14. Are there any contextually relevant media that might be appropriate to link your target consumers with the media they consume and your brand?
15. Have you considered any timing issues for the brand?

Chapter 3

Developing Optimal Media Objectives

Setting objectives is something we are all familiar with in our day-to-day lives: "I will get an 'A' on this test;" "I'll lose 10 pounds by Christmas;" "My goal is to become the CEO of the company by the time I reach 35." Whatever the objective may be, if you didn't have one it would be difficult to know what you've achieved!

In the media planning context, you need to establish firm objectives for your plan in order to demonstrate how it will help your brand achieve its marketing goals. Although you may feel that in order to execute a media plan you must keep returning to your starting point, moving one step back for every two you go forward, it cannot be overemphasized that *everything* you do on the media planning side must be coordinated with the overall marketing strategy. Therefore, in order to establish your media objectives—what you intend the media plan to achieve—you must first reaffirm and clarify the goals of your complete advertising program to ensure that your media objectives fit in with the goals set in your brand's marketing objectives.

How the Marketing Objective Leads to the Media Objective

The media specialist is likely to be presented with the marketing objective rather than having to develop it on his or her own. It is usually stated in some quantifiable form, such as "sell x thousand more widgets in 2010 than in 2009," or "increase awareness of Brand X to 75 percent within calendar year 2010." It may relate to any of the major marketing functions, such as increasing shelf space in the store, or increasing the number of distribution channels for your product. And frequently it is expressed in terms of specific volume and share goals, such as "within calendar year 2010, bring Brand Z's total volume sold to 25 percent of the total category, raising its market share from 35 percent to 38 percent."

If the marketing objective is vague or ill-defined, simply "increasing awareness" or "improving distribution," then at the end of the year (or whatever time period has been set to achieve the goal) there is likely to be considerable debate over whether the plan was successful or not. It is also going to be more difficult for the media specialist to devise a plan that satisfies those objectives; even if awareness does improve, how much higher must it go in order for the media plan to be considered a success?

Along with understanding the marketing objective, the media specialist should also look at *how* that objective will be achieved, because that will affect what the media plan is supposed to do. Examples might be to increase product penetration among potential users by taking sales away from competitors or bringing new users into the marketplace. Alternatively, the strategy might be to encourage people to use your brand more frequently, perhaps offering new uses for it. In order to increase the sales of Sara Lee deli meats, the marketing objective might be to get current users to buy additional packs of the product for use in new and different ways besides just in a sandwich. For the media plan, this could lead to an objective of increasing the frequency with which target users are exposed to the message to remind them of the various ways they can use the product by demonstrating the uses in recipes.

For a hospital with the marketing objective of introducing a new children's critical care unit and encourage more people in the community to choose that facility for their pediatric medical needs, the media objective could be to reach 75 percent of people who live within a ten mile radius to inform them of what is now available. Clearly, the marketing objective has a major impact on how the media plan develops, affecting the target audience, communications used, and media selected.

Media and the Advertising Objective

As we noted earlier, the marketing objective may relate to any of the four major areas of the marketing mix (product, promotion, distribution, or price). Therefore, before establishing specific media objectives it is also essential to focus on how the media affect your advertising goals. While your ultimate *marketing* goal for most goods is to sell more product (or services or image), unless your audience finds out about the product through the media that you use, that goal is unlikely to be reached. You need to be aware, at the same time, of the other marketing mix elements. If the product is no good, your media advertising will have little impact. Similarly, if you advertise your product heavily but it isn't available in most stores, sales will not improve.

Frequently, the objective of your advertising is tied in to the stage at which the target audience is in the decision-making process. As we noted earlier, this process breaks down into three very broad areas: Think, Feel, and Do (or, in research-speak, the *cognitive*, *affective*, and *conative* stages). Once you have decided that you need a new TV set, you will *think* about what brands are available. Then, you will consider how you *feel* about each one of them. And finally, you will select a particular brand and take action (*do*) and buy it.

This process can be better understood by revisiting the eight main stages of the consumer decision-making process introduced in Chapter 2:

1. Need.
2. Awareness.
3. Preference.
4. Search.
5. Selection.
6. Purchase.
7. Use.
8. Satisfaction.

Need

Before you can hope to sell any more widgets, people have to have a reason to buy them. Contrary to what many advertising critics maintain, advertising cannot persuade people to buy something they do not want. Indeed, it is often easier to think of this first stage in the decision process as reflecting people's *wants*, for in today's industrial society most people are able to satisfy their basic needs, such as food and shelter.

Even when people buy products that seem pointless or silly, such as chia pets or hula hoops, they may feel they have a *need* to indulge in it just for fun. And while you might argue that no one really has a *need* for a $150,000 BMW, the person who chooses to purchase one clearly feels that he or she deserves this luxury automobile. Defining what the need might be for the product helps the marketer to understand the motivations behind why people might buy it, which in turn may provide some clues as to ways of reaching those people through the media. Though everyone buys shampoo, if you can segment the target into different groups according to their motivation for use, you could reach each one through a variety of media forms. People who are most concerned with how their hair looks may be reached in fashion and beauty magazines. Those who want a shampoo with built-in conditioner to help in their busy lives may respond to ads in women's magazines that offer advice on juggling multiple roles. For the ones who are looking for the most natural ingredients in their shampoo, then print ads in titles that are eco-friendly might be most appropriate. And all of that is just within magazines. Research conducted directly with target consumers may reveal that different segments have different media habits altogether, leading you, as planner, to determine what those media options should be. This is covered in greater details in subsequent chapters, but you should understand how different needs can often lead to different media choices.

Awareness

Once the consumer has determined that she needs a particular product, it is the job of marketing to make her aware of the choices that are available. For the media specialist, this means reaching that consumer in the right place and often enough so that your brand's message is the most relevant and convincing. And it is not enough to simply make people aware of your *brand*; the real goal here is to make them aware of your brand's *message*. You might well be able to reach 95 percent of all cat owners to make them aware of the new cat food that you sell, but unless they also learn that your product provides 100 percent of a cat's daily nutritional requirement, which is more than any other competitor, your advertising is unlikely to increase sales. Of course, keep in mind that while you are promoting *your* message, every other cat food company is also trying to boost awareness of its own brand.

Preference

Based on the various choices the consumer sees and hears, he or she will then develop specific brand preferences. Ideally, the marketer would like that consumer to develop *brand loyalty* to his brand so that every time Julie Smith needs to buy more running shoes, for example, she always chooses Saucony. A media plan to enhance preference might include opportunities for the target audience to try your brand at home, perhaps by offering a free sample in magazines or via the Internet.

Search

Once the target audience decides it might prefer your brand over others, the audience's next task is to find out where to purchase the item. Here, media advertising can be a big help, by notifying people of the places that sell your product. You have probably seen or heard this yourself in local or regional TV and radio ads that list which stores in your area stock the item. Billboards can be used, too, to display the retailers' or dealers' name. A web ad can link directly to a local seller of your product and/or contain a store or dealer locator that will find the closest one to you. If your audience cannot find the product when it wants to buy it, then not even the best advertising placed in the most appropriate media will help increase sales.

Selection

Brand selection may seem like an easy stage for the consumer. If she has decided already that she prefers Cover Girl nail polish over others, and has learned that it is sold in Wal-Mart stores, then isn't it obvious that she will buy it? Not necessarily. Today's consumer is faced with so many different brands that, once in the store and standing in front of the shelf, she may decide to go with your competitor's offering, because it is on sale, or packaged more attractively, or comes in larger bottles. So the selection process is a crucial stage for the marketer and the media specialist to consider. From a media perspective, the nail-polish user may be encouraged by in-store vehicles such as in-pack premiums or point-of-purchase radio. Personal contacts can also be very important at this stage. Someone who has come into the store in order to buy a mid-range computer may be encouraged to select your more expensive model by being offered one year of free parts and service by the dealer.

Purchase and Use

Clearly, the ultimate goal of marketing and media plans is to persuade consumers to purchase the product. But if they buy it and never use it, then there is no reason for them to ever buy another one. No marketer can remain successful by continually targeting new product users. Often, one marketing and media objective is that of encouraging consumers to *use* the brand. In media planning terms, this might involve increasing the message frequency so that users are reminded of the different ways in which the brand can be used. A good example of this, in past years, has been Campbell's soup, which often places recipes in its print ads and on its website to encourage people to use more of the product, and hence purchase it more frequently.

Satisfaction

The final stage in the consumer decision process is really a feedback loop into the earlier ones. If people come to your restaurant but are dissatisfied with the quality of the food or friendliness of the staff, then their dissatisfaction will likely mean they won't return to your venue again. What is worse, they may tell their friends about their bad experience and decrease your potential sales even further. So customer satisfaction is extremely important for future success. *Satisfaction* is generally not listed as the primary marketing or media objective of a plan, but should nonetheless be kept in mind when deciding where and when to place your advertising message. It is perhaps harder to achieve through the media, because it is ultimately up to the user to decide whether he or she is satisfied. But many advertisers promise "satisfaction guaranteed or your money back" as a way to reassure consumers that they will, indeed, be content if they buy your brand.

Advertising Objectives and the Consumer Decision Process

To see how advertising objectives might fit in with each stage of the consumer decision process, let's take an example. If your client is the city's professional soccer team trying to increase the number of people who attend home games, you may not have to create a "need" for your offering, since anyone who likes sports feels the "need" to attend live games. It is very likely, however, that you would want to increase awareness of your team. So your advertising objective might be to boost awareness of the Soccer Stars from a baseline measure of 40 percent to 70 percent among young people under the age of 25 within a 50-mile radius of the city.

It could be that many people have heard about your team, but are still choosing to attend baseball games instead. Here, your advertising objective would be to improve *preference*, so that instead of two out of ten under 25s choosing to go to a soccer game over baseball, three out of ten do so. Setting advertising objectives for the subsequent stages in the decision process is somewhat less common, because it is believed that advertising has a less direct role to play here. But you still want to encourage your target to *use* your team, by attending games, setting as your advertising objective to boost visits to your games from an average of one time per year to four, perhaps by promotional tickets or special events at the stadium.

Media and the Consumer Decision Process

The advertising media will also affect each of these stages in the consumer decision process. To continue with the Soccer Stars example, you might boost *awareness* of the team through widespread local TV and radio ads or outdoor billboards in the communities where you believe there are high concentrations of young adults. Consumer *preference* could be encouraged by sending direct mail or emails to potential visitors offering them two tickets for the price of one. They could be helped in the *search* process by putting ads that provide maps to your stadium in local newspapers or by buying search keywords on local or regional tourist websites. *Selection* might be helped by bringing some of the bigger soccer stars in from out of town and offering the opportunity for fans to meet them. These special events could then be promoted in local media and perhaps receive additional publicity through press releases. Finally, to get current team supporters to *use* the team and attend more games, you might create a monthly online newsletter that tells them about the exciting events coming up at future games.

Let's take another example. Say you are in the market for a new automobile. That puts you in the initial stages of *needing* a new car. You see some TV ads for various makes and models, which increases your awareness of what is available. Three of the cars that interest you are the Toyota Yaris, the Ford Fusion, and the Chevy Aveo. You read several automotive magazines, check out their resale value on Edmunds.com, and pick up the *Consumer Reports* issue on new cars and decide that these models fit your needs. Now you have developed a *preference* for these particular models out of the hundreds that are available. Your next step would be to visit some car dealerships to *search* out the cars themselves. Here, your interaction with the salespeople is likely to play a major role in influencing your decision. You will also probably talk to friends and colleagues and return to the Internet to look in greater detail at each car's specifications. Faced with all of the information you have gathered, you *select* the Aveo. You negotiate a deal and drive the car home; now you can *use* it and, based on your experiences, you will develop a degree of *satisfaction* with your new purchase. If you are happy with the car, you may well buy another Chevrolet the next time you are in the car market.

The media's role is important at several points in the process. Television advertising is frequently used to create or enhance *awareness*, informing people of the qualities of the brand and what it has to offer. Both TV and magazines can help develop consumer *preference*. Here, you might see ads that compare the Chevy Aveo to other cars in the same class, or that cite the awards and rankings the car has received in automotive competitions. And as we noted above, personal contacts and the Internet may be critical too. Retail or local ads on spot radio and television and outdoor billboards help reach consumers who are *searching* for your brand; sometimes you will see a brief message from the local dealership tagged on to the end of a commercial.

To encourage people to *select* your offering, the media may emphasize special discounts or added features, such as a 60,000 mile warranty or $1,000 cash back. Getting people to *use* the product is also important. While this is not an issue in the case of an automobile, it can be for other consumer products. Nestle, for instance, uses print ads that feature recipes for foods made with its Toll House chocolate chips in order to encourage people to take the product off the shelf.

As with the marketing objective, the more measurable the advertising objective is, the easier it will be to determine whether it has been achieved. This can be done either through specific testing after the ads have run for a while, or by setting up some kind of market test and determining the effect of advertising on sales.

Consumers, Brands, and Media

Both advertising and media objectives require a clear understanding of how consumers connect with brands and with media. This relationship can be thought of as a Venn diagram, or a series of connecting circles. That is, consumers relate to certain brands, and are more likely to be receptive to those brands' advertisements when they appear in the media forms that the consumer likes and/or responds to. Exhibit 3.1 displays this relationship.

What some advertisers and agencies have realized in recent years is that the advertising industry has typically focused on just two of the three circles at any one time. That is, the media department has zoomed in on the relationship of consumers to media, while the agency account planning and client brand management departments have concentrated efforts on exploring consumers' relationships with brands. To truly fulfill advertising and media objectives, however, those three elements must be examined together.

As noted in Chapter 2, this practice—known variously as consumer context planning, the consumer-centric approach, or communications planning—involves in-depth research (qualitative and/or quantitative) to understand in greater detail who the target audience is, and how they relate to both the brands they use and the media they consume. The approach has been embraced by large marketers such as General Motors and Procter & Gamble, each of which spend significant funds on learning about that relationship of brand–media–consumer for their products, whether that is the Cadillac luxury vehicle or Kotex panty-liners. The concept will be examined more closely as we go through the rest of the media planning process.

Media Objectives and ROI

Another important consideration before you develop any media objectives is that of ROI, which stands for Return on Investment. This financially ori-

Exhibit 3.1 Relationship of Brands, Media, and Consumers

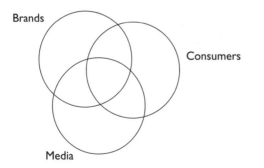

ented term is used to help those at the top of the company (Chief Executive Officer, Chief Financial Officer, etc.) understand how the money being spent on media is helping to generate profits. That is, for every dollar spent in media, how much is *returned* to the company in terms of sales or awareness or customer goodwill? As the media specialty has grown increasingly sophisticated (through the use of computers and far deeper analysis of available data), marketers have put greater pressure on those working in media to prove that those dollars are well spent.

One of the ways this is done is through econometric modeling (described further in Chapter 7). This combines an analysis of economics with the use of statistical metrics, or models. The idea here is that statistical models can be created to explain, mathematically, the value of each dollar spent in media by comparing the amounts invested in each media form to the results achieved. These results may be in terms of product sales or consumer awareness or brand preferences.

This is not an easy process, in part because not everything is easily quantifiable. How can Cover Girl "prove" that its product integration into the popular TV program *America's Next Top Model* is what causes sales of its mascara or eyeliner to go up? Perhaps it was the concurrent TV or print advertising that caused it. Or possibly it was the absence of its competitor, Almay, on-air during the same time period. Or maybe it was the introduction of Ellen De Generis as its celebrity endorser that helped sales. These econometric models attempt to parse out all the causes of changes in sales. When sales are increasing, everyone wants to take credit for it. The harder challenge is explaining what is *not* working—what causes sales to decline? Often it may be far broader economic trends, from the recession of 2008, to drastic weather patterns. An unusually warm (or wet or cold) period is often cited as the reason for sales of products to go down. A colder-than-normal summer can cause havoc on sales of suntan lotion, while a sudden freeze will cause a rapid halt to Starbucks' chilled coffee drinks. While the media specialist cannot be held responsible for all these external events, he may be required to help demonstrate the accountability of the media included in the plan.

Establishing Media Objectives

Armed with clear and concise marketing and advertising objectives, that are in sync with how your brand's consumers think about and respond to the brand and to media, you are now ready for the most important part of the media planning process—setting media objectives. As with the other goals, once you have a clearly defined course set for you, it becomes much easier to figure out how to get there. There are three main elements involved in the media objectives:

- Defining the target audience.
- Setting broad communication objectives.
- Considering creative requirements.

Defining the Target Audience

Although you haven't yet started to put a plan together, you are probably beginning to realize that much of the most important work needs to be done beforehand to establish the media objectives. Defining the target audience is one key step you must take in the objective-setting process, for only by knowing who you wish to reach through the media will you be able to put together a schedule that will convey your brand's message to the right people.

Ideally, the target audience for your media plan should be identical to the audience for the overall marketing plan. Since most of a brand's sales are typically generated by its current users, the target audience definition is likely to include some product usage qualification. A marketing plan that is intended to increase sales of Pantene shampoo-conditioner combinations might have as its target audience "women 25 to 54 who currently use shampoo-conditioners, with an annual household income of more than $50,000." Life stage can be a crucial factor too. A plan geared toward increasing awareness of your new Sony digital camcorder might have as its target "adults 25 to 49 who have had a child in the past year."

Often, however, you will find that the media target may be both more and less precise than the marketing target. This is largely because the media themselves have traditionally been bought and sold on the basis of fairly basic demographics, such as age, sex, income, education, or race. For example, while your brand of Carr's crackers may be aiming to sell 20,000 more packets this year by expanding its user base and capturing more sales from "young adult gourmet lovers who enjoy entertaining and eating out," when it comes to creating your media objectives, your target may be "adults 18 to 34 with college education and an annual household income of more than $30,000." This is a more precise definition in that it specifies a particular age category as well as particular income and education levels, but it does not take into account (at least definitionally) the lifestyle variables (like eating out, entertaining, and fine foods).

As technology improves, however, we are likely to see the development of more precise and lifestyle/product usage-based targeting. Much of this is driven by what happens in television. Currently, the age/sex target standards dominate. But in the not-too-distant future (and already being tested by cable and satellite companies, as well as Internet-based companies such as Google), household-level information from data companies such as Experian or Acxiom will be used to deliver ads to those homes who are known to have certain desirable characteristics or product habits. For example, Purina will be able to send its dog food ads only to homes known to have a dog. This practice, referred to as *addressable advertising*, was tested in 2007–2009 and found to deliver significantly more in terms of the message effectiveness (greater relevance leads more people to watch the commercial) and media efficiency (money saved by only paying to reach homes of interest to the advertiser). Further down the road, ads could even be selected by the consumers based on product categories of interest to them.

One element that will be as true tomorrow as it is today is that the media target should be identical to the creative target. While this may seem blatantly obvious, occasionally, the research and account teams will develop a complex and precise target audience, but the creative team will march forward with their own ideas of who the message should speak to. That leaves the media department in confusion. So just as the media specialists should have seen and understood the marketing objectives, they should also be familiar with the creative brief, a document that lays out for the copywriter and art director the fundamental information about who or what the brand is, what the communication goals are for the campaign, and, importantly, who the message is directed at. Ideally, all of the target definitions will match!

As far as media definitions of targets are concerned, the syndicated data sources of audience information are usually the first port of call. Depending on the target, these resources may provide armloads of information, or they may offer up next to nothing. In particular, if you are dealing with a non-consumer target, such as retailers or dealers, you may find yourself without much syndicated information at all, relying more on your experience and judgment. You can assume, for example, that if you are trying to promote your refrigeration equipment to restaurants, one place to put your message would be *Restaurant News*.

One important consideration for defining your media target is whether it should be broad or narrow. Because everyone in the country uses laundry detergent, does that mean your media plan should be aimed at "all adults in the United States who use laundry detergent?" Increasingly, the answer will be "no." Today's brands are becoming more and more segmented. So we don't just have one box of Tide on the store shelf, but 27 of them, including powder or liquid Tide, Tide with Bleach, Tide Total Care, or Tide Cold Water Wash. There are six different sizes of 2X Ultra Tide Liquid alone, aiming to suit the needs of diverse groups, from singles living alone to large families. Each of these groups is likely to have different media habits and preferences—and trying to create a media plan that would reach everyone would ignore the needs of different population groups in terms of both product benefits and media usage. There might be one plan aimed at mothers with young children, another for those with large families, another with an environmental slant, and a fourth promoting the smaller size for urban apartment dwellers. Each plan has a different target audience.

There is also the opposite danger, however. That is, you might define your target audience so narrowly that it would be almost impossible to reach them. You might, from previous research into who buys your plasma TVs, find that they are most likely to be college-educated graduates of private colleges, professionals working in high-tech industries, living in the mid-Atlantic region in urban areas in homes worth $150,000 or more, who use the Internet frequently, and with at least three TV sets in their homes (Exhibit 3.2). But there may only be a few hundred of them!

There are two major problems to note here. First, most traditional media will not only present your message to *your* target, but also to many others for whom the product is probably irrelevant. This is a problem that currently can only be alleviated by careful consideration of exactly who your target should be and which media will best reach that audience. As noted above, in the future, addressable advertising will allow marketers to send messages to a more selective and relevant group of households. And Internet advertising is able to be more precise also, delivering ads dynamically based on where the user has been on the Web. But for now, thinking of all three parts of the connecting circles—Consumer–Brand–Media—will help you here, for with a thorough understanding of

Exhibit 3.2 Profile of Plasma TV Owner

People who own a plasma TV are:

more likely to	*less likely to*
be . . .	**be . . .**
Age 18–24	Age 65+
College educated	High school graduates
Male	Female
Urban	Rural
Living in Mid-Atlantic region	Living in South region
Non-White	
read magazines on	*read magazines on*
Cars	Hunting and fishing
Travel	Science and technology
listen to . . .	**listen to . . .**
Adult contemporary	Classical
News radio	Rock
watch . . .	**watch . . .**
College sports	Movies on TV
Sitcoms	Early evening news on TV
Late night talk shows	
Go to movies	watch broadcast TV
Use the Internet frequently	not subscribe to additional TV services

Source: Mediamark Research, 2009.

how your target relates not just to your brand but also to the media they consume, your media plan is not only more likely to reach that target but also do so more effectively.

A second consideration in establishing media objectives is the cost effectiveness of the plan. It may well be the chief concern of you or of the top executives of your company. You could come up with an extremely elaborate and highly targeted media plan, with a clearly defined target audience and appropriate communication objectives, but if it is going to cost twice as much as is in the marketing budget, you are unlikely to be able to execute it. When defining the target audience, you must be sure that the audience will be reachable at an affordable cost. As the maker of Oral B toothbrushes, you cannot hope to reach everyone who brushes their teeth on a budget of $10 million.

Having defined your target audience, your next step should be to find out as much as possible about the individuals who make up that audience. Ideally, you should not only know their basic demographic characteristics (age, sex, education level, income, profession, etc.), but also learn more about the kinds of products they use and the media they tend to hear or see. Again, depending on the target, you can often obtain this information from syndicated data services. Or you may have to rely on your own judgment and experience. So if your target for the iPod Touch is young adults 18 to 34 who listen to music, you should also know that they are more likely to have a cell phone and a DVD player.

Communication Objectives

When it comes to writing down what you expect the advertising message to do for your brand, you will start to find that all of a sudden you are dealing with the art, rather than the science, of media planning. These objectives are measurable to some degree through communications tests with the target audience that find out what information the audience is taking away from the message. In addition, media calculations can be made to estimate what the plan should achieve. But many of the criteria you need to use to establish what the goals should be are far more evaluative and rely on your judgment and subjective response to everything that you know about the brand, its advertising, and the marketplace. These objectives must also be in line with the overall marketing strategy for the brand. If you are trying to increase your market share in the athletic shoe category by 2 percentage points by increasing distribution into mass merchandise outlets, then your communication objective might involve increasing awareness of your brand among your target audience by 15 percent within the first three months of the campaign.

Communication objectives will vary, depending upon the kind of product you are promoting. For launching a new brand of cat litter, you probably want your advertising to generate awareness of the product. If you are advertising Charmin toilet paper, in contrast, which has been around forever, your message will more likely serve as a reminder to consumers of the qualities of the product such as its softness or strength. These differing objectives will also affect your reach and frequency goals. For a new product, you would want to establish some initial awareness levels and then sustain them (for example, generate awareness of the product among 75 percent of the target group within the first three months of the campaign).

Don't forget to consider your competition, too. You might set as your objective to achieve, within the first six months of your new campaign, awareness levels for your Cannondale mountain bike that are equal to or greater than those of your closest competitor. Geography is another factor. If your bike is the number-one brand in the category with the highest awareness levels in the Northeast and Pacific, but falls to number two or three in the South, then you might set different objectives in different parts of the country, broadening your reach in areas where awareness levels are currently lower.

There are three main factors to consider when developing communication objectives: campaign timing, category and brand dynamics, and media reach and frequency.

Campaign Timing

Here you should consider what stage your campaign is at—are you launching a new product or changing the strategy for selling it, or is this the third or fourth or twentieth year of an ongoing campaign? Also think about the specific timing of the campaign. Are you trying to communicate a seasonal message to warn young adults about drinking and driving during the holidays? Or maybe it's April and people are starting to think about summer vacation, so it's the perfect time to begin promoting your park district's swimming pool. Thinking of your communications objectives within a specific timeframe will help to ensure that your media plan stays focused on that period.

Category and Brand Dynamics

If you study the trends for your brand in particular as well as trends within the category overall, your communication objectives will be firmly fixed in reality. That is, if research shows that users of lawn-care products are extremely brand loyal, it makes little sense to say the objective for Scott's weed-killer is to gain 15 market-share points from your competitors in the next 12 months. Related to loyalty, you should think also about what degree of consumer involvement with the category can be reasonably expected. It's hard to get people excited about staplers or canned tomatoes, no matter how wonderful your creative message or media plan. Try to be objective about your brand's positioning too. Is your advertising message really very different from competitors', or is it in fact just another version of the same idea? If you look at the advertising for most products, you'll see that the latter is far more common than the former. Almost all banks tout their low financing rates, while nearly all beers talk about great taste, and most garbage bags emphasize their strength. None of this should be too surprising; you wouldn't want to buy a beer that didn't taste good, or a garbage bag that wasn't strong.

Reach and Frequency

Having stated earlier that communication objectives tend to be more subjective than objective, more art than science, there is still a role for some numbers here. But they should only be included if you will have some way of measuring them. The two key concepts to consider here are *reach* and *frequency*. These are the two most commonly used media terms in the whole planning process. The *reach* of the plan refers to the number (or percentage) of the target audience that will be reached by the brand's advertising in the media. As we shall learn in Chapter 6, that number is determined by calculating what percentage of the target audience will be exposed to the media in which your ad appears. Along with knowing how many people will have the opportunity to see or hear your ad, you also need to state how many times they need to do so in order for the message to have some effect. This is the concept of *effective frequency*. You should identify some reach and frequency goals as a way of measuring whether your communication objectives were achieved. If the communication goal is to "increase awareness of the brand by 10 percent among the key consumer target," then that can be measured by establishing what percentage of the target was actually reached with the message and how many times they saw or heard it, and whether brand awareness levels did in fact go up. More will be said on this topic in Chapter 6.

Creative Requirements

The last area that should be considered in preplanning discussions is any special creative requirement that will affect the media selected. As noted above, this should be made evident in the Creative Brief, and provides another reason why it is critical for media specialists to be exposed to that document. If, for example, you are introducing a new hybrid car and want to talk about its advanced engineering and environmental benefits through long copy and details, you will have to think in terms of the media that can allow you to do that. Or, if your task is to promote the Florida Keys as a vacation destination for families, then the creative requires media that convey the desired image by depicting many different sights or sounds from that area, such as print or the Internet, TV or radio. The message will, in part, determine where you choose to place it. Yet another example might be introducing a new Pillsbury cake mix. Your ads will showcase the delicious results of using the product, so the visual element is going to be particularly important. Immediately, this leads you in a certain direction when starting to consider your media plan strategies and tactics.

Summary

In order for a media plan to be successful, it must be tied directly to the broad marketing objectives for the brand, usually defined in terms of sales and market share. The goals for media should also be derived from the advertising objectives, which show where the advertising fits in to the consumer's decision process, such as increasing awareness or improving customer satisfaction, or generating additional use of the product. Both marketing and advertising objectives are tied to the media objectives by considering the relationship that exists between consumers, brands, and media. Media objectives should be developed with a consideration of how they might tie to the brand or company's return on investment (ROI), demonstrating how each media dollar spent contributes to sales. The media objectives state to whom the message is to be delivered (the target audience), when it is to be distributed (timing specifics), and how many times a given proportion of the target will, ideally, be exposed (media reach and frequency). Special creative requirements for the brand's communications should also be taken into account, in part by ensuring that media specialists are able to review the Creative Brief.

Checklist—Developing Optimal Media Objectives

1. Do you know your brand's marketing objectives?
2. Are they stated clearly and explicitly, in an actionable way?
3. What is the advertising objective for the brand?
4. Have you considered where the advertising might fit in with the eight stages of the consumer decision process—need, awareness, preference, search, selection, purchase, use, and satisfaction?
5. What have you learned about how consumers relate to your brand and the media they consume?
6. In which stage of the consumer decision process does your advertising objective fit?
7. Have you clearly defined your target audience, or audiences?

8. Are your target definitions in line with those developed by the marketing team and the creative team?
9. What are your communication objectives, in terms of a specific timeframe, given the competitive situation?
10. What are your media reach and frequency goals?
11. Are there any specific creative requirements for the brand's message?
12. Have you seen the Creative Brief?

Chapter 4

Exploring the Media, Part I
Traditional

We are all familiar with television, radio, the Internet, newspapers, social networks or magazines from the consumer's standpoint. That is, we don't think twice about checking our social network site every morning, listening to the radio on the way to work, going online to catch up on the news, watching TV when we get home at night, and leafing through a magazine in bed before going to sleep. For advertisers, each of those points of contact we make with the medium represents an opportunity to communicate with a potential target for their product or service. So, for example, the local car dealer will place his ad for a GMC Envoy in the daily newspaper in the hope that you will see it in the morning and stop in at the dealership on the way home from work or at the weekend. The First National Bank might put an ad on the radio in the morning hours to reach commuters on their way to work to alert them to the bank's favorable interest rates on savings accounts. And an organic foods company that offers delivery of fresh local foods might buy a keyword so that if someone searches for "organic" and lives in the zipcodes served, the company's ad will appear. When you sit back and relax in the evening to watch television, a wide range of advertisers will remind you of their brand of beer, cookies, pet food, or coffee. They do so either in traditional commercials or by placing their products within the programs themselves, hoping that when you next visit the grocery store theirs is the brand you will select. And finally, right before you fall asleep, advertisers in magazines will try to persuade you that their credit card company will be there when you need it. In this chapter, we will focus on the traditional media forms of TV, radio, newspaper, magazines, Internet, and out of home. The next chapter discusses advertising opportunities to reach consumers through media that go "beyond traditional."

Media vs. Communications

The task of today's media planners has become much broader than in times past. Instead of just considering the traditional media (TV, radio, magazines, newspapers, outdoor), the planner now must evaluate all forms of "brand contact," wherever or however they occur. Should Kraft Macaroni and Cheese sponsor the local Little League teams? Can Columbia Sportswear be the official sponsor of an Olympic ski team? Would it make sense to put Powerbar ads along running trails? Should the doctors in *Grey's Anatomy* be seen to be drinking Coca-Cola? Or could Campbell Soup ads pop up on the website weather.com when the temperature falls below freezing in the location being viewed? The key with all of these communications is that they must be integrated into the plan. That is, Powerbar's trail's message should look and feel like its magazine ads, and should appear in the plan as another regular line item, scheduled in conjunction with all other media. And as with all media planning elements, the selections must tie fully into the brand's marketing and media objectives.

Media Categories

Once you have clearly defined media objectives, the next step will be to decide which media types, and vehicles within those types, will best help you achieve your goals. Before exploring that further, we need to think about what the different media can offer you as an advertiser conveying an advertising message. Here, we will consider the six major media categories: television, radio, Internet, magazines, newspapers, and out-of-home. The many forms of new or "alternative" media will be covered in the next chapter.

There are various ways of categorizing the media. We can contrast the *print* media of magazines, newspapers and outdoor billboards with *electronic* media—radio, Internet, and TV. We can also make an important distinction between media that are predominantly *local* (newspapers, outdoor billboards, and radio) and those where most ads are placed on a *national* basis (TV, Internet, and magazines). And increasingly, we can classify media based on the level of consumer *control* involved in their use, from magazines, TV via DVRs, and the Internet, which require active involvement, to radio and traditional TV, which are more passively consumed. Here, we will start by looking at the major characteristics of each traditional media form. As a point of reference, Exhibit 4.1 shows how much was spent in advertising in each major media form in 2007.

A Television in Every Home

Almost every household in America has a television set, while eight in ten (82 percent) have two or more. The average household owns 2.4 TV sets. Television is the largest mass medium available for advertisers. In 2008,

Exhibit 4.1 Adspend by Medium Spend in 2007

Direct Mail	$59,622
Broadcast TV	$43,734
Newspaper	$35,788
Cable TV	$21,440
Radio	$17,535
Yellow Pages	$13,844
Consumer Magazines	$12,960
Internet	$11,371
All other	$54,473
	$270,767

Source: Ad Age, May 2009.

about $70 billion was spent promoting goods and services this way. Households in the U.S. have their TV sets on, on average, 7.5 hours each day, which is one of the highest viewing figures of anywhere in the world. One in five (18 percent) are watching in high definition. The average household can receive 130 channels, thanks to the presence of cable, while two-thirds of all homes (74 percent) receive 100 or more channels. That figure continues to rise, increasing by 11 channels in just one year. It will keep going up since, as of June 2009, all U.S. households have to receive television digitally, either via cable or satellite, or by adding special converter boxes to their TV sets to bring the digitally transmitted signals onto their old analog sets. The digital transition results in clearer pictures on the TV set, and frees up much-valued bandwidth that the government has already sold to major telephone companies Verizon and AT&T to use for their services.[1]

Broadcast television programming is traditionally divided up in two ways: by *daypart* and by *format*. The daypart refers to the time of day the program airs. There are nine standard dayparts, which are shown in Exhibit 4.2.

Program formats are also standardized into twelve main types, which are given in Exhibit 4.3.

Again, it is worth emphasizing that these breakdowns are really only the concern of the programmers and advertisers; you don't choose to watch "situation comedies" or "reality-based programs," but rather decide to watch *Dancing with the Stars* on ABC on Tuesday nights.

The popularity of different program genres changes over time. Typically, the two most popular types are dramas and situation comedies. In the late 1990s, reality shows (such as CBS's *Survivor* and NBC's *Deal or No Deal*) became extremely popular, in part as a result of networks realizing they were a far less expensive form of TV program to make. The average prime time drama can cost more than a million dollars per

Exhibit 4.2 Dayparts

Early Morning	M-F	7:00–9:00 a.m.
Daytime	M-F	9:00 a.m.–4:30 p.m.
Early Fringe	M-F	4:30–7:30 p.m.
Prime Access	M-F	7:30–8:00 p.m.
Primetime	M-S	8:00–11:00 p.m.
	Sun	7:00–11:00 p.m.
Late News	M-Sun	11:00–11:30 p.m.
Late Night	M-Sun	11:30 p.m.–1:00 a.m.
Saturday Morning	Sat	8:00 a.m.–1:00 p.m.
Weekend Afternoons	Sat-Sun	1:00–7:00 p.m.

Source: Nielsen Media Research, 2002.

Exhibit 4.3 Television Program Formats

Animation/children
Daytime serials
Drama/adventure
Game shows
Late-night talk
Movies
News
Newsmagazines
Reality-based
Sitcoms
Specials
Sports

Source: Nielsen Media Research, 2002.

episode, compared to a few hundred thousand for a reality show. Today, the reality genre is a staple of the prime time TV line-up.

As always happens, soon every network was jumping onto this band-wagon, leading to a slew of copycat programs that created a glut of that program type. While those programs continue to do well, viewers grew bored with seeing too much of just one format, and the networks developed more dramas and sitcoms that found favor with viewers, such as *Desperate Housewives* and *30 Rock*. The challenge for media planners and, particularly, media buyers is to predict which shows will be popular several months or even one year from now, buying them at a less expensive cost and enjoying higher-than-predicted ratings. We will explore this further in Chapter 9.

How people watch TV has been changing, however, as more viewers acquire digital video recorders (DVRs) that allow them, in effect, to become their own program scheduler. By making it easy to record favorite shows, and fast-forward or pause both live and recorded programming,

DVR providers (such as TiVo and the cable or satellite companies) have helped turn television from a passive medium where viewers watch what is shown when it appears, to a much more active experience where people can watch whatever they want whenever they wish to do so. Currently, about one-third of U.S. households have this device. The consequences for advertising will be explored further in this chapter.

What people watch is also impacted by who owns the various TV networks. For example, Disney's ownership of ABC, Lifetime, and ESPN networks is not only evident in ESPN announcers on ABC sports programming, but leads to "Wonderful World of Disney" on ABC. Exhibit 4.4 shows the ownership of the major networks.

There are four main types of television to consider: network, syndication, spot (local) and cable. Beginning in the mid-1990s, the ownership of these various entities became more and more consolidated, so that today just a handful of large media companies have majority control of all four types of TV, squeezing out the independents or mom-and-pop operations that flourished in the first 50 years of television. The viewer is not really aware of who owns what, and does not differentiate, for the most part, between network or cable or syndication. He or she chooses to watch a certain program, regardless of how or where it airs, or who created it or owns it. So the distinctions we draw here are purely for media purposes.

Network Television

Network television consists of four major broadcast networks: ABC, CBS, NBC, and FOX. There is also one smaller network: The CW, owned jointly by CBS and Warner Brothers. A "network" is actually made up of hundreds of local stations that become "affiliates" of the national organization. There are a total of 1,461 network affiliate stations, about half of all TV stations on air (2,847). Each station receives a set amount of money every year from the network in return for which they agree to air national programs for a given number of hours every week, though as the networks have looked for ways to cut their costs in recent years, they have attempted to cut or eliminate these payments. Network programs air at the same time in every market within a given time zone. So CBS's "60 Minutes" appears at 7 p.m. on Sunday night in the Eastern zone, 6 p.m. in Central markets, and 5 p.m. in the Mountain zone. Programs in the Pacific time zone are shown at the same time locally as in the East (i.e., "60 Minutes" airs at 7 p.m. Pacific time).

Network shows come with several minutes of commercial time both within and between programs that are sold by the network. The local station is then able to sell an additional one to three minutes of commercial time in the hour to local or regional advertisers, depending on the daypart. Historically, local commercials always had to appear in the commercials that aired between programs, but that rule has been relaxed, allowing local or regional advertising within the program too. The research findings have been mixed on the relative effectiveness of ads appearing between or within programs. The local station also decides what to air when it is not showing network programs. This might include locally produced shows, such as local news or current affairs programs, or programs purchased from independent producers, known as syndicated programming (see below).

Stations not affiliated with a network are known as *independents*. Today, there are only 88 stations in the U.S. who are not affiliated with any broadcast network. Several hundred others have part-time affiliations with a smaller network (primarily CW). Most of these stations broadcast on the lower-frequency, locally based UHF signal. Each one decides which programs to air throughout the broadcast day, and is responsible for selling its own commercial time.

Syndication

One of the major sources of programs for independent stations is syndicated programming. Here, an individual program (or package of several programs) is sold on a station-by-station basis, regardless of that station's affiliation. It may be of any type or length. There are two main types—original shows, and off-network fare. The former are filled with game shows, such as *Wheel of Fortune*, and talk shows such as *Oprah* or *Ellen*. They are sold either by the program's producers or by syndication companies such as Viacom's King World that puts together packages of properties. The distinction between syndication and network shows is that syndicated programs can air at different times in different markets as well as on different networks. This leads to syndicated shows having to be "cleared" by each local station that chooses to buy them. The clearance figure refers to the percentage of markets across the country that can view that particular show. So, for example, if a syndicated talk show is "cleared" in 70 percent of the U.S., it means that broadcast TV stations seen by 70 percent of all TV viewers have purchased that program. Syndication clearances generally range anywhere from 70 percent to 99 percent. It is worth noting, too, that some network programs do not have total (100 percent) clearance because an affiliate station may refuse to air them, or will put them on at a different time than the rest of the network. For example, early on in its airing, ABC's police drama, *NYPD Blue*, received good ratings and won numerous awards, but could still not be seen by viewers of the ABC affiliates in several Texas markets because they felt the program was too offensive. That state also had several network affiliates who would not air the broadcast premiere showing of Steven Spielberg's graphic war

Exhibit 4.4 Media Company Ownership

Rank	Company Name	Net Media Revenue	TV	Print	Cable/Satellite	Internet	Radio	Outdoor	Cinema	Other
1	Time Warner	35.64 billion	Turner Broadcast System, Home Box Office, CW Network	Time Inc. magazines, Southern Progress Corp, Time4Media	Time Warner Cable	America Online			Warner Brothers, New Line Cinema	
2	Comcast Corp.	26.94 billion	Golf Channel, Outdoor Life, E! Networks, Versus, Style Network, G4, AZN Television		Comcast Cable					
3	Walt Disney Co.	17.49 billion	Disney Media Networks (ABC TV, ESPN, Disney Channel, ABC Family, SoapNet, Toon Disney), A&E, Lifetime	Buena Vista Magazines (FamilyFun, Disney Adventures, Wondertime), US Weekly, ESPN The Magazine			ESPN Radio, Radio Disney		Walt Disney Studios	Disney Stores, Disney Theme Parks, Baby Einstein, Disney Cruise Lines
4	News Corp.	15.7 billion	Fox Broadcasting, MyNetworkTV, Fox Cable Networks (Fox Sports, FX, Fox News, Speed Channel, Fox Soccer Channel), National Geographic	New York Post, Wall Street Journal, News America Marketing, Weekly Standard, TV Guide					20th Century Fox, Fox Searchlight	HarperCollins Publishers
5	DirecTV Group	13.74 billion			DirecTV					
6	NBC Universal	12.16 billion	NBC TV, Telemundo, NBCU Cable (USA Network, CNBC, SciFi, Bravo, MSNBC), Ion Media Networks			iVillage			Universal Studios	Universal Studio Theme Parks

#	Company	Revenue						
7	CBS Corp	12.1 billion	CBS TV, CW Network, Showtime, CSTV			Westwood One, CBS Radio	CBS Outdoor	Paramount Pictures
8	Cox Enterprises	10.39 billion	Cox TV stations	Cox Newspapers		Cox Radio		Cox Auto Trader
9	EchoStar Communications Group	9.46 billion			DISH Network			
10	Viacom	8.44 billion	MTV Networks, BET Networks	Advance Publications (Conde Nast, Advance Newspapers, Parade, American City Business Journals)	Bright House Networks			Paramount Pictures

Source: Advertising Age, 12.26.08.

Note: As this book went to press, Comcast made a bid to buy NBC Universal. At this time, the deal is still undergoing legal scrutiny.

movie, *Saving Private Ryan*, because they deemed it too explicit for network television.

The goal of many network programs is to produce enough episodes to go into the syndicated marketplace (usually 100 episodes). This is known as off-network programming, and helps fill up the hours of airtime that stations have when network shows aren't running. Programs that have been popular on the networks can continue to air for many years in syndication. Hits from the 1970s and 1980s, such as *MASH, Cheers*, and *Cosby* can still be seen on TV during the early evening or late night hours in syndication. Today, there are about 1,055 hours of syndicated programming produced each year for 153 different programs. Exhibit 4.5 shows the top programs in syndication.

Spot Television

Spot television is another way to purchase television time. Here, instead of contracting with the network to distribute a commercial to all of that network's affiliate stations across the country, an advertiser can pick and choose which programs and stations to use, placing the message in various "spots" across the country. As noted above, fewer than 100 of all TV stations are not affiliated with a network, a number that will continue to diminish as networks (and their multimedia conglomerate owners) buy up independents as regulation is relaxed on station ownership. The spot TV buy could be as small as a single station in one market, to a couple of hundred stations across a region. While the actual cost of placing spots on local stations is lower than a total network buy, once you start including a large number of markets it can become quite expensive.

Spot TV time is sold either by the individual station and/or by station representative firms, or *rep firms*. These firms put together packages of

Exhibit 4.5 Top 10 Syndicated TV Programs

Rank	Program	Rating %
1	Friends	9.0
2	Everybody Loves Raymond	7.1
3	Oprah Winfrey Show	7.6
4	Will & Grace	6.9
5	Entertainment Tonight	5.9
6	That 70's Show	5.7
7	Sex and the City	5.5
8	Judge Judy	5.5
9	Seinfeld	5.2
10	Malcolm in the Middle	5.2

Source: Adage.com, 2009.

stations, known as *unwired networks* (because they are not physically linked together, or wired). Rep firms can usually customize buys, allowing the buyers to pick only those stations in which they are interested in a given number of markets.

Cable Television

Cable television is sometimes thought of as a newer way to distribute programs and commercials, but in fact it has existed as a means of conveying television signals since 1948. Because it does not depend on over-the-air signals, but comes into the home via wires laid underground (or sometimes on poles on the street), reception is much clearer in many areas. That was the original reason behind its growth—so that people in Eugene, Oregon, or Lancaster, Pennsylvania could receive the signals of the broadcast networks more clearly. While the broadcast networks distribute their programs from a central location to each of their affiliates, cable programs are sent via satellite from the cable network to individual cable operators (franchises) within each market, who then distribute the signals to the subscribers' homes. There are more than 10,000 separate cable systems operating today, although the majority belongs to one of the large Multiple System Operators (MSOs) that have cable systems in numerous markets. In 2008, the top two players were Comcast and Time Warner. Together, these two operators serve 70 percent of all cable viewers in the country.

Another difference between broadcast TV and cable TV, from the consumers' standpoint, is that they must pay a monthly subscription fee to receive cable service. The average monthly cost of cable in 2008 was about $80. For an additional monthly fee, consumers can receive one or more of the pay cable networks, such as Home Box Office (HBO), Showtime, or Cinemax, which do not show any advertising at all.

Cable TV is made up of a wide variety of different networks, many of which specialize in certain kinds of programs or appeal to certain types of people. This was originally called *narrowcasting*, in contrast to the more diverse or broad-based programming found on broadcast TV. Cable News Network (CNN) shows 24 hours of news and information programming, while ESPN airs sports all the time and Comedy Central has 24 hours of comedy. There are several cable networks, such as USA Network and TBS, which are more similar to the broadcast networks in their programming, airing a variety of different types of shows, from adventures to situation comedies to movies and dramas. In recent years, most of the cable networks began producing their own original programming, rather than simply rebroadcasting old TV shows or movies that had already aired. Today, it is not uncommon for some of these "originals" to garner audiences that are not that much smaller than those for broadcast shows and, at times, the highest-rated cable programs are larger than many on broadcast TV. In the week of June 22, 2009, for example, the top two programs on cable TV, Discovery Network's *Jon & Kate Plus 8* and the *BET Awards Show* each generated higher ratings than any of the top ten programs on broadcast TV.[2]

Exhibit 4.6 describes the biggest cable networks currently available, together with the number of subscribers to each one. The number of networks available varies by system. In recent years, most cable companies have spent large sums of money upgrading their physical plant to provide digital cable services which allow them to offer hundreds of different channels, rather than the 50–100 that were most common in the 1980s and 1990s. Exhibit 4.7 shows how the number of stations and channels available to viewers has increased over the past 25 years.

The development of cable TV as an advertising medium began in the early 1980s and has grown steadily ever since. Today, more than $26 billion of total TV advertising dollars go to cable television, representing nearly one-third of the total amount advertisers spend in television. Most of cable's ad dollars are purchased on a national basis, although the medium has been growing rapidly at the local level too. If you manage a local restaurant or a bank, you can run your commercials throughout the area, or can confine your messages to a particular cable system's area. National advertisers can use local cable, customizing their messages down to the neighborhood (system) level.

Advertisers can also purchase time on several systems at once by going

Exhibit 4.6 Top 15 Cable Networks and Subscribers

Rank	Network	Subscribers (000)
1	Discovery	98,000
2	TNT (Turner Network Television)	98,000
3	ESPN	97,800
4	CNN	97,500
5	USA Network	97,500
6	Lifetime Television	97,300
7	Nickelodeon	97,300
8	TBS	97,300
9	The Weather Channel	97,300
10	The Learning Channel	97,300
11	ABC Family	97,000
12	ESPN2	97,000
13	C-SPAN	96,500
14	HGTV	96,500
15	Food Network	96,300
15=	MTV	96300

Source: Kagan Research, LLC, as reported by NCTA, 2008.

Exhibit 4.7 Number of Channels and Stations Received

Number of Stations:	0–14	15–19	20–29	30+	Average number of stations per household
1985	78%	18%	4%	0%	11.0
1995	65%	25%	9%	1%	13.0
2005	48%	22%	26%	4%	16.3
2008	42%	21%	28%	9%	17.7
Number of channels:	0–14	15–19	20–29	30+	Average number of channels per household
1985	50%	15%	16%	19%	18.8
1995	17%	9%	6%	68%	41.1
2005	5%	4%	7%	84%	96.4
2008	5%	2%	4%	88%	130.1

Source: Nielsen Media Research 2008.

through a central sales office, known as an *interconnect*. This is similar to a rep firm—you select the cable systems on which your ad will appear. Most interconnects operate on a metropolitan or regional basis, such as Greater Chicago, or the Bay Area.

As noted in Chapter 3, advertisers are starting to test sending different ads to individual households, depending on the characteristics of each home. This practice, known as *addressable advertising*, allows companies making dog food, for example, to send ads only to homes known to have a dog, while makers of diapers can deliver ads just to the households with infants and toddlers. Tests conducted by Comcast Cable and Starcom Mediavest Group in 2007 and 2008 indicated that this type of advertising was not only more effective, by delivering more relevant ads to viewers in those homes, but also potentially far more efficient. As this technology is deployed in larger numbers, it is not hard to imagine a time when advertisers will only have to pay to send ads to homes they care about, rather than having to bear the cost of sending ads to all households. In this way, television can become a far more targeted, less "mass" medium.

Satellite Television

Although listed here as a type of television, satellite TV is more of a means of distribution. From being a way for rural inhabitants to receive any kind of signal via large C-band dishes, today's far smaller satellite dishes can be seen perched on the outside of houses all across the country, and are as common in urban markets as rural or suburban. By delivering TV signals directly from the satellite and eliminating the cables that have to be laid under the ground or above ground on poles, satellite services are able to offer a far larger number of channels to viewers. There are two major satellite providers: Dish Network (owned by EchoStar) and DirecTV network. About 25 percent of the country now receives television via satellite (31 million homes), and the battle between that form of distribution and cable is increasingly fierce. Without much of the high cost of transmission incurred by cable, satellite providers have been far quicker in offering new or high technology services to customers, such as two-way interaction with the TV set and the functionality of digital video recorders (see below).

Television Becomes Video

The development of new forms of television began in the early 1990s, but it was not until the latter part of that decade that technology began to catch up with the pipe dreams of the inventors. One of the first to be available was *video on demand* (VOD). Here, several channels are allocated to special programs, such as movies or sporting events, purchased by the cable subscriber on an individual basis. They may cost as little as a few dollars, or as much as $100 for a special boxing match, for example. In order to be able to receive this form of programming, the cable linking the television to the cable system operator must be two-way, or *addressable*, allowing the operator to deliver the program to individual households on demand. At present, more than half of all homes are VOD-enabled, allowing viewers to order up any program that they want to watch, at any time. While its availability has become quite widespread (about 35 percent of all homes), the number of people using it remains fairly small, in large part due to the lack of "content," or programming that people want to buy. It is something of a chicken-and-egg situation. Programmers or cable operators do not want to invest heavily to create programs if there are not enough people willing to pay for it, but until there is a sufficient variety of good programs available, people will not want to buy it.

VOD's expansion has occurred largely due to the growth of digital cable, which is now in about 37 million homes. All of the major cable system operators have been rapidly upgrading their systems in recent years, seeing great potential in enhancing their revenues not only by offering more channels to viewers, but also by selling numerous ancillary services, from Internet access through the TV set to special channels featuring local news and weather to phone services. With some of these enhancements, for example, viewers can call up sports statistics as an overlay on the screen while viewing a football or baseball game.

Another way that television has been significantly altered is through the video recorder. The introduction of digital video recorders (DVRs) at the tail end of the 1990s promised to revolutionize the way people watched

TV and, as a result, the advertising business for that medium. DVRs, now in about 32 percent of all U.S. households, allow people to program the device to find programs to record on a regular basis either by title (all new episodes of *CSI*, for example), or by actor/director (find anything with Brad Pitt). What happens as a result is the official program schedule evaporates, and every consumer becomes his or her own program scheduler, timeshifting to watch whatever programs they want, whenever they choose. More importantly for advertisers, DVRs let viewers fast forward through most, if not all, commercials. Statistics from TiVo, one of the more advanced forms of DVRs, show that during prime time programming on the broadcast networks, viewers are skipping about 60 percent of the commercials when they watch in this "timeshifted" mode.

The implications for advertising are potentially huge. As we will see in Chapter 8, television is planned to a large extent based on program dayparts. What happens when there is no such thing as "primetime" television anymore? And what if the viewership of a program no longer occurs simultaneously because large numbers of people are recording the program for viewing at a later date? What should the program rating be based upon? There has been much deliberation in the industry over this question, resulting in the "official" national rating now being based on "Commercial + 3 Days" or "C3"—that is, the audience for those watching the average commercial in the program as it airs, plus any viewership of that program in the 72 hours following the original telecast.

The use of the TV to connect to the Internet, and the computer to view television, has been expanding quite rapidly, although the two devices are far from interchangeable. TV viewing remains, by and large, a more passive, "lean back" experience, in contrast to the active involvement required of the "lean forward" computer activity. Nevertheless, we are likely to continue to see new attempts to somehow merge the two media in the future, with more Internet functions (such as searching or pop-up ads) appearing on the TV screen, and more TV offerings (programs and TV commercials) migrating to the small screen. All of the major TV networks now make either segments or whole programs available on their websites for viewing via the Web, where an estimated 140 million people watched programs in 2008. When consumers choose to watch them there, it is primarily to catch up on missed episodes or prior seasons, or to take advantage of the convenience of the "anytime, anywhere" viewing. For advertisers, the online video experience is almost wholly positive, with results from studies undertaken on these programs showing upwards of 80 percent ad recall among consumers watching TV shows on the Web. In addition to going online to watch TV programs, viewers are also consuming large quantities of short-form programming, primarily clips on sites such as YouTube. This form of online video, sometimes referred to as user-generated content, or UGC, is particularly popular with teens and young adults. More is covered on this in the Internet section later in this chapter.

Another significant shift in the use of television has been taking place on the advertising side with the growth and development of brand integration (also referred to as product placement or embedded advertising). Here, advertisers pay the program producer to put their brands into the storylines or content of TV shows. This began back in 2001, when contestants on the reality show *Survivor* were shown happily consuming cans of Pepsi's Mountain Dew. Sometimes the product is overtly written into the script, such as the challenges on *The Apprentice* to sell a product such as Dove soap or create a marketing campaign for Pontiac's G6. In 2008, there was even talk of airing a new program called "Jingles" where the purpose of the show was to have people compete to write commercial jingles. The success of a brand placement is not guaranteed. Three brands were placed in the hugely popular show *American Idol*: Coca-Cola, Ford, and Cingular (then AT&T). While consumers readily accepted and remembered the soft drink (consumed by the judges) and the phone company (linked to the text messages they sent in), there was no clear connection with a vehicle. As a result, Ford's brand equity actually declined during its time on the program.[3] A research analysis to assess placement techniques, prevalence, and trends showed that this is going to become an increasingly important area for marketers, and for consumer researchers to understand more about how it works.[4]

Of course, placement is nothing new. It was how commercial TV got started, with the product sponsorship of the Texaco Star Theater or daytime dramas brought to you by Tide and Dreft (i.e., soap operas).[5] In 2007, on the top ten broadcast shows alone, it is estimated there were an estimated 26,000 product placements[6]. The difference between integration and placement is that in the latter, the product appears more or less as a "prop," such as a character being seen to open a box of General Mills' Wheaties cereal rather than Brand X. Another example of integration was for Head and Shoulders shampoo, which ran a six-week campaign inviting consumers to try the "mystery brand." After four weeks, TV ads told them to tune in to the daytime talk show *Ellen*, where the host, Ellen De Generis, revealed what the brand was.

One of the more prominent efforts at paid product integration occurred in September 2004, when GM gave away its newly launched Pontiac G6 vehicles to every member of the studio audience in Oprah Winfrey's daytime talk show. In keeping with the theme of the program to fulfill people's "wildest dreams," Oprah gave away 276 vehicles, each of which had an estimated value of $28,400. The event generated enormous publicity for the company, most of it favorable, and Pontiac registered a record number of visits to its website in the days following the show.[7] In another case, Burger King paid between $2 million and $3.5 million to appear in the hit TV show *The Apprentice*, with the contestants charged to run a franchise restaurant in New York while a new sandwich was being launched. That allowed viewers to see how the restaurant really worked, and to get lots of exposure to the new product. In the weeks following the episode appearing, sales of that sandwich rose to 1.2 million, 20 percent higher than expectations. At the same time, the promotion was featured on the BK website, generating 600,000 visits to find out more and enter a sweepstakes.[8] A report by the Federal Communications Commission in 2008 noted that the popular Fox program *American Idol* had a stunning 3,291 product placements during just the first three months of that year! While no new legislation exists specifically for this newer type of TV advertising, questions are being asked about how the public should be informed when a product has been placed directly in a program, or not.

For some companies, their advertising can become a program. That is, they purchase time on local TV stations or, more often, on cable networks, for direct response TV (DRTV). This time could be anywhere from a two minute "infomercial" to a 30-minute program. What the consumer sees is an informational message, with an immediate opportunity to purchase (usually via telephone). The direct-to-consumer approach works well for certain types of marketers, and has typically been used by smaller or independent companies offering unusual products, such as the Snuggie "blanket" or Nordictrack fitness equipment. The media rates can be up to 75 percent lower than the cost of buying "regular" commercial time. Bigger companies occasionally use DRTV, to good effect. Johnson & Johnson's Neutrogena skincare line launched SkinID products via DRTV. One of the biggest benefits of this approach is that it is instantly measurable, whether through phone calls logged and products sold, or visits to the website.[9]

Benefits of Television to Advertisers

Whichever type of television advertising you choose, you will enjoy a number of benefits unavailable from any other media. Among these benefits, television's ability to imitate real-life situations, its pervasiveness, and its broad reach are most noteworthy.

True to Life

The most obvious advantage of television advertising is the opportunity to use *sight, sound, color,* and *motion* in commercials. This form of advertising is generally considered the most lifelike, re-creating scenes and showing people in situations with which we can all identify. That does not mean we don't see cartoons or animated commercials, or fantasies on the screen; today's electronic wizardry lets TV ads show us everything imaginable. But of all the media available, TV comes closest to showing us products in our everyday lives. This is not only important for package goods advertisers—firms such as Kellogg's Anheuser-Busch, or Unilever, who are able to show us what their products look like and how they are used or enjoyed—but also for service companies such as Marriott Hotels or American Express, which can offer us ways to use their amenities. As the Internet continues to expand, and bandwidth grows, more TV-like ads have appeared there too. American Express was one of the first advertisers to launch a TV ad (starring comedian Jerry Seinfeld) on the Internet before it appeared on television.

The Most Pervasive Medium

Television advertising is the most pervasive media form available, given that the average American is watching about 133 hours or so of TV every month. Several slogans from TV commercials have entered the mainstream of conversation, such as Bud Light's "Whassup?" or Wisk detergent's infamous "ring around the collar" line. Characters in commercials have also become part of our lives, such as the lonely Maytag repairman, or Tony the Tiger for Kellogg's Frosted Flakes. From time to time, advertising characters are developed further, such as the Geico "cavemen" who starred in their own (ill-fated and short-lived) TV show.

Reaching the Masses

Another important advantage of television from an advertising perspective is the wide *reach* of people it offers at any one time. Even in programs with ratings of eight or ten, you are reaching about nine million individuals! While there is generally a smaller audience for the commercials than for the programs themselves, nevertheless, television remains a truly mass medium. Moreover, by buying time on several different programs shown at different times and/or on different days, it is possible to reach a wide *variety* of individuals. And although each ad appears for a short time (usually 15 or 30 seconds), if it is repeated on several occasions more people are likely to be exposed to it, often more than once. This helps build brand awareness, which in turn may lead to the formation of favorable attitudes or intentions to purchase that brand.

Drawbacks of Television Advertising

Unfortunately, television advertising has unique drawbacks as well as the unique benefits just discussed. Four of the most commonly encountered drawbacks are cost, limited exposure time, cluttered airwaves, and poor placement of ads within or between programs.

Dollars and Sense

Perhaps the biggest disadvantage for advertising on TV, particularly at the national level, is the high cost. The average 30-second during prime time on the six main broadcast networks in fall 2008 cost $130,000, with a wide range from about $30,000 at the low end to $435,000 at the top.[10] Even that cost pales in comparison to television's most expensive ad opportunity. An ad in the 2009 Super Bowl cost about $3,000,000. For many advertisers this is far beyond their budget, leading them to cable or spot TV as cheaper alternatives.

Quick Cuts

Another drawback to this medium is its brief exposure time. Although many ads are seen several times within a short period of time, unless the commercial is particularly inventive or unusual it is likely the viewer will ignore it or be irritated by seeing it after the first few occasions and deliberately try to avoid the message.[11] Controversy remains over just how many times people can be exposed to spots without getting bored or annoyed, a phenomenon referred to as commercial *wearout*. In the future, this drawback may be avoided through *addressable* or *interactive TV*, where viewers receive ads considered more relevant to their needs, and/or select the kinds of messages they are more interested in, finding out more about a specific brand or product in detail. The key here is that this self-selected audience is more interested and involved in the message.

Cluttering the Airwaves

A related factor that is becoming an increasing concern for advertisers is the sheer number of ads appearing on TV. This leads to clutter of spots, again believed to reduce the effectiveness of individual commercials.[12] There is evidence to support this fear. From 1990 to 2008 there was a nearly 300 percent increase in the number of spots shown on primetime network TV. Part of the explanation for this is the increase in the number of TV networks. But another major reason is the growth in the number of shorter-length commercials. For many years, the standard television spot lasted a full minute. Then, in the mid-1960s more and more advertisers started using 30-second commercials, finding them more cost-efficient and no less effective. As costs continued to increase during the 1970s and early 1980s, advertisers tried the same tactic, shifting to even smaller commercial lengths. Today, the 15-second spot accounts for 36 percent of all primetime network TV commercials. The total number of spots aired on English-language broadcast TV in a given month is close to

13,000.[13] Exhibit 4.8 shows the trend in TV ad clutter in Prime Time, while Exhibit 4.9 displays the expansion of 15-second commercials. The result of clutter on consumers is questionable, but research suggests that it hinders the communication, sometimes considerably.[14]

Placing Spots

Another area that has provoked a good deal of discussion is where commercials should be placed for optimal effectiveness. For network TV, you can buy time either within the program (*in-program*) or between two shows (*break*). While some believe there is no difference in viewer attention between these two options, others feel that you are likely to lose more viewers during the breaks than within the program itself. On spot TV, the break position used to be the only timeslot available, though in recent years the "rules" have been relaxed, as commercial breaks have slid a few minutes into the program rather than only at the top or bottom of each hour.

Related to this placement issue is where to position your commercial within the series, or *pod* of spots being shown. Evidence suggests that the first ad to appear will receive the most attention, followed by the last one; those in the middle are likely to suffer from viewers switching channels, not looking at the screen, or leaving the room. The advertiser, however, does not routinely get the choice of where in the pod to air his ad. Some

Exhibit 4.8 Commercial Clutter Trend: Prime Time

	Number	Percent Change (Yr on Yr)
1990	2,059	
1995	3,177	54.3%
2000	4,751	49.5%
2005	5,300	11.6%
2008	5,688	7.3%

Source: Nielsen Media Research 2008.

Exhibit 4.9 Growth of 15-Second Commercials in Prime Time

	1990	1995	2000	2005	2008
:15	36%	34%	35%	35%	36%
:30	62%	64%	62%	58%	57%
:60	1%	1%	2%	5%	5%
Other	1%	1%	1%	2%	2%
	100%	100%	100%	100%	100%

Source: Nielsen Media Research 2008.

advertisers will pay a premium to ensure their ad appears first, but this is not always permitted.

Research on Television

Much of the research literature on television has focused on two key issues: the impact of a life-like message and the effects of program environment. Buchholz and Smith found that the more "involved" consumers are in the medium, the stronger their cognitive responses to ad messages.[15] Kamins et al. examined how TV ads are evaluated depending on the mood created by the program in which the ads appear.[16] Several other research articles are also available.[17]

Radio—The "Everywhere" Medium

Radio is the oldest electronic advertising medium. It first became popular in America in the early 1920s and since that time has managed to hold its own against all other media forms. Although families no longer sit around their radios as they once did to listen to the most popular programs of the day, they still rely on this medium for both information and entertainment. Indeed, almost every home in America has at least one radio, and most have several of them. People listen to the radio, on average, for 2 hours 39 minutes every day, and the medium reaches 71 percent of everyone 12 and older each day (92 percent each week). Most listening (84 percent) occurs between 6 a.m. and 10 a.m. More and more, that listening occurs outside of the home. Almost all cars (95 percent) are fitted with radios now, and people can carry the medium with them wherever they go. About one-third (36 percent) of radio listening occurs in the car, while 39 percent happens at home and 25 percent is at work or elsewhere. Radio accounts for nearly one-third (28 percent) of the estimated time consumers spend each day with major media.[18]

There are more than 14,000 radio stations across the country. Of those, about one-third operate on the AM (Amplitude Modulation) wavelength, while two-thirds are FM, or Frequency Modulation, stations. The primary differences between them are in reception area and audience. AM stations can broadcast over a wider distance, but because the soundwaves are impeded by any kind of obstruction (hills, tall buildings) the sound quality is inferior to FM stations, which broadcast in a narrower listening area but AM tends to be listened to more by older adults, reflecting the fact that more AM stations offer news and talk programs rather than the music formats which dominate the FM wavelength. Radio stations are either commercial, accepting advertising as their chief source of revenue, or non-commercial, funded by public monies and/or audience sponsorships. Commercial stations will, on average, air anywhere from

9 to 20 ads per hour, frequently concentrated in blocks of three minutes or more.

As with television, radio is classified by both daypart and format. The different formats that are available for the advertiser are not defined the same way by the listener. Radio dayparts and formats are shown in Exhibits 4.10 and 4.11.

Today, radio represents a little over 7 percent of all advertising expenditures, with about $18.6 billion spent on the medium in 2008. The two main types of radio advertising are network (national) and spot (local). The way programs and ads are distributed is similar to that of network and spot broadcast TV.

Network Radio

Unlike television, network radio is less important to advertisers than is local radio. It currently receives about 4 percent of all radio dollars and

Exhibit 4.10 Radio Dayparts

Day of Week	Time Period
Monday–Friday	6:00am–10:00am
Monday–Friday	10:00am–3:00pm
Monday–Friday	3:00pm–7:00pm
Monday–Friday	7:00pm–Midnight
Saturday–Sunday	6:00am–Midnight
Monday–Sunday	6:00am–Midnight

Exhibit 4.11 Top Ten Radio Formats

Rank	Format	Number of Stations
1	Country	2,037
2	News/Talk	1,359
3	Latin/Hispanic	721
4	Oldies	720
5	Adult Contemporary	631
6	Sports	553
7	Contemporary Hit Radio (CHR/Top 40)	474
8	Classic Rock	459
9	Adults Standards	372
10	Hot Adult Contemporary (AC)	369
		7,695
	Percent of all commercial radio stations in U.S.	73%

Source: Arbitron, 2009.

reaches about seven out of ten people 12 and older each week. Like TV, however, a message placed on network radio is distributed via satellite to each network's affiliate stations. These stations are paid an annual sum to take, or "clear," the network's programs. Perhaps surprisingly, almost two-thirds of all radio stations are affiliated with one network or another. The kinds of programs they receive from the network may be aired every day, such as the Westwood One newscast, or periodically, such as *Casey Kasem's Weekly Top 40* show. There are presently four major radio networks, each of which has subdivisions based on the programming and the demographic make-up of their listeners. Altogether, there are about 50 different networks. So Westwood CBS Radio News is aimed primarily at listeners from 25 to 54 years old through news radio, while the stations that are part of Crystal Media's Smooth Jazz Network include stations playing that format across the country. Exhibit 4.12 lists the major networks.

From an advertiser's perspective, one key benefit of using network radio is that you can go through a single source to place your ads across a region or across the country. The downside of this form of radio, however, is that you have less flexibility in choosing the stations you wish to be in. If you buy the CBS Spectrum Radio Network, you may get the Number 1 station in Biloxi, Mississippi, but a distant fourth station in Little Rock, Arkansas.

Spot Radio

About 96 percent of radio's advertising dollars are spent in spot markets, where you buy time on individual stations on a market-by-market basis. Here, if you were placing the advertising for Coldwell Banker realtors, you could buy time on individual stations in a market, regardless of which network they belong to, and choose which markets you wished to target. The advantage of purchasing radio in this way is that you can select the exact stations and/or markets in which you wish to

Exhibit 4.12 Radio Networks

American Urban
Citadel
Crystal Media
Dial Global
Premiere
United Stations
Westwood One

Source: Arbitron, 2009

Note: Data are for Monday–Sunday, 6AM–12 Midnight, Persons 12+.

advertise your product. This also allows you to customize the message to each location, so that Home Depot home improvement stores can mention the address or phone number of different locations in each market's ad.

Some stations are linked together only for the purpose of selling advertising time. They constitute an "unwired" network, allowing you to select which stations within the group you wish to use based on your demographic or geographic preferences. Typically, an advertiser buys time through a representative, or rep firm, rather than dealing with every station individually. So if you are trying to target teens with the Nintendo Wii, you could go to a rep firm that offers you stations that do well against that group. Examples of unwired networks include the Wall Street Journal Radio Network, which offers classical music and performs well against adults over 25. Again, for the advertiser, using a network of this kind provides you with a single invoice for all of the stations. But, as with wired network radio, you may end up buying time on less-attractive stations as part of the package deal.

Satellite Radio

In 2001, satellite radio services were introduced to the U.S. marketplace. Two companies, XM Radio and Sirius Radio, each delivered about 100 different channels via national satellites. In 2008, they merged to form Sirius XM. Today, 55 percent of vehicles on the road have satellite radio capability. Consumers need special receivers in order to tune in to these services, and must also pay a monthly subscription (about $10–$15/month) for the privilege. One incentive for them to pay is that about half of the stations air without commercials. Even on those channels that include advertising, the amount will be far less than on regular radio stations—6 minutes per hour, compared to 15–20 minutes on terrestrial stations.

The content offered by satellite radio ranges from niche forms of music to college radio stations that let alumni keep up with their favorite college sports teams to syndicated talk show hosts such as Howard Stern or Rush Limbaugh or Oprah Winfrey. This type of radio resembles cable TV, in that there are so many channels, they can afford to be highly specialized (e.g., a Nascar channel, several baseball channels, or a channel offering bluegrass music). The satellite radio company has deals with the major U.S. auto manufacturers, who have built satellite radio capability into more and more of their models and are offering it as a standard piece of equipment in their luxury vehicles.

As of mid-2009, about 4 percent of adults 18+ were subscribing to a satellite radio service. The jury remains out, however, as to whether consumers will be willing to pay for something they are used to getting for free. While they "learned" to do so for television back in the 1980s, the perceived value of the radio medium versus television may not be as high among most radio listeners.

Streaming Audio

As the Internet develops further, more and more people are listening to the radio via their computers through a technology generally known as streaming audio. Radio signals are digitized, and then sent through the Internet. Many traditional, land-based stations offer simultaneous signals on the Web, while other stations have been created solely online. While still accounting for a small proportion of total listening, about 69 million people age 12 and older listen to the radio online each month (42 million each week), and streamed audio accounts for up to 15 percent of some station's listenership now. The growth is due to two factors—more online listening in the workplace, and greater usage of streamed audio via handheld devices (such as iPhones). One problem for the sector is that advertisers typically think of radio as a local medium, but streaming audio is currently sold nationally. Another hindrance is lack of ongoing audience measurement, but that is likely to change as the segment grows.[19]

Benefits of Radio to Advertisers

As an advertiser, you cannot afford to ignore the many benefits of radio advertising. Although it does not offer the visual power of television advertising, it does provide the opportunity to reach targeted audiences frequently, at a reasonable cost. These and other benefits of this medium are discussed below.

Local Appeal

As we mentioned earlier, most advertising dollars in radio are spent at the local or regional level rather than on the networks. Radio is therefore listened to primarily as a local medium, allowing you the opportunity to tie in to local events, news, or celebrities.

Reaching the Right Audience

Because of the way radio stations are formatted, the medium provides you with targeted, specific audiences. If you run a local health club, you can reach women 25 to 54 by placing your message on light rock stations. Or, as the owner of a religious bookstore, you can promote your store by advertising on the local religious radio station. Radio also offers good opportunities for reaching ethnic groups. In areas with sizable Black or Hispanic populations, you are likely to find at least one station which appeals to each of these minorities. It will generally have a very loyal following. For a baby-clothing manufacturer, for example, advertising to Hispanics may turn out to be very profitable because they tend to have larger families than non-Hispanic households. And in 2005, radio audience measurement company Arbitron released its first-ever survey results of Chinese listeners in both New York and Los Angeles. The results showed that 56 percent of all listening done by these consumers was to Chinese language radio.

Imagery Transfer

For many advertisers, radio is seen as a secondary medium, used in conjunction with a major print or television campaign. The good news here is that research has shown the power of radio ads to create a visual image in listeners' minds from the TV commercials they have seen for that same brand[20]. This process, known as imagery transfer, gives radio ads far more impact than the auditory stimulus alone and, therefore, greater potential influence on consumer response.

Keeping Costs Down

Compared with television, radio is an extremely inexpensive ad medium. A 30-second spot in prime time on a broadcast TV network may run as high as $500,000, while the price for that same length commercial on a local radio station will be closer to $15,000. Of course, these costs are linked to the number of people you will be reaching.

Building Frequency

With a TV buy, you are usually looking for high reach numbers. In order to gain frequency, you need either a very large budget or inexpensive dayparts. On radio, however, because the costs are so low, it makes sense to buy a lot of time and build up frequency against your target audience. It also makes sense to do this for strategic reasons; people tend to listen to a particular station for a fairly brief period of time, so you want to ensure you reach them while they are listening. You should keep in mind that listening habits are not seasonal, so frequency can be built up year-round.

Radio and Purchasing

Research shows that the time between media exposure and purchase is shorter for radio than for any other traditional medium, as shown in

Exhibit 4.13. This means that your potential consumers may well be listening while they are making their purchase decisions.

A study undertaken by the Radio Advertising Lab (RAL) on behalf of the Radio Advertising Bureau, in 2005 found that in a controlled test, consumers exposed to radio ads along with TV were more likely to buy the advertised product than those who were only exposed to an equivalent amount of TV ads.[21]

Flexible Messages

Compared to the high production costs and long lead times of television, radio is extremely flexible. If your ad is read live on the air, as is often the case, you can change the message at very short notice without much difficulty. You can vary the message for different dayparts or station formats, perhaps using different music backgrounds depending on the type of music played on that station. Radio also offers the flexibility of tie-ins to local retailers or other promotional opportunities, such as local contests or events.

Drawbacks of Radio Advertising

In addition to the numerous benefits of radio advertising, there are a few drawbacks to keep in mind, as well. Each of these can be seen as a challenge; most can be overcome with some planning and creativity.

In the Background

When we listen to the radio, we are usually doing something else at the same time, making it a background medium. Ads on radio must therefore work a lot harder to grab—and keep—our attention.

Exhibit 4.13 Time Between Media Exposure and Purchase

	Percent exposed to medium within an hour of purchase
Radio	59%
Outdoor	27%
TV	20%
Magazine	11%
Newspapers	10%

Source: Radio Advertising Bureau, 2001.

Sound Only

Radio can only offer sound, rather than the sight and motion of television. However, the medium can still be used to great effect because it offers the possibility of inspiring the listener's imagination. You can hear the waves crashing against rocks, or breaking glass, or party chatter, and conjure up images in your mind of what the scene looks like. Radio advertisements also tend to feature humor fairly often both as a way to get attention and because the audience is less likely to be distracted by any visuals and can listen to the words. And as noted above, if used in conjunction with similar TV commercials, listeners will often transfer the TV images to the radio spot.

Short Message Life

Because we listen to radio in the background, for the most part, ads on this medium have a very short message life. Like TV, and unlike newspapers and magazines, once the ad has aired, the opportunity for exposure has disappeared. This makes it all the more critical to grab the audience's attention right away with a message that is relevant, involving, and interesting.

Fragmentation

One of the drawbacks for radio is the fragmentation of the medium. We no longer just have "rock" stations, but "active rock," "classic rock," and "album-oriented rock" formats, among others. Each one appeals to slightly different kinds of people so if you wanted to reach them all, you would have to buy each type of rock station in a market. Audience shares, particularly in major markets, may be very small, which makes it harder to use the medium as a reach vehicle.

Research on Radio

Although radio is considered a "second cousin" to television in the realm of electronic ad media, research has been done to compare the two forms. In addition, the power of sound, and of music in particular, has been studied to see how that impacts radio ad effectiveness. Legal issues in the radio business are noted here, because the legal policies adopted by radio stations as far as which ads are accepted or not have a direct impact on the kinds of radio commercials that are broadcast.[22]

In 2003, the radio industry started to fund significant research studies under the umbrella of the Radio Advertising Lab, or RAL. This consortium of advertisers, agencies and radio station groups helped fund and design several major studies that examined the impact of radio advertising on consumers. Its first work looked at radio's psychological role in consumers' lives. Its study, "Personal Relevance, Personal Connections," found that radio listening is considered by people to be a personal and emotion-driven experience. They listen for personal gratification more so than for entertainment or pure information. As noted earlier in this section, another study looked at the benefits of synergistically mixing radio ads with newspaper or TV ads. It exposed consumers to two radio ads or one TV + two radio ads, and did the same substituting newspaper for TV. What they found was radio ads alone performed better than either the single exposure to TV or newspapers (in terms of brand recall). When radio was used together with TV, brand awareness and brand recall were higher than either medium alone.[23]

In an online research study that compared two Internet ads with one Internet and one radio spot for the same brand, the Radio Ad Lab program found that combining the two media produced far more effect on consumers than simply using two web ads. Unaided brand recall was four times greater for the Internet–Radio combination, while most brands saw greater impact also for purchase intent and emotional connection.

Another study looked at the emotional power of radio ads compared to those on TV. This project used electromyography—the measurement of facial muscles—while consumers were exposed to program content that included either radio or TV ads for the same brands. Negative and positive emotions were measured and found to be equivalent across media, in contrast to conventional wisdom that would suggest TV is a far more powerful emotional indicator.

In a follow-up to that study, consumers' responses to the radio ads were examined in greater detail to determine what factors lead to greater impact for the commercials. Key elements were identified: a strong start to the spot, the inclusion of words (not just music or sound), strong branding for the advertiser, and maintaining listener interest throughout the spot.

All the News That's Fit to Print—Newspaper Advertising

Newspapers are one of the oldest media forms in this country and perhaps one of the most troubled in the early part of the 21st century. They were also one of the earliest media to accept advertising. In fact, the first advertising agencies were established to handle the purchase of space in this medium. Some of the earliest ads were for "medicinal" remedies, such as Lydia Pinkham's Compound.

In contrast to many other countries that have national newspapers, in the U.S., the majority of newspapers are written for and distributed to a primarily local audience. As a result, most of the advertising is placed on a market-by-market basis. You can also choose which section of the paper to appear in, such as news (local, national or international), sports, entertainment, business, fashion, food, home, and travel, among others.

There are currently 2,329 newspapers published in the U.S. This figure includes both weekday and Sunday editions (1,422 and 907 respectively). That number has remained relatively stable over time. In 1970, for example, there were 2,334 papers published. Newspaper audiences are measured in terms of *circulation*, or the number of people who subscribe to or purchase the newspaper. Exhibit 4.14 shows the top ten papers across the country based on their circulation.

The past decade has witnessed a decline in the percentage of the adult population that says they read a paper daily. Currently, about 50 percent claim they do so, in contrast to the 78 percent who read a paper back in 1970. What is perhaps more worrying for the newspaper industry is that the readership figure is lower among younger people, who constitute the medium's future readers (among 18 to 24 year olds, only 34 percent read a daily paper, although 61 percent do so during an average week). Several papers have introduced daily low-priced tabloid papers to entice younger people to develop a newspaper reading habit. The *Chicago Tribune*'s *Red Eye*, for example, sells about 90,000 copies of its daily tabloid, primarily to readers under 40, at the low cost of $0.50. Another way to capture readership of younger audiences is on the Web; two-thirds (65 percent) of 18 to 34 year olds visit a newspaper website each week.[24]

Circulation, especially at large newspapers, continues to decline. From March to September 2008, the total number of readers for the country's 507 measured weekday papers fell about 5 percent, on top of a 3 percent decline in the six months prior to that. Among the top 25 daily papers in 1990, nearly all have seen their circulation fall. The *Los Angeles Times*

Exhibit 4.14 Top 10 Newspapers by Circulation

Rank	Newspaper	Circulation (000)
1	USA Today	2293.1
2	Wall Street Journal	2011.9
3	New York Times	1037.8
4	Los Angeles Times	794.7
5	New York Daily News	681.4
6	New York Post	667.1
7	Washington Post	635.1
8	Chicago Tribune	559.4
9	Houston Chronicle	502.6
10	Newsday	387.5

Source: Audit Bureau of Circulations, as reported in *Editor & Publisher*, 3.1.2008. Data for 6 months ending September 2007.

has experienced a 38 percent drop in papers sold while the *Minneapolis Star-Tribune* fall is 21 percent.[25]

Another problem the industry faces is the demise of the two-newspaper town. Most large cities used to have at least two competing newspapers; today, due to the high costs of running a newspaper, that is the exception rather than the rule. Only in the largest cities (New York, Los Angeles, Chicago) are there still two or three daily papers. This not only harms the newspaper industry, it is not particularly good news for advertisers either. Without competition, the paper can set its advertising rates wherever it wants them, as long as it can still compete with other media alternatives.

As major cities have dropped competing papers, as was seen in Seattle and Denver in 2009, some of the readership has moved to suburban or weekly newspapers. The growth here is not too surprising, given population shifts from city to suburb in the past few decades. The focus of these titles is far more local, writing about high school sports scores or local ordinances rather than national or regional news. For advertisers, it offers the opportunity to bring the message down to the truly local level. National advertisers such as Gap Stores can announce the opening of a new store in Arlington Heights, Illinois, in the *Arlington Heights Post*, instead of a zoned or regional edition of the *Chicago Tribune*.

Perhaps the only bright spot for newspapers is growth in their online readership. In 2008, an estimated 73 million people visited a newspaper online per month. They spent an average of 45 minutes per month on such a site. Overall, 42 percent of Internet users visit a newspaper website in an average month. The problem remains how to make money from that audience, since most papers do not charge readers anything for the online content, but cannot generate sufficient ad revenue to make up the lost subscription money.[26] But realizing the potential of digital assets, several newspaper companies have created or purchased web-related divisions or companies. Perhaps the biggest is News Corporation (owner of *The London Times, The New York Daily News*, and *Newsday*) which bought leading social network site, MySpace, in 2008. Another big publisher, Gannett Corporation, has focused its efforts on start-up ventures such as Pointroll (technology behind rich media ads), ShopLocal (newspaper inserts online), and MomsLikeMe (local parenting sites around the country). One of the biggest classified websites, Careerbuilder, has three of its four primary owners from the newspaper industry (Gannett, Tribune, and McClatchey, along with Microsoft).[27]

Newspaper Advertising Revenue

The largest part of newspaper advertising revenue (45 percent) comes from retailers. This includes large companies, such as major national department stores like JC Penney and Nordstrom, to regional banks such as National City or First National, down to Joe's shoe repair shop around the corner. Second in importance as far as newspaper ad revenues are concerned is classified advertising (40 percent). The most important classified sections are for real estate and automotive, which together account for the majority of classified ad dollars.

The third type of newspaper advertising is that which is placed on a national basis so that it appears in all (or most) papers across the country. This type of advertising represents only 17 percent of total advertising revenues for the medium, despite the efforts of many newspapers to position themselves as valuable national vehicles in the face of increased competition with other local media, such as spot TV and radio, regional magazines, or billboards. The main problem that advertisers have with using newspapers on a national basis is the considerable premium that it costs to run their ads in all markets. Most are reluctant to pay that premium, which can cost up to 75 percent more than a local or regional ad.[28]

Newspapers also offer a medium within a medium, in the form of *freestanding inserts*, or FSIs. These are pre-printed sheets that are usually distributed within the Sunday paper. Most of them carry coupons. On Sunday, too, most newspapers carry a special magazine supplement, either produced by the paper itself or coming from one of the nationally syndicated Sunday supplements, *Parade* and *USA Weekend*.

At one point it seemed that newspaper classified advertising would be greatly diminished by the Internet. Automotive and real estate classified ad sites were very popular at first, and threatened to take revenues from the printed newspapers. It did not take long for newspapers to set up their own Internet-based advertising sites, either as part of their own individual newspaper sites (bostonglobe.com) or, as noted above, in concert with other newspapers (Careerbuilder.com, FrontDoor.com). Today, about 1,500 North American newspapers have websites, while 5,000 papers do so globally.

Not only are newspapers competing with the Web for readers, they are also losing their premiere position as the carrier of coupons. In addition to FSIs, many papers carry coupons in the ads that they print, but consumers can now seek out coupons on specific websites (e.g., coupons.com or fatwallet.com), while some people are starting to sign up to receive coupons via their mobile phones. In each case, they can specify or request the categories or brands for which they wish to receive the coupon.[29]

Another issue that newspaper advertisers are increasingly trying to deal with is the "sacred" line between the advertising and editorial departments. General Motors, for example, pulled its advertising from the *Los Angeles Times* newspaper after a journalist for the paper wrote a critical review about the automaker's Pontiac G6 vehicle. GM claimed there were mistakes in the article.[30] This may be the start of a trend, with major advertisers attempting to put clauses in their contracts that overtly state they will pull their ads if unfavorable editorial content appears. This is a slippery slope, potentially leading to a blurring of the "church" and "state" separation of editorial and advertising departments.

Benefits of Newspapers to Advertisers

As Exhibit 4.14 illustrated, the top ten newspapers in the U.S. reach nearly ten million consumers every day. Add to that the circulations of the other, smaller, newspapers in the country, and you'll begin to see just what kind of exposure is possible with newspaper advertisements. But, in addition to reach, newspapers offer advertisers a number of important benefits which are discussed below.

Timeliness

During the stock market crash of 2008, ads appeared in many newspapers each day reassuring consumers and stockholders that everything was still all right at their institution. Financial services companies reacted similarly after the terrorist attack on the World Trade Center in 2001. And McDonald's quickly responded in newspaper ads when it discovered that someone at one of its agencies had stolen winning game cards to several of its "instant-win" promotions. The company immediately created newspaper and TV ads to apologize to the public, and then added a new game with daily prizes awarded randomly to customers in the store.[31]

Unlike magazines or even television, newspapers are by their very nature filled with "news." People turn to them for the latest information on products, prices, and availability. The role that newspaper advertisements play in purchase decisions may be critical. A survey found that 79 percent of respondents agreed with the statement that they had "visited retail store or showroom due to newspaper ads." And 46 percent said they preferred to use the medium to receive advertising information, compared to 10 percent for radio and 18 percent for direct mail.[32] Another survey found that more consumers said they turned to newspapers for advertising information than to any other source, with 41 percent citing newspapers versus 21 percent for the Internet (the next most mentioned).[33] In addition, electronic scanner devices in most supermarkets and retail stores are now able to assess the link between advertising and sales more directly and rapidly. Data suggest that newspaper ads can triple the sales volume for items that are advertised at reduced prices.

Desirable Audience

In the battle to attract advertisers, newspapers can offer highly desirable audiences. A newspaper reader is more likely to be better educated, have a higher income and be more involved in upscale activities than non-readers. People with a household income of $75,000 a year or more are more likely to be newspaper readers. Exhibit 4.15 gives a profile of the newspaper audience.

In contrast to other media, readers spend a considerable amount of time with the newspaper, although that varies by age. Older readers (age 65+) spend about one hour a day with the paper, whereas the youngest adults (age 20 to 29) read daily for only 20 minutes[34] (most likely because they are going online for their news). On average about two-thirds (67 percent) of all newspaper pages are actually opened, a figure that depends in part on the number of pages in the issue. In thinner papers (10–32 pages), 78 percent of all pages are opened, but when the paper becomes much bigger (81–204 pages), only 63 percent are opened.

Another consequence of the time readers spend with the paper is that it offers the media specialist more opportunity to provide detailed information. If you are trying to sell a new home equity loan program, you need the space to provide details on the terms of the deal, as well as on bank locations so interested consumers can find you. While you might worry that so much fine print will be boring or encourage page-turning, those people who are in your target audience will probably be interested enough to read through the entire ad (assuming the copy is inviting and attention-getting).

Impact of Editorial

An obvious advantage of newspaper advertising is that you can choose which section of the paper your ad is placed in, putting food ads in the Food Section, or offering investment advice in the Business pages, for example. This effectively narrows your reach to those consumers most likely to be interested in your product or service.

Exhibit 4.15 Profile of The Newspaper Reader

Professional/executive
Graduated college/post graduate
Age 45+
Household income $50,000+
Married
Own home
Northeast region
Lived at present address 5+ years

Source: MRI, 2007.

Local and Regional Possibilities

Although advertisers are reluctant to use newspapers on a national basis, they rely on them heavily for local or regional marketing. If Procter & Gamble wishes to test a new detergent in Peoria, Illinois, it can advertise in the *Peoria Journal Star* and feel confident that the message will only reach those people able to buy the product, thereby creating awareness for the new item. They might also test the effects of advertising on sales this way. For regional operators, such as Friendly Restaurants—located only in the northeastern part of the country—ads can be placed in newspapers in the selected markets where the restaurant is found.

Even within a market, an advertiser can buy space in only those papers being sold in a certain area. The *Chicago Tribune*, for example, offers eight zoned editions of its daily paper within the Chicago area.

Drawbacks of Newspaper Advertising

As with every medium, newspapers have several drawbacks. The three most critical are short issue life, the challenge of grabbing the reader's attention, and the constraints of using a largely black and white medium.

Today or Never

While magazines can often prolong their issue life and reach more people by being passed around or picked up on several occasions, at the end of each day the newspaper is usually discarded. If the reader misses your ad that day, you are not given a second chance. So, although newspapers are available every day, their issue life is very short.

Active Readers

The issue life of the newspaper is closely linked to how people read it. Although more than half of all pages are likely to be opened, it is up to the reader to actively choose what to look at. If your headline doesn't attract Jane Doe's attention, she won't look at it at all; if the copy isn't intriguing and relevant to her, she can simply turn to another article or page. It is therefore crucial that newspaper advertisements get the reader's attention. When people sit in front of the television or listen to the radio, they are generally a "passive" audience with no choice but to attend to the ad (even if fleetingly) or turn off the radio or TV set. Exhibit 4.16 shows how the newspaper advertiser must fight for attention.

Exhibit 4.16 Elements That Get Newspaper Reader's Attention

Colour
Full Page
Photography and illustrations
Product in use
Sale price

Source: Roper Starch Study conducted on behalf of Newspaper Association of America, 2001.

Black and White

In the 1980s, it was rare to find a color ad in a newspaper. Then along came the Gannett Corporation with its national newspaper *USA Today*, which offers full-color capabilities. The quality of newspaper color reproduction has been improving ever since, although it is still a long way from looking as sharp as magazine pages (due primarily to the poorer quality of the paper it is printed on). Even so, newspapers charge a premium for use of color, generally about 17 percent extra for a one-page four-color ad. For many advertisers, particularly those who wish to show "life-like" qualities such as food manufacturers, it remains more effective to use magazine or television ads. Newspapers have become increasingly creative, however, in order to attract advertisers, offering "glow in the dark" or scented ad pages within the paper, or attention-getting features surrounding the paper when it is delivered.

Research on Newspapers

While the newspaper industry, through its trade association, Newspaper Association of America, conducts annual research on the size and strength of the industry, and periodic studies on the medium's effectiveness, academic research has been more limited in recent years. Some studies have been done on the impact of ad size on consumer responses, including work on different promotional formats for the ads.[35]

Magazines—An Explosion of Choice

Although magazines have a long history in the U.S., with the earliest publications appearing in the middle of the eighteenth century, they are also a medium that may be said to have had two very distinct life stages. Originally, most magazines catered to a very general audience, offering a mixture of news, stories, and features aimed either at the total population or, in the case of titles such as *Ladies' Home Journal* and *Good Housekeeping*, at women. The strength of publications such as *Life, Look,* and the *Saturday Evening Post* is reflected in the fact that an ad placed in those magazines in the 1950s would be likely to reach about 60 percent of the total population.

But with the rise of television in the 1950s, general interest magazines found they could not compete effectively either for advertising dollars or for readers. Rather than simply disappearing, magazines began to move toward greater specialization in their targeting and their editorial content. This trend continues today, with extremely narrowly focused magazines devoted to topics such as tropical fish (*Tropical Fish Hobbyist*), cross-stitching (*Simply Cross Stitch!*), or aircraft (*Affordable Aircraft*). And while there are still some general offerings, such as *Atlantic Monthly* or the *New Yorker*, their readership is considerably lower than the audience of their general interest forebears. Because of this increased specialization, there are today more than 7,000 different consumer magazines available, most of which also have websites. In 2008, 195 new titles were introduced.[36]

Magazines Today

Despite this specialization, magazines as a medium reach a broad range of the population. Indeed, 85 percent of all adults read magazines in any one year, buying about 11.5 different titles every month. The places they purchase them include supermarkets (accounting for 37 percent of all magazines sold individually), discount stores, book stores, and drug stores. Each magazine copy is looked at for an average of 45 minutes.

There are three main types of magazines available: consumer, farm, and business-to-business. Consumer magazines are usually categorized according to their editorial content, such as business, men's, women's, sports, news, and entertainment. This category includes titles enjoyed by all segments of the population, from *Time* to *Sports Illustrated* to *Cosmopolitan*. Farm magazines are geared toward that particular industry. Some may be crop-specific, such as *Cotton Farming,* while others deal with the technical aspects of agriculture. The third type, business-to-business, cover all titles aimed at the industrial user, everything from *Chemical Age* to *Offshore Drilling* to *Information Week.*

Taken together, magazines account for 5 percent of all ad dollars spent in the U.S. Most magazines are considered as national vehicles for advertising, although city or regional publications are also classified within the consumer segment, such as *Milwaukee* or *Southern Living.* More and more, however, national magazines offer geographic breakouts of their circulation allowing an advertiser to place a message that will, for example, only reach southerners, or people who live in the northeast states, or in the Los Angeles metropolitan area. They are also developing more demographic "splits," so that Fidelity Investments can advertise its mutual funds in the edition of *Bloomberg's Business Week* that is read by people earning $75,000 or more per year.

Magazines are sold in one of two ways—at the newsstand or by subscription. For most titles, it is the latter that generates the most sales, accounting on average for 68 percent of a title's circulation. As with newspapers, magazines are assessed in terms of their circulation. Today's top ten circulation magazines are shown in Exhibit 4.17.

The newsstand sales have seen a big drop in sales in recent years, with the 70 largest titles losing 31 percent of such sales, due to the combination of the economic recession and an increased readership on websites. It is the latter that has been the one bright spot for magazine companies. In 2008, several mainstream titles, such as *Time* and *Martha Stewart Living* saw 5 to 10 percent of their ad revenues coming from digital sources.[37] For some more specialized magazines, such as *PC World* and *Entrepreneur*, more than one-third of the ad revenue was digitally based.[38]

Benefits of Magazines to Advertisers

To an advertiser, three of the most attractive qualities of magazines are their high-end audiences, the enthusiasm of those audiences, and the long issue life of the medium.

Upscale and Niche Audiences

One of the incentives to using magazines for your advertising message is the favorable demographic profile of magazine readers. Similar to newspaper readers, the heaviest user of this medium is in the age range 18 to 44 years, with a college education and household income over $75,000,

Exhibit 4.17 Top 10 Magazines by Circulation

Rank	Title	Circulation
1	AARP The Magazine	24,444,293
2	Reader's Digest	9,322,833
3	Better Homes & Gardens	7,687,533
4	National Geographic	5,042,682
5	Good Housekeeping	4,632,531
6	Family Circle	4,011,530
7	Woman's Day	3,930,566
8	Ladies' Home Journal	3,911,188
9	People	3,618,718
10	Prevention	3,383,408

Source: Adweek Hot List, 3.31.08, p. 23.

and employed in a professional or managerial job. At the same time, given the fragmented and targeted nature of magazine titles, they are able to reach a variety of audiences, from youth to multicultural to people at different life stages (parents, seniors, etc.).

Getting Attention

Another benefit of placing your ads in magazines is reader involvement. While this concept is rather difficult to define (and even harder to measure), it generally refers to the interest that the reader has in the material, both editorial and advertising. Since most magazines today focus on a particular subject or interest, they can tie in more readily with the personal needs and lifestyles of the audience, enabling advertisers to do so as well. In this way, automakers can target car enthusiasts or prospective buyers in *Car and Driver* or *Road and Track*; detergent manufacturers can promote their new or improved products in magazines aimed at homemakers (*Better Homes and Gardens, Good Housekeeping, Ladies Home Journal*); while financial services companies can offer their mutual funds to interested investors in *Fortune* or *Money*.

Consumers also seem less resistant to seeing ads in magazines. One study conducted for the magazine industry in 2004 found that whereas 62 percent of those surveyed agreed that the advertising on network TV gets in the way of their enjoyment, for magazines the figure was only 28 percent of respondents. Moreover, nearly half (48 percent) said that advertising in fact adds to their enjoyment when reading magazines, a proportion that was higher than for any other medium. These findings are in part due to the fact that as a reader, you get to select what ads you read, whereas with television the ads are more or less forced upon you (the remote control notwithstanding). Internet advertising is seen, by most users, as mere "clutter" on the screen.

Reactions of readers to magazine ads also differ to their reactions to ads on television. Information seen in magazines tends to be retained longer because people can read up to five times faster than they take in the spoken word. They tend to trust magazine ads more, placing greater faith in the authority of the printed word. And in many instances, reading a magazine can be considered a pre-shopping experience, allowing consumers the chance to compare products and services and learn new information about your Apple iPhone prior to purchasing it.

Hanging Around

Another important, and unique, feature of magazines is their *long issue life*. While the television program is over in half an hour, and the newspaper is thrown out after one day, you will probably keep a monthly magazine in your home for four weeks or longer. This not only gives you opportunities for additional or repeat exposures to the advertising, it is also likely that other people, known as the *secondary* audience, may see the issue too. The importance of this *passalong* readership is shown by the fact that the average magazine is seen by four different readers, with each one spending about 61 minutes with the issue.

Drawbacks of Magazine Advertising

Magazines, too, have their drawbacks. Among the most significant obstacles to keep in mind are the considerable lead time necessary and the relatively high cost of reaching your targeted audience.

Long Planning Cycle

For most publications, ads have to be completed and at the printer well in advance of their publishing date, a factor known as the *lead time*. This makes it difficult for advertisers to create particularly timely or newsworthy ads of the kind seen in newspapers. Moreover, despite the generally excellent color reproduction quality, the magazine remains two-dimensional (aside from pop-up displays or inserts, discussed further below). This prevents the magazine ad from offering the truly life-like qualities of a television spot.

Reaching Readers

The increasingly targeted nature of magazines means that the cost of reaching one thousand members of the audience (the *CPM*, explained in greater detail in Chapter 7) is higher than that of a broader, mass medium such as television. Even some of a magazine's benefits can be viewed as potential disadvantages for you as a media specialist. The notion of readers' involvement with the magazine also means that if they are not very interested in a particular product or ad, they can very easily ignore it by simply turning their attention to the next page.

Research on Magazines

Studies on magazines as a medium have focused on similar areas as broadcast research. The value of the context in which an ad is seen was found, by Norris and Colman, to impact consumer recall and recognition of the ad.[39] The same topic was explored further by Yi to see what happened when readers were given additional information prior to seeing the magazine ad in its context.[40] Meanwhile, the magazine industry has itself sponsored several studies showing the impact of magazines on sales.[41]

In 2004 the magazine industry sponsored a study undertaken by Northwestern University to examine the motivations for reading magazines. The top ten reasons included statements such as "I get value for my time and money," "it does not disappoint me," and "it makes me smarter." Several other studies conducted on behalf of magazines have attempted to show how magazine ads provide a better return on advertisers' investment than do other media.

Outdoor Billboards and Beyond—From Cairo, Egypt, to Cairo, Illinois

There are some in the outdoor industry who like to claim that billboards are the oldest medium in existence. They date it back to Egyptian times, when hieroglyphics were written on roadside stones to give people directions to the nearest town or village. Whether you agree with that or not, outdoor billboards are certainly well established, having been around in this country since the 1800s. At that time, companies began leasing space on boards for bills to be pasted (hence the term *billboard*). There are two main types of billboard—poster panels and painted bulletins. Panels come in several sizes, named according to the number of sheets of paper originally needed to cover them, such as 8-sheets and 30-sheets. Posters are found mostly in populated areas, in or near cities and towns. Painted bulletins are larger boards situated along highways and major roads. Their name refers to the fact that they were originally painted by hand at the site.

Putting messages on outdoor boards used to be extremely labor-intensive. The sheets for poster panels were pasted onto the board while bulletins were hand-painted. Both were created either at the board site or at a central location within the market or region. Since this had to be done in each market, differences resulted in the look of the message from one market to another (and even one site to another within the market). Today, thanks to computer technology, poster panel messages are created electronically and then shipped either in one piece or in sections to the board site. Bulletins still tend to be hand-painted, but computers are now used to make sure that the finished product looks identical across boards. Today, bulletins are often created using other materials, such as lithography or special stretch vinyl.

In the past 40 years the industry has come under increased criticism from environmentalists who claim that the boards are a blight on the scenery. Many cities and several states have introduced bans on putting up new boards and, in certain cases, demanded the removal of existing structures. So you won't see any billboards in Hawaii or Vermont, for example.

Unlike other media that have editorial material too, outdoor billboards exist solely for advertising messages. They are primarily a local medium, bought on a market-by-market basis, but are used by both national and local advertisers. The type of business using the medium has changed considerably in the past 20 years. For many years, the biggest category of advertiser was the tobacco industry, but in 1999, legislation was passed prohibiting the advertising of tobacco messages on any outdoor billboards. This not only had a significant impact on the tobacco industry, it freed up many high-profile and well-positioned billboards across the country for other advertisers who had never been able to buy that space because the tobacco companies had long-term deals with the billboard companies. Today, you are far more likely to see billboards from local retailers, the travel industry, or healthcare providers than you would have even five years ago. Exhibit 4.18 shows the top categories that spend on outdoor advertising.

For many years, outdoor billboard audiences were calculated from manual traffic counts conducted by each system operator of how many cars passed by a given billboard, multiplied by government statistics that are updated periodically on how many people are present in the average car. That became the estimated audience viewing a billboard. In 2007, the Traffic Audit Bureau (TAB) announced a major new measurement initiative to update and improve outdoor audience measurement, moving from estimates of "opportunities to see" a billboard to a system to get closer to "eyes on" ratings. The measurement combines the broad "impressions" a billboard can deliver based on traffic, with an adjustment for how visible the sign is, and an eyes on impression (EOI) factor for the number of people who in fact saw it, by age, gender, household income, and race or ethnicity.[42] The TAB also commissioned travel surveys in 15 markets to collect information on how people travel, and why they are traveling, in order to calculate the reach and frequency metrics for the medium.[43] The TAB employs statistical modeling techniques to combine all the data

Exhibit 4.18 Top Outdoor Advertising Categories in 2007

Rank	Category	Dollars in thousands
1	Services & amusements	$588,407.9
2	Commercial insurance & real estate	$395,461.1
3	Public communications	$357,935.5
4	Public transportation, hotels & resorts	$337,902.8
5	Media & advertising	$330,691.5
6	Retail	$322,400.2
7	Restaurants	$238,852.6
8	Financial	$232,136.9
9	Automotive dealers & services	$198,746.1
10	Automotive, automotive accessories & equipment	$187,591.0

Source: Kantar Media 2007.

sources into a system that can provide estimated audiences to the ads on individual outdoor boards across the country.

In addition to new forms of measurement, outdoor billboards have become increasingly electronic. Digital billboards offer advertisers the opportunity to create messages that can change by the touch of a button from a central location, altering the ad based on conditions outside, for example, or simply to create a more engaging environment. These boards also allow the outdoor company to sell ads to multiple marketers at one time, with different messages appearing on different days or times. And of course the marketers must pay more for the more sophisticated technology. The digital element even allows marketers to send personalized messages. Mini Cooper, for example, created a promotion that involved sending owners of the vehicle a special key fob. After the recipients answered a few questions on a special website, when they drove by specially enhanced outdoor billboards, individual messages would appear on the sign, such as "Motor on Jim!"[44]

Indeed, the outdoor industry is far more expansive than it used to be. For example, outdoor messages are now quite commonly seen painted on the sides of buildings, on telephone kiosks and bus shelters, or in sports stadiums. More is said on this in the following chapter.

Benefits of Outdoor Billboards to Advertisers

The advantages of billboard advertising have contributed to the medium's popularity over the past two centuries. Four of the most consistent and important benefits are size, mobility, effective reach, and cost. Each of these advantages is discussed below.

Big is Better

The size of the poster panel or painted bulletin means that outdoor advertising gets noticed. In fact, at a typical busy location in the center of a city, more than 10,000 people are likely to pass an 8-sheet poster panel within a given month. In addition, the message is there constantly, for 12 to 24 hours (and many posters are illuminated at night).

Mobility

Not only can painted billboards be moved around an area to expose more of the target to the message, but the outdoor messages can also be designed for specific locations, audiences, or activities. So you could place ads for Samsonite luggage aimed at businesspeople at airports to catch them when they travel, or advertise Chiquita bananas near the A&P supermarket where your target audience shops.

Reaching Ethnic Groups

With outdoor billboards you can tailor your message to members of a particular ethnic group using their own language or culture yet still reach a mass audience within a specific market. You can buy space in areas with heavy concentrations of Hispanic people, for example, reaching them where they live, work, and shop. It is harder to reach a large portion of these groups with traditionally "Anglo" television or magazines. Furthermore, it is valuable to be able to reach non-native English speakers in their first language, whatever language that might be.

Reinforcing the Message

Outdoor advertising is a good supplementary medium, helping to add reach and frequency to a media schedule at reasonable cost. A fairly typical outdoor buy could reach over 80 percent of adults in a given area in a month. In addition, the fact that the billboard is there all the time means that frequency builds up and the message can be a constant reminder. Because many panels are situated in shopping areas, an advertiser can present his message very close to the point of purchase.

Drawbacks of Outdoor Billboard Advertising

In considering what part of your advertising budget to commit to outdoor billboard advertising, you will need to keep in mind the two drawbacks of the medium: short exposure time, and the potential for criticism from environmentalists.

Brief Message Exposure

Since the average outdoor message is only seen for between three and seven seconds, the copy needs to be extremely concise and compelling. For products that need a lot of explanation, outdoor is clearly not the right medium. One way to gauge whether there is too much copy on a billboard is to estimate how quickly people are going to pass by it. You can try the exercise yourself, and see how much of the message you can take in as you drive or walk by. Because most of the viewing is done at high speed, especially for bulletins situated along the highway, the advertisement must also be eye-catching and interesting enough to attract the driver's (or passenger's) attention.

Environmental Criticism

The outdoor industry, as noted earlier, has come under increasing criticism for cluttering up the environment. Advertisers might shy away from the medium to avoid legal or ethical disputes, especially in areas with a recent history of environmental controversies.

Research on Outdoor Billboards

The outdoor industry is one of the least researched of any mass medium. Studies have focused mostly on proving that the medium works, as shown by Bhargava et al.[45] More recently, a study in the Netherlands looked at what factors enhance recognition of outdoor ads. More information on how the medium has been researched can be found on the website of the Outdoor Advertising Association of America (www.oaaa.org).

Internet—The Ultimate Choice

The rapid growth of the Internet as a consumer medium in the 1990s was unprecedented in the history of media. Internet penetration rose faster than any other medium (or appliance), reaching the critical mass of 50 million users in five short years (it took radio 36 years to get to that point). Today, with nearly three-quarters (70 percent) of the country accessing the Internet from home, work, school, or some other location, the medium's capabilities continue to expand and develop. That is due, in part, to the ability of users to access the Web through high-speed (broadband) technology. Today, about four in five of all users can do so, allowing them easier and faster access to full video offerings.

The Internet was first devised as a means of communication for the academic community, more than 30 years ago. It was a fairly arcane and complex system, relying on a lot of computer language and processing. The Hypertext Markup Language (HTML) that formed the basis of the Web is now seamlessly (and invisibly) connected to everything we do on the computer. That was not the case originally. It was not until the late 1990s that the Internet came to be seen as a genuine medium (as opposed to computer tool), and one that offered users far greater control than with any other existing medium. Even more so than print media, the Internet lets you select exactly where you want to go, and what you want to see. You choose where to click, and how long to stay there. Although you can browse through a magazine or newspaper, you generally have to look at each page (or a table of contents) to find what you are most interested in. On the Web, you can type in a web address (www.mediahandbook.com) and be taken straight to that specific piece of information, without having to wade through other pages in which you have no interest. At the same time, the computer is keeping track of your every movement, capturing each site you visit, and each page within that site. This information proved invaluable in the development of the medium for advertising.

Indeed, as companies began setting up websites (a fairly inexpensive proposition), they saw huge potential for advertising to help generate revenues. Analogies to the direct response industry are common. Companies were immediately able to track visits to their sites (by computer address only), and offer advertisers more information on who was not only visiting their sites, but also looking at the ads—and clicking through to the advertiser's site—than any other mass medium. They did so by placing special software, known as *cookies*, on a user's computer, to monitor the path that user takes as they browse different sites on the Internet. Internet ad revenues doubled each year for several years in a row in the late 1990s, surpassing total ad revenues for the outdoor and syndicated TV industries, and by 2008 had reached $11.4 billion.

At first, Internet ads consisted of banners—billboards on the Web— that did little more than offer a brand name or teaser, and a link to another site. Companies began to consider using web advertising for brand-building purposes, rather than simply to offer information. And before long, the ability to purchase via the Web became mainstream rather than exceptional. Today, according to eMarketer, 74 percent of the online population age 13+ has made a purchase over the Web. Before long, advertisers started to get more creative, changing the size of the ad message, and incorporating (as technology advanced) more sound, motion, and visual stimulation (animation, for example), a phenomenon known as *rich media*. Not surprisingly, the research findings showed that these kinds of ads had greater impact (recall, awareness) than the plain-vanilla banners. But it became more and more clear that as fast as advertisers moved to surprise consumers, those consumers became increasingly disenchanted with web ads.

Today, when most consumers are asked about web advertising, their response is primarily one of irritation. They talk about the "clutter" of websites, the irrelevance of most ads that appear, and their techniques for avoiding them. In particular, annoyance with ads that pop up, or pop under, a website is considerable. At the same time, if an ad appears on the Web that is relevant and informative, consumers will click on it to find out more. For many, the line between the "editorial" material and the "advertising" is a narrow one on the Web, which is viewed by most people as an information cornucopia.

As more marketers have embraced ads on the Internet, they have moved to online video ads, which primarily consist of 30-second TV commercials (sometimes transferred directly from television). These appear before, during or after what is known as long-form content, such as TV shows or movies available over the Web. For shorter clips, such as those found on YouTube, the video message tends to be proportionately shorter. Research has been conducted to demonstrate the immediate, short-term impact of ads seen prior to or during online video.[46]

Online video advertising is not simply a consumer phenomenon, however. Companies have begun to use it for other reasons. Sun Microsystems has used online video to create and foster a sense of community between its software developers, employees, and customers. They can all go to the website to explore a video library, as well as talk to each other. Online video can be used for educational purposes too. The plumbing accessories company Kohler uses online videos to help people see their products in action and gain a better sense of the full range of products available.[47]

According to Nielsen, time spent watching video on the Internet is still fairly small relative to the hours spent watching TV on a regular set. In the fourth quarter of 2008, the average monthly time viewing online was less than 3 minutes, compared to 151 minutes watching TV at home. But it is expected that online video viewing will grow rapidly, especially as the speed of content delivery increases and improves. Indeed, one indicator of that is that among 18 to 24 year olds, the time spent was nearly double the average, at just over five minutes.[48] Indeed, eMarketer forecasts that by 2012, 190 million people will regularly watch online video in the U.S.[49]

Another Internet phenomenon that has had an increasing impact on how advertisers think about and use the Web has been the growth of search advertising. Inspired by sites such as Google, which allow users to type in any word and find out what is available throughout the Web, advertisers started to realize that they could "buy" keywords or links, and deliver ad messages to consumers when they requested those words. So, for example, if you do a search on Google for the words "razor blades" to find out if your product with a built-in counter is available, at the top of the screen you might see sponsored links from websites such as drugstore.com, or connecting you to manufacturers such as Gillette or Braun.

Today, search has become the most popular way for advertisers to reach online consumers. In 2008, advertisers spent an estimated $14 billion on search alone. They now spend more on search than on "regular" display online ads; indeed, four in every ten online ad dollars go toward search.

There are various forms of search marketing. As noted above, the most common is paid placement, which appears when the consumer types in a particular word. Second is contextual advertising, where links appear next to related content on the website, such as an ad for Hyatt Hotels appearing on Travelocity.com. Third is paid inclusion, which guarantees that a marketer's website is included in a site's directory. Last but not least is search engine optimization, or SEO, which helps a marketer's site or link appear on the list when a related word is typed in. In 2008, paid search accounted for nearly two-thirds of the dollars spent (see Exhibit 4.19).

Exhibit 4.19 U.S. Search Marketing Spending by Type

Paid search advertising	61.2%
Contextual advertising	14.7%
Paid inclusion	4.8%
Search engine optimizations	19.3%
Total spend	$13,625,000

Source: eMarketer, January 2008, as seen in Advertising Age Search Marketing Fact Pack 2008.

There were an estimated 11.8 billion searches made in the U.S. in 2008. Google still accounts for the majority of search traffic (about 63 percent), followed by Yahoo and MSN. Worldwide, the search number is a staggering 82.8 billion, with Google still commanding more than half of the total (about 59 percent). Notably, the number two on the list is a Chinese search engine, Baidu. One area of growth within the U.S. is local search, estimated to account for about $3.7 billion of total U.S. spend in this area. With this, advertisers can ensure that the search results will be linked to the zipcode in which the consumer lives. For example, if someone lives in Urbana, Illinois, and does a search for "dog collars," PetSmart can pay to ensure that the listings that result will include information on its store in the 61801 area.

The benefit of search marketing is that it is possible to measure its impact. That is, if someone clicks on the results of a search, their subsequent web behavior can be tracked to see if that search led to a sale. In this way, search can be assessed in terms of its return on investment, or ROI. For every $x spent on search marketing, how many dollars are returned through increased sales? In one survey, when advertisers and agencies were asked which metrics they tracked related to spend on search, two-thirds or more said that they measured the click-through rate and return on investment.[50]

One increasingly important use of the Web is to build communities around products or brands. When Kodak wanted to start selling inkjet print cartridges in early 2007, it knew that it was late to the game, even though it believed its product was superior to the competition. Working with a research company, Kodak created an online community of cartridge users, recruited through media, and then used surveys to find out more about their target audience, and let them talk to each other, share user experiences, and ask the company questions directly. Not only was the result a fairly large group of happy users, but the company is also able to maintain communications with them and continue to improve its products.[51]

The notion of community is paramount to the explosive growth of the Internet-based social networking. Websites such as MySpace (now owned by Google) and Facebook give users the ability to connect with friends and family locally and globally to exchange messages, video, music, or photos. It is estimated that about one in four (43 percent) of U.S. Internet users accessed a social networking site in 2009. And if you look only at those under the age of 35, the figure is 70 percent.[52] One source indicates that, globally, this phenomenon now accounts for 16 percent of total time spent online. It has replaced email for younger web users, giving them far more flexibility and creativity than a text-based email can do. And increasingly, this use of the Web is becoming highly influential in people's lives, considered almost as important as talking to others as a source for information.[53] Advertisers are just starting to think of ways to create a presence on these sites.

A growing attraction of social networking sites is their ability to allow users to post widgets, or software applications that anyone can use (often at no charge) to complete a task more easily. These may be as simple as putting your local weather forecast on your Facebook page or news updates on your latest favorite band. They are migrating beyond the Web to mobile phones (especially the iPhone), and the concept is likely to spread to traditional media too.

It is hard, if not impossible, to discuss today's Internet without covering YouTube. This global phenomenon, which started as a way for people to share videos with each other, is estimated today to be seen by more than 250 million people around the world in a year. The key benefit it offers viewers is that they can search for whatever or whomever they want, whether that is Aunt Betty's New Year's Eve party or clips from past episodes of *Saturday Night Live* to live streaming of sports events. It accounted for about one-third of all video viewed online in the U.S. in 2008. It has rapidly become the destination for online video content. According to Nielsen, those who watch online video (including the viewing of TV programs online at sites such as Hulu.com or nbc.com) spend about 2.5 hours per month doing so. And the "prime time" for this media form is between noon and 2 p.m., suggesting there are a lot of people taking their lunch breaks in front of a computer screen!

Benefits of Internet to Advertisers

In many ways, the benefits of this emerging medium for advertisers are still being explored. Four of the current advantages are flexibility, personalization, reach, and measurability. Each is examined below.

Flexibility

There are many forms of Internet advertising. Unlike other mass media, where choices come down to 15- or 30-second commercials, or full page

versus half-page ads, on the Internet, there really is little limit to the imagination. From traditional banner ads to pop-ups to search, ad messages
can appear in numerous forms. Beyond that, advertisers are increasingly
trying to communicate with prospects via email, asking people to *opt-in*
and be willing to receive messages that way, offering them cut-price travel
deals on Travelocity, or the best-seller list on Amazon. Advertisers can
also engage in affiliate marketing, where one site promotes another site's
products or services in exchange for some commission on the sale.

Targeted Message

The Internet is the first mass medium able to offer a targeted, personal
advertising message. Although direct response has been doing so for
many years, it was not possible in TV, radio, newspapers, magazines, or
billboards to talk to anything less than a sizable audience. With the Internet, however, advertisers are actually able to send messages to named
individuals (via opt-in email marketing). It is assumed that such messages,
by being more relevant to that individual, are more likely to be accepted
and absorbed.

Reach

Although the Internet does not offer as broad a reach as television,
campaigns that appear on a range of websites (particularly the gateway
or portal sites many people have as their home pages, such as msn.com
or yahoo.com) can indeed reach a high proportion of everyone on the
Internet. In addition, the reach on the Internet can be given against
specific advertising messages, not just the sites on which those messages
appear (i.e., ad exposure not just opportunity to see).

Measurability

For advertisers, the Internet's ability to measure who is doing what on
the Web would seem to be answering one of the "holy grail" questions of
the industry. But because the measurement is computer-based rather than
person-based, the measures are in fact not as precise and valuable as they
might appear. Having said that, Internet measurement is certainly far
more detailed than for any other mass medium, where at best the media
specialist can look at opportunities to be exposed to the ad, rather than
actual viewer, reader, or listener behavior. Several advertisers have undertaken cross-media studies of ad impact on the Web compared to other
media (using statistical modeling) and found that the Internet ads are
usually more effective at enhancing brand image and consideration than
other media types.[54] Initially, web advertising was sold based on *click*

throughs (users clicking on web ad to link to advertisers' sites), but it soon became clear that if Internet advertising was to be comparable to other ad media, the cost metric had to be the same. Today, most sites price their advertising based on cost per thousand (CPM). Web measurement services provide data on the demographics and lifestyles of web users, as well as web traffic to individual sites and/or ads.

Drawbacks of Internet to Advertisers

As powerful as the Internet is, it still cannot provide advertisers with everything they would want to reach their desired targets. Here is a summary of the downside to Internet advertising, in terms of consumer irritation, confusion, and non-standard metrics.

Consumer Irritation

The plethora of advertising on the Internet is not always appreciated by consumers. Although users have the option to click on an ad to find out more information, there are more and more messages that appear on a site that the user has to actively remove if he or she does not want to look at it. Moreover, since people tend to use the Web to look for specific information (rather than passively consuming a TV program or browsing a magazine's pages), the irritation level with the high number of ad messages on a web page (banners, buttons, sponsorships) can become overwhelming, detracting from the impact of any one particular message.

Clutter

When the Internet was first developing as a consumer medium, there were only a few banner-type ads that appeared occasionally. Today, that is far from the case. An estimated 4.5 trillion display ads appeared on the screens of U.S. web users in 2008![55] And what constitutes advertising, to a consumer, has changed too. Is it a company's website (such as nike.com)? Or are the pages that pop up in moving from one page to another (so-called *interstitials*) ad messages or actual sites? While some of this may benefit advertisers (putting out messages that users see as information rather than advertising), the likely reaction is for consumers to see all of these ad messages as "clutter," which will lead them to avoid them as quickly as possible.

Non-Standard Metrics

Despite its use as an advertising medium for more than ten years, the Internet has not yet developed fully standardized measurement metrics.

Each measurement service uses slightly different methods (not always fully revealed) to measure a different list of websites. Some sites try to sell advertising based on audience impressions, others on site visits (clicks), and yet others on actual sales. The Interactive Advertising Bureau has worked hard, however, to standardize the ad unit sizes, so that there is consistency for the consumer, and for the creative developers, on rectangular billboards, or pop-ups, or skyscraper ads. The guidelines include not only the size (in pixels), but also recommendations on the size of the file that has to download onto the page it appears on, along with the duration of the ad.[56]

Research on the Internet

A study conducted on behalf of the Online Publishers Association (OPA) in 2005 found that when Internet users were more engaged in the content, they not only spent more time with a site, but also were more likely to recommend it to their friends. Through both qualitative and quantitative studies, and segmentation of the data, the OPA uncovered 22 distinct online user experiences, ranging from "connection with others" to "worth saving and sharing." The experiences most likely to increase online usage were that the content was entertaining and absorbing, and that it was personalized ("looks out for people like me").[57]

Others have started to try to model the uses and gratifications of Internet use, finding that those looking for information tend to interact more with messages on websites, whereas those looking for social interaction turn to the Web for human-to-human communication.[58] Research has also been undertaken to look at what factors encourage interactivity with websites. One study found that the more personalized the message on the site, the more likely users were to interact with it.[59]

Which Media Should You Use?

Now that you have some basic information on each major media category, we can start to consider why you might or might not wish to include them in your media plans. To make this process less cumbersome, we'll recap some of the most important advantages and disadvantages that each medium offers. These are summarized in Exhibit 4.20.

Summary

Before deciding which media might best be suited to achieving your plan objectives, it is important to consider the advantages and disadvantages that each type of media can offer. Issues to be incorporated into your analysis include the reach and/or frequency of the medium, length of

Exhibit 4.20 Pros and Cons of Major Media

	Pros	Cons
TV	True to life; pervasive; high reach	Expensive; brief message; clutter; ad positioning
Radio	Local appeal; targeted reach; imagery transfer; low cost; high frequency; flexibility	Background; short message life; fragmentation
Newspaper	Timeliness; desirable audience; editorial impact; local/regional benefits	Short issue life; attention span; black and white
Magazine	Upscale audience; selective exposure; long issue life	Long lead time; high targeted cost
Outdoor	Large size; mobility; low cost; ethnic reach; complement to other media	Brief exposure; environmental issue
Internet	Flexibility; reach; personalization; measurability	Consumer irritation; confusion; non-standard metrics

message exposure, audience involvement, clutter, targetability, and cost. For each media category, an examination of the benefits and drawbacks will help determine whether—and to what extent—it should be included in the final plan.

Checklist—Exploring the Major Media

1. Do you want primarily national or local media in your plan, or a combination of both?
2. Will the benefits of television (mass reach, closeness to reality, and pervasiveness) help achieve your media objectives?
3. Have you considered the drawbacks of television (cost, brief exposure time, advertising clutter, and uncertain pod positioning)?
4. Should you use traditional TV ads or explore some of the new forms of TV advertising, such as on DVRs, or through brand integration?
5. Will the benefits of radio (local appeal, targeted formats, low cost, high frequency, and message flexibility) help achieve your media objectives?
6. Have you considered the drawbacks of radio (its background nature, audio-only message, brief exposure time, and fragmented market)?
7. Will the benefits of newspapers (timeliness, editorial affinity, local and regional capabilities, and upscale audiences) help achieve your media objectives?
8. Have you considered the drawbacks of newspapers, such as brief exposure, poor color capabilities, and selective readers?

9. Will the benefits of magazines (upscale audiences, involved and interested readers, and long issue life) help achieve your media objectives?
10. Have you considered the drawbacks of magazines (long lead time, two-dimensional message, and higher costs per thousand)?
11. Will the benefits of outdoor billboards (large message size, rotating message, ethnic targetability) help achieve your media objectives?
12. Have you considered the drawbacks of outdoor billboards (brief message exposure and environmental impact)?
13. Will the benefits of the Internet (flexibility, targeted message, reach, measurability) help achieve your media objectives?
14. Have you considered the drawbacks of the Internet (irritation, confusion, and non-standard metrics)?

Chapter 5

Exploring the Media, Part 2

Beyond Traditional

Increasingly, advertisers have come to realize that traditional media are not as effective in conveying messages to consumers as they once had been. This is true for various reasons, including consumers taking greater control of their media consumption, as well as their ever-busier lives making it harder to reach them through the traditional media covered in Chapter 4. At the same time, many advances in technology have led to the development and growth of several new forms of advertising communications. In this chapter we will explore some of these less traditional disciplines that today's media specialist needs to know about. Once relegated to specialized units of divisions within an agency, these communication forms are now considered as important (and in some cases more important) than the 30-second TV commercial or full-page magazine ad. We call them "beyond traditional." They include point-of-purchase (retail or in-store), sponsorship, word of mouth, Yellow Pages, mobile and social networks. They encompass forms that have been around for decades as well as those just recently introduced. They are tangible or intangible, electronic or not, focused on consumer or trade audiences. And while each brings its own distinct set of benefits and drawbacks to the consumer and the advertiser, what they all share is a different way of conveying brand messages that go beyond simply displaying an ad in a medium.

Yellow Pages: When Your Fingers Do the Typing

Although placed in the Beyond Traditional category, Yellow Pages advertising has been in existence for almost as long as the telephone directory itself. Offering advertisers (and consumers) another type of classified advertising, the Yellow Pages generated nearly $14 billion in advertising revenues in 2008. There are nearly 7,000 different Yellow Pages directories in the U.S., distinguished not just by location (Chicago versus New York) but also by target (the "silver" pages targeting senior citizens or the gay/lesbian directory for that consumer group). This can sometimes make it harder for advertisers because of the lack of standardization in terms of ad sizes or guidelines.

People use the Yellow Pages to look up information and services. More than one-fifth of the time, the search is related to business needs. The top three categories that people turn to are food, dining out and entertainment, and automotive. The top three headings in Yellow Pages directories in terms of the number of listings are restaurants, physicians and surgeons, and auto parts.

According to Mediamark Research, Inc. (MRI), 11 percent of the population has used the Yellow Pages in the past seven days, while more than half (57 percent) have done so within the past 12 months. But 61 percent of the 4 percent of the country who used a moving van in the past year used the Yellow Pages to look up information about moving and storage, as did 27 percent of the 99 percent of the country who ordered a pizza. The "average" profile is someone who is between the ages of 25 and 49, has been to college, and has an annual household income of $60,000 or more.[1]

Within the past few years there have been some new developments in Yellow Pages advertising. First, the industry has attempted to attract more national advertisers, who accounted for just 15 percent of total revenues in 2004. For most consumers, the Yellow Pages are usually considered a means of finding local information. In 2004 the Association of National Advertisers (ANA) hired one company to provide measurement for a new syndicated Yellow Pages service that uses telephone surveys to estimate usage of the medium and recall overall and in key product categories.[2]

Today, there are other places to go for Yellow Pages information. Most prominent among these is the Internet, where sites such as switchboard. com or 411.com let people search for what or who they want, online. For most people, however, the Internet and printed copies of the Yellow Pages are not mutually exclusive. One survey found that 80 percent of the people who had shopped online in an average month had also looked at the printed version in that same timeframe.

The most popular categories looked up online are given in Exhibit 5.1.

The availability of color in the Yellow Pages has helped some advertisers gain additional attention from consumers. In a study conducted by Fernandez and Rosen, ads were seen as more informative and noticeable when color was included.[3] Research by Laband and Abernathy looked at the impact of different sized Yellow Pages ads and, as expected, larger size ads generate more response, though not in an exponential fashion, while the number of competitive advertisers under the same heading has a negative impact on response.[4]

Exhibit 5.1 Top Categories Searched in Yellow Pages Websites

Rank	Category
1	Restaurants
2	Physicians & Surgeons
3	Hotels
4	Auto Repair and Service
5	Florists

Source: Yellow Pages Association, 2008.

Benefits of Yellow Pages to Advertisers

The two key benefits for advertisers of the Yellow Pages are consumer selection and measurable response.

Consumer Selection

Unlike many media, especially traditional forms, consumers are almost always *choosing* to look at ads in the Yellow Pages. Whether it is simply an alphabetical listing of plumbers' names and addresses, or the display ads that appear on the pages, the person whose drain is blocked is seeking out the ad in order to solve a problem or find information—so that message is desired by the consumer, leading to greater impact.

Measurable Response

The fastest way to determine if your Yellow Pages ad is working is to measure the response. Whether in print or online, the use of distinct phone numbers or web addresses allows the advertiser to know precisely how many calls or emails he received directly as a result of placing that ad. That makes it a lot easier to calculate his return on investment.

Drawbacks of Yellow Pages to Advertisers

Drawbacks for Yellow Pages advertising include clutter and infrequent usage.

Clutter

When you open almost any page in a Yellow Pages book, or search within a Yellow Pages website such as 411.com or yp.com, you are likely to be rapidly overwhelmed. You want to order a pizza? Which of the 50 listings should you choose? How do you find the best auto body shop when your car's bumper gets damaged? Online, you are either looking for a specific company (in which case you will really just be looking for a phone number to call or website to go to), or if you are in need of a particular type of business, you'll search within a category, and likely face the same kind of dilemma as on the printed page.

Infrequent Usage

The downside of the Yellow Pages medium always being there is that you generally only turn to it at a time of need. Unless your carpets need cleaning, you won't turn to that page filled with carpet cleaning companies. So while it is a very measurable medium, the measures may show such infrequent usage that it is questionable whether the investment is worthwhile. But it is typically a low-cost medium, so that even the few calls or sales generated may be cost-effective advertising.

Retail: Closest to the Point of Purchase

Just like Yellow Pages advertising, the notion of placing advertising messages inside stores is not especially new. Signs and promotions have been available in stores for more than 25 years. Today, however, more and more advertisers are including in-store media explicitly in the media plan, acknowledging this as advertising rather than simply a promotional expense. Advertisers have doubled their spending in this venue since 2004, although it still only represents about 6 percent of total advertising spend. The in-store industry moniker covers various forms such as point of purchase, point of sale, or below the line. Indeed, research suggests that nearly nine in ten consumers make an unplanned purchase when they are in a store.[5]

One of the main reasons for the increased popularity of this media type is that it is the most measurable of all media. Thanks to electronic scanning at the cash register, advertisers are able to see what happens at the checkout counter when their messages are in the store. Some of the most popular locations for in-store messages are on the shelf displays, on TV screens at the checkout, or "floor signs" next to the freezer cabinet or in the aisles. In addition, messages or coupons can be generated at the checkout counter when people pay for their goods, tailored to the purchases that have just been made. This form of advertising has moved from grocery stores to a wide variety of retail outlets, large and small, including Wal-Mart and Einstein Bagels.

In-store advertising effectively eliminates the time between seeing the message and buying the item. Drawbacks include the possibility that the target misses the ad somehow, either by not paying attention or by its being covered up in some way. In addition, in-store advertising is not especially cheap. It tends to have its greatest effect among current brand users rather than persuading buyers of the competitor's brand to switch. The time for message exposure is very short, so messages tend to focus on price and be extremely brief.

In 2008, the industry tried to launch an in-store measurement service, using Nielsen to capture consumer exposure to in-store advertising offerings. The venture, known as PRISM (Pioneering Research for an In-Store Metric) involved major marketers such as Procter & Gamble and Wal-Mart. The venture failed to gather sufficient industry support, however, and was shut down in early 2009.

There is fairly limited research available on the impact of retail advertising, though it is becoming a more popular area of study as recognition grows that the variety of media forms within the store provide interesting opportunities to better understand what influences consumer purchases.[6]

Benefits of Retail Advertising to Advertisers

Retail advertising offers the benefits of being closest to purchase and visual stimulation.

Closest to Purchase

There is no form of communication closer to the point of purchase than in-store advertising. Seeing ads for grocery products in the grocery store or sporting equipment in the sporting goods store can act as the final reminder to consumers of why they should purchase that particular brand rather than any other, even if they have seen many TV or magazine ads for the competing brands right up until the moment they stepped into the store to make the purchase.

Visual Stimulation

Although a retail ad can be as simple as a sign with the brand name placed at the end of an aisle, more often than not it is something more striking and distinctive. It could be a life-size picture of a Sara Lee frozen cheesecake staring at you on the freezer door, or a three-dimensional version of a Nike running shoe sitting on the display table of Sports Authority. In either case, such forms of communication are difficult to miss and may make a crucial impression on consumers minutes before they make the purchase decision.

Drawbacks of Retail Advertising to Advertisers

The drawbacks to retail advertising are that it may come too late to be useful, and it can be costly.

Lack of Influence

Although proponents of retail advertising claim that its location is inherently persuasive to consumers, there are others who argue that at the point someone walks into a store, their mind is already made up and no number of pretty pictures or displays will make a difference to her decision. If you go to the grocery store to buy Kraft cheese, will the picture of Sargento's brand in front of your face really make you switch brands? There has been too little research on this to know for sure, but it is something to consider before embarking on a widespread retail campaign.

Costly to Implement

It may not seem like it would cost much to put stickers on freezer cabinets or create cardboard cutouts of products. And it is not. The expense comes in the form of "allowances" that must typically be paid to the retailer to allow those items to be placed in the store. While such costs may come out of a promotions budget within the marketing mix, rather than the advertising budget, you as the media specialist should know how much they would cost before recommending them to your client.

Sponsorship: Making Your Mark in the Mind

As advertisers have had to work harder to reach their target consumers, one of the beyond-traditional forms of communication they have turned to is sponsorship. This involves paying an organization a fee to put a company or brand name at the head of an event or as the key sponsor of that event. Examples include State Farm Insurance's sponsorship of an Ice Skating competition, to Visa's sponsorship of the U.S. Olympic team, to the renaming of sports stadiums after companies (e.g., Pepsi Center in Denver, Philips Arena in Atlanta, and Staples Center in Los Angeles. The practice of sponsorship is now estimated to be worth $9.5 billion.

The majority of sponsorship spending (69 percent) goes toward sports-related events, followed by entertainment tours and attractions (9 percent), and festivals, fairs and annual events (8 percent). A rapidly growing area within the sponsorship area is cause-related marketing, where companies link up with non-profit groups and become "sponsors" of their causes. Examples include Avon's support of an annual three-day walk to raise funds for breast cancer research, and Tanqueray's sponsorship of a bike ride each summer to raise money for AIDS. Even though sponsorship is generally considered to be undertaken to reach a national audience, there are often significant local opportunities too. Sponsorship of local sports teams can enhance a business' reputation in those particular markets, while companies that choose to sponsor a local annual festival often receive positive coverage in the local media. There are also benefits to be gained by sponsoring grassroots or community festivals and fairs, especially among ethnic audiences.

The reasons companies choose sponsorship instead of (or more likely in addition to) traditional advertising are many. They include the opportunity for heightened visibility for their brand name, thereby increasing the chances of shaping positive consumer attitudes ("I like ice skating, therefore since State Farm sponsors a skating competition, I like State Farm more too"). Sometimes, sponsorship works well for smaller companies. While they may have smaller ad budgets compared to bigger competitors, their sponsorship of a key event or attraction can make them seem an equal in consumers' eyes. MillerCoors Brewing Company spends far less on advertising than Anheuser-Busch, but when both companies are sponsoring racing cars at Nascar events, the viewer or attendee does not see one company as a "better" or necessarily bigger sponsor than another. One of the potential downsides of sponsorship was seen in 2002 when the giant energy trading company Enron found itself bankrupt and subject to numerous criminal investigations for its financial practices. The company's earlier purchase of the naming rights for Houston's arena, now called the Enron arena, no longer seems as smart a decision as before.

In economic downturns, however, sponsorship can suffer. For example, Nascar, one of the sports that is most heavily sponsored by corporations, started seeing many of the 400 firms that had spent $1.5 billion as race sponsors try to pull out during the 2008 recession partly as simple cost-cutting measure, and partly out of fear that, as attendance declined, their logo-covered cars would be seen by fewer people.[7]

The media are getting more actively involved in creating sponsorships for advertisers. *Cooking Light* magazine created a "healthy" house filled with products of its sponsoring companies, such as Reebok (exercise equipment), Lennox Industries (air conditioning), and Whirlpool (appliances). The magazine promoted the house in its pages, and attracted thousands of visitors to its Birmingham, Alabama location. After the promotion ended, the magazine was able to sell the home privately. Sponsorships are not only aimed at adults these days. Procter & Gamble sponsored a shopping mall tour featuring the singer Rihanna to promote the launch of a teen body spray brand, Secret. A MySpace page was created, linked to the tour and the brand, which let people purchase concert tickets and get product information.[8]

Benefits of Sponsorship to Advertisers

For advertisers, sponsorship offers the opportunity to surround consumers with a brand and enhance brand image and associations.

Surrounding the Consumer

Whether you attend the Sprint Cup Nascar race or watch it on TV, you can't help but notice that Allstate is the sponsor. From the brief "billboard" messages that appear on the TV airing, to the signage at the racetrack to the mention of the insurance company every time the race is talked about, Allstate's sponsorship surrounds the consumer. Promotions tied to the sponsored event can enhance the value of the sponsorship even more, such as online competitions to meet a Nascar driver. All work to connect the company with the sponsorship in a way that, it is hoped, will lead the consumer to feel more positively about that brand.

Enhanced Image and Associations

When you see or hear that Bank of America has sponsored your city's annual marathon, the desired response by the advertiser is that there is a positive association made between event and brand. That is, consumers may be grateful for the corporate support of a charity race or pleased that "their" chosen brand or company has decided to associate itself with an event or sport or charity that they like. Research has indeed demonstrated that such positive associations do in fact lead to greater purchase consideration.

Drawbacks of Sponsorship to Advertisers

A mismatch between sponsoring company and event, and imprecise measurement are two of the drawbacks for advertisers involved with sponsorships.

Sponsor Mismatch

For sponsorship to truly make a difference, it needs to change a consumer attitude or behavior, or influence opinions on the brand or company. If not done right, the sponsorship can actually backfire. Having a cooking festival, for example, sponsored by an indigestion product might lead people to feel worse, not only about the festival ("these recipes will give me indigestion") but also potentially about the brand ("Are they encouraging me to eat so much I feel ill?").

Imprecise Measurement

You can tell sponsorship works—when it works! Event attendance may increase, perceptions may improve, sales may even go up. But proving that it was caused by the sponsorship is a tricky proposition. Some research has been done to assess the financial fundamentals of a company employing sponsorship, but even here, it can be challenging to determine cause and effect. Did the company's fortunes change due to the sponsorship, or was the sponsorship the result of the company's situation?[9]

Word of Mouth: Who Says What?

While considered by many to not be a true "medium," per se, word of mouth is becoming an increasingly popular way for advertisers to promote their brands. It is sometimes referred to as "viral" marketing, using the metaphor of spreading good words about a brand the way that a virus can spread among people. In particular, products that are new or are targeting specific groups may lend themselves to this form of promotion. At its simplest, word of mouth involves getting the (positive) word out to people who are considered opinion leaders in a particular category, so that they will then influence others to consider the brand. Some marketers take it further, and plant people in key venues where the brand is being used (such as a new vodka in a bar), and have them talk to the people around them about the wonders of this product. Those consumers are unaware that the individual has been paid to promote the brand, so critics have complained that this is a deceptive, or even unethical practice.

The use of word of mouth marketing has spread to cell phones. The goal of viral mobile messages is to have the message spread from person to person. Some ringtones have actually spread this way, particularly among teens and young adults. However, there is the danger that these messages will be considered "junk" or "spam," and ignored or discarded.

Perhaps the most important venue for word-of-mouth advertising is online, on blogs (originally referred to as "web logs," then abbreviated). Whatever the topic, someone somewhere will have created a web page and filled it with content that others can read and, in most cases, comment on. For some these are an online equivalent of a written diary, while others like to share their knowledge on a topic (electronics, fashion, finance). Advertisers are only starting to determine how best to put paid messages on these sites, whether overtly through banner ads, or clandestinely by paying the author to promote an item on their blog.

Benefits of Word of Mouth to Advertisers

The primary benefits of word of mouth are consumer-driven communications and minimal cost.

Consumer-Driven Communications

When people are asked if they are affected at all by advertising, a majority always responds no. But when questioned on what made them choose a particular product or brand, the answer is often the recommendation of a friend or relative. This benefit, the fact that the "advertisement" was, in effect, from someone they know, clearly works to the advantage of word of mouth.

Minimal Cost

Due to the viral nature of word of mouth, it is an extremely cost-efficient means of communication. If done correctly, word of mouth acts like a pebble dropped in a pond, with ripple effects that go far beyond where the brand mention started. And the marketer only has to pay for that initial mention!

Drawbacks of Word of Mouth to Advertisers

Two drawbacks of this type of communication are lack of control and weak measurability.

Lack of Control

It is always serendipitous for a brand to generate positive word of mouth without even trying (as happened to BlackBerry when President Barack Obama announced he could not give up the device), but there is no guarantee that the reverse will not occur, with celebrities or even regular consumers creating a negative "buzz" about the product. Either one is hard if not impossible to control, and this should be taken into consideration when implementing a WOM campaign.

Weak Measurability

There is an increasing effort on the part of research suppliers to provide measurement of word of mouth, but it remains nascent. The two main forms are panels of consumers who report on what they are talking about, and with whom, and online passive data capture from blogs which automatically monitors the online "conversation." While the latter can track vastly more data, it cannot necessarily get to the nuances of human conversations. The former can do so, but typically with smaller samples and the unreliability of self-reported data.

Research on Word of Mouth is just starting to build.[10]

Mobile: Location, Location

Within the past few years, the mobile phone (cell phone) has moved from being a way to make phone calls to a full-blown communications and advertising medium. Today's mobile marketing, as it is generally called, includes text or picture messaging, video, television, and downloadable applications such as games, podcasts, or ringtones. With the growth of Internet access, improvements in screens, the addition of keyboards, today's mobile phone is seen by both consumers—and increasingly, by advertisers—as a mobile computer that delivers messages to target audiences wherever they are, with the ability to generate a direct response. Indeed, in 2008 it was estimated that there are a total of 3.4 billion mobile phone subscribers worldwide, a figure more than three times greater than the 1 billion who have access to a PC.[11] Forecasts for mobile phone growth suggest that by 2013 more than 5 billion people will own the device.[12] The phone can reach many consumers in places where PCs have not yet penetrated broadly, such as the high-potential global markets of China and India.

Initial use of the mobile phone for advertisers focused on interactive voice response (IVR) where phone subscribers can respond via their phone to marketers' promotions or contests. This includes voting on popular TV shows such as *American Idol*. Right behind IVR in terms of popularity, and growing fast, is text messaging, or SMS. Here, consumers can respond to marketers by sending a text to a special phone number. In Brazil, 46 radio stations combined together for a promotion that generated 1.3 million text messages in a three-month period in 2008. For Adidas, text messages were used during the National Basketball Association that encouraged those who saw the Adidas ads during NBA games to send a text and hear a message from one of the basketball players that told them to go to a special website. There, they could send messages to their friends recorded by the players. Then to create a retail element, Adidas could send texts to players and get recommendations on the products.[13]

This example demonstrates how mobile marketing can work in an integrated way with the Internet. This may in fact be the greatest value of the mobile phone for advertisers. An estimated 40 million mobile phone subscribers had browsed the Internet from their mobile phones in the U.S. in an average month in 2008. This might include checking emails (14 million do that with Yahoo! Mail each month), or keeping track of sports scores during the World Cup soccer tournament or Olympics, or watching short-form TV programs from subscription services such as MediaFlo.

Another use of the phone for advertising is to deliver coupons. Companies such as Borders or CVS let members of their "rewards" programs sign up to receive mobile messages to get coupon promotions that can then be taken into the store and redeemed. And in late 2008, several airlines began offering passengers mobile boarding passes that permitted them to check in by showing their phone at the gate.

Mobile search is also on the rise. In August 2008, an estimated 44 percent of mobile subscribers in a survey said they had used Google search on their phones.[14]

Benefits of Mobile Marketing to Advertisers

Advertisers considering the use of mobile marketing can benefit from its ubiquity and direct response mechanism.

Ubiquity

Although mobile marketing is still in its infancy, the ubiquity of the phone holds out huge potential for ad messages. It is the only video-based advertising medium that is geographically specific; that is, ad messages can be sent based on the location of the phone user. This makes the phone an "everywhere" ad medium.

Direct Consumer Response

As a two-way communications device, the mobile phone allows advertisers to generate immediate behavioral response from consumers. That is, Starbucks could send someone a text message offering them $0.50 off a coffee if he goes to his nearest store in the next 48 hours. When he presents the coupon, via his phone, the company can quickly tally just how effective that advertising was. And as noted above, mobile phones play a very significant role these days in viewer response to reality shows on television, making it easy for people to text or call in with their opinions and choices.

Drawbacks of Mobile Marketing to Advertisers

When advertisers are considering mobile marketing, they must keep in mind that there remain technological limitations and consumer irritation may be high.

Technology Limitations

While there are many articles about the promising future of mobile mar-keting, the reality right now is that most consumers do not have phones that are technologically advanced enough to take advantage of the many features under discussion or development. That, in turn, becomes a catch-22 situation, because advertisers are less likely to invest in creating custom-built ads or applications for the phone until there are enough consumers able to utilize them.

Consumer Irritation

Research has been conducted with consumers to determine how open they are to the idea of receiving advertising on their mobile phone. While published results always indicate an openness and willingness to see it (especially if it offsets any costs incurred in phone use), it remains to be seen whether that will turn out to be the case, or whether the public will ignore or avoid any marketing messages that appear, out of irritation at yet more commercialization in their lives.[15]

Guerilla Marketing: The Element of Surprise

What many of this chapter's communication forms have in common is that they are not restricted to a particular page or screen or location. Perhaps the ultimate version of going "beyond traditional" is what is variously referred to as guerilla or ambient media or, on occasion, ambush marketing. It may be as simple as staging an event around a brand or as complicated as creating virtual landscapes that consumers believe to be real.

One version of this type of communication is to recreate a scene or an experience so that consumers can touch or feel the product. When Ikea opened a new store in Japan, the company took over a train and outfitted the cars with items that could be purchased in the new store, including price tags. In addition to the benefit of having consumers look at the products, Ikea was sticking to one of its strategic objectives of demon-strating how it can help people furnish small spaces.

A very different way to use a subway was seen in Toronto, where the tourism bureau of the province of Alberta, to encourage visitors to travel there, recreated scenes from its rocky mountain scenery, changing rail seats into ski lifts and surrounding commuters with photos of the idyllic landscape. Visits to the bureau's website more than doubled during the two months of the campaign.

A variation of guerilla marketing is ambush marketing, where brands that cannot get into "official" sponsorship or communications use alternative means to spread their message. This has been a common tactic during the quadrennial Olympics. Nike, for many years, purchased so much local media in whatever city the Games were held that, despite not paying for or being an official sponsor of a country or team, survey after survey would show that consumers believed them to be one. Even small businesses can use these tactics. A coffee brand in Hawaii that was forced out of being an official sponsor of the Ironman World Championship found a creative solution to communicate to the participants by creating a coffee bar on the water offshore from the island of Maui where the competition was held. Not only was the bar floating in the ocean but billboards placed 20 feet under the sea's surface could be seen by swimmers during their practice, directing them to the non-sponsoring coffee brand.

Sometimes these marketing campaigns are not even real. To launch a new car model in the U.S., BMW created a pseudo-festival called Rampenfest that featured video of a BMW car driving on an enormous ramp in a tiny town in Austria. Except that the ramp, and the town itself, were not real, and neither was the festival. But the buzz that surrounded the campaign certainly was, with an estimated 10 million visitors to the vehicle's website.[16]

Benefits of Guerilla Marketing to Advertisers

There are two main benefits guerilla marketing offers: consumer surprise and cost flexibility.

Consumer Surprise

If done well, consumers can be pleasantly surprised by guerilla tactics, whether seeing people dressed up on the street handing out product samples, or more elaborate recreations similar to those mentioned above. That good feeling toward the effort can translate to more positive attitudes toward the brand, as well as a willingness to purchase or repurchase it.

Cost Flexibility

Guerilla marketing, by virtue of its very wide remit, allows marketers great flexibility in expenditure. It costs relatively little to hire college students to perform street theater related to your brand. Building a platform out in the middle of the Pacific Ocean is a more costly proposition. Either way, the marketer is able to manage those expenses as necessary.

Drawbacks of Guerilla Marketing to Advertisers

The two key disadvantages of guerilla marketing are strategic weakness and cool factor overload.

Strategic Weakness

There are often lots of ideas brainstormed by client or agency teams for "cool" or "unusual" promotions or events; the danger is in executing them for those reasons rather than because they are strategically aligned with the brand's meaning and message. Ikea's takeover of Japanese subway cars would not have been nearly as impactful (though still attention-getting) if they had not been trying to show how they could furnish a small space. So it is critical that any guerilla ideas are examined through a strategic lens.

Cool Factor Overload

Perhaps the biggest potential drawback for guerilla marketing is an extension of strategic weakness. That is, ideas are approved simply because they are novel and capture the imagination of the brand's decision maker. That was probably the case a few years ago when TNT Network created fake manhole covers on the streets of Boston to promote a new program. The covers were certainly cool and attention-getting, but they had large Xs on them that quickly caused a major panic that this was some kind of terrorist plot, practically shutting down the city for several hours while police were called in to investigate.

Which Media Should You Use?

Now that you have some basic information on each major media category, whether traditional, as described in Chapter 4, or beyond traditional, as outlined here, we can start to consider why you might or might not wish to include them in your media plans. To make this process less cumbersome, we'll need to recap some of the most important advantages and disadvantages that each non-traditional medium offers. These are summarized in Exhibit 5.2, including the traditional media discussed in Chapter 4.

Summary

In going beyond traditional media, the specialist must still focus on how each media type will enhance and achieve the plan's strategic objectives. Whether looking at Yellow Pages, retail, sponsorship, word of mouth,

Exhibit 5.2 Pros and Cons of Traditional and Beyond Traditional Media

TRADITIONAL	Pros	Cons
TV	True to life; pervasive; high reach	Expensive; brief message; clutter; ad positioning
Radio	Local appeal; targeted reach; imagery transfer; low cost; high frequency; flexibility	Background; short message life; fragmentation
Newspaper	Timeliness; desirable audience; editorial impact; local/regional benefits	Short issue life; attention span; black and white
Magazine	Upscale audience; selective exposure; long issue life	Long lead time; high targeted cost
Outdoor	Large size; mobility; low cost; ethnic reach; complement to other media	Brief exposure; environmental issue
Internet	Flexibility; reach; personalization; measurability	Consumer irritation; confusion; non-standard metrics
BEYOND TRADITIONAL		
Yellow Pages	Consumer selection, measurable response	Clutter, infrequent usage
Retail	Closest to purchase, visual stimulation	Lack of influence, costly to implement
Sponsorship	Surrounding the consumer, enhanced image and association	Sponsor mismatch, imprecise measurement
Word of Mouth	Consumer-driven communications, minimal cost	Lack of control, weak measurability
Mobile	Ubiquity, direct consumer response	Technology limitations, consumer irritation
Guerilla	Consumer surprise, cost flexibility	Strategic weakness, cool factor overload

mobile, or guerilla marketing, media experts need to assess the benefits and drawbacks of each, and how to incorporate them seamlessly into the overall media plan.

Checklist—Exploring Beyond Traditional Media

1. Is there a need to go beyond traditional media in your plan?
2. Are the benefits of Yellow Pages (consumers selecting your ad and a highly measurable response) important to your brand?
3. Would the drawbacks of Yellow Pages (clutter and infrequent usage) potentially detract from the usefulness of the medium for your brand?
4. Does your brand have a retail presence that could be enhanced by the benefits of retail advertising (closest to point of purchase and visual stimulation)?
5. Do the disadvantages of retail advertising (lack of influence and cost to implement) suggest that this may not be the best use of your advertising dollars?
6. What potential events or causes could your brand sponsor?
7. Would the advantages of sponsorship (surrounding the consumer and enhanced image and associations) be significant contributors to your brand's success?
8. Do the disadvantages of sponsorship (risk of sponsor mismatch and imprecise measurement) lead you to not recommend sponsorship for your brand?
9. How and why could you generate word of mouth for your brand?
10. Can you justify how the benefits of word of mouth (consumer-driven communications and minimal cost) would enhance your brand's performance?
11. Do the downsides to word of mouth (lack of control and weak measurability) pose too great a risk for your brand?
12. Would the addition of mobile advertising, with its benefits of ubiquity and direct consumer response, provide value to your media plan?
13. In what ways might the drawbacks of mobile advertising (technology limitations and consumer irritation) be detrimental to your media plan?
14. How might the advantages of guerilla marketing (consumer surprise and cost flexibility) help you achieve your marketing, advertising, and media goals?
15. Have you considered how the disadvantages of guerilla marketing (strategic weakness and cool factor overload) might negatively impact your ability to achieve your objectives?

Chapter 6

Terms, Calculations, and Considerations

Defining Key Media Terms

Just as computer programmers talk about bits, bytes, and RAM, and car enthusiasts dwell on RPM, jerk, and lateral acceleration, so do media specialists converse in their own language. Before moving on to the actual media plan development, it will be helpful to review some of these definitions.

Understanding Ratings

Most of you are probably already familiar with the weekly release of the Nielsen ratings that show which are the most popular television programs. The size of the audience is usually given in two ways—in absolute terms (i.e., millions of people), and as a percentage of the population. It is this latter figure, known as the *rating*, that is used as the baseline measure for all media concepts.

Rating Point

One rating point equals one percent of a particular target group. That audience can be defined in various ways—by household, by geographic market, or by a given demographic group, such as men 18 to 49 or women 25 to 54, or by product usage or ownership, such as people who own a digital camera. The television program *CSI* might receive a household rating of 11.3 in Memphis, which means that 11.3 percent of homes in that city watched the show. The magazine *Entertainment Weekly* might get a rating of 9.6 among females ages 18 to 34, meaning that 9.6 percent of all women in that age group read that particular issue of the magazine. More recently, Nielsen began releasing ratings that represent "Live" only (watched at the time of airing) and "Live + 7 days," which includes programs recorded and watched within one week of airing. The company also calculates average commercial ratings that include the Live audience together with up to three days of delayed (timeshifted) viewership. That metric is called the C3 rating.

Gross Rating Points

By adding up all the rating points we wish to achieve, we end up with a concept known as gross rating points, or GRPs. For media planning purposes, we set as our goal a given number of total, or "gross," rating points to achieve and then figure out which vehicles to use to obtain that number. We might want our plan to have a total of 100 gross rating points each week against our target of working women. These could come from any media.

The reason these rating points are considered "gross" is that they do not take into account any duplication of exposure. That is, there are probably many people within our target who see our ad for Special K cereal in *Fitness* and also hear the same message on the local morning talk show. So while our total number of rating points placed in the media each week is set at 100, each person will be exposed to a different number of them and in different vehicles. This is shown in Exhibit 6.1.

In today's complex media world, where our targets are becoming more and more narrowly defined, the term GRP is often altered to TRP, or "target rating point." This makes explicit the fact that we are planning our ratings against a specific *target*, rather than the whole world. The concept is the same, however.

Exhibit 6.1 Diagram of GRPs and Duplication

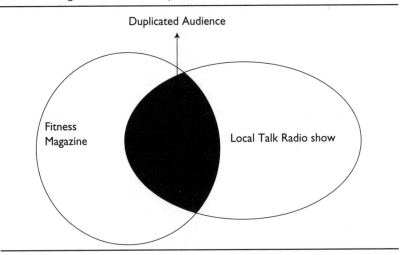

Gross Impressions

This term simply converts the gross rating points into a number by dividing the number of rating points by 100 and multiplying that figure by the size of the target audience. So if our plan calls for obtaining 200 GRPs against a target audience of 500,000 people, then we are aiming to achieve 1,000,000 gross impressions $(200/100 \times 500,000)$.

Reach and Frequency

Although many would argue that advertising is more art than science, we still need some way to assess whether the messages we place in the media are having any impact. It is not enough to know how many impressions are made with one ad, or what percentage of the target audience is exposed to a given program or magazine. As media specialists, we also need an estimate of the cumulative effect of our media plan. That is provided by the concepts of reach and frequency.

Reach

Reach refers to the number or percentage of people in the target audience who will be exposed to the medium where the message appears. You should note that we can only estimate exposure to the *media vehicle*, not to the ad itself. If you think about your own media habits, there are many intervening variables that easily prevent you from seeing or hearing an ad. You might deliberately ignore it, turning the page of the magazine or changing the TV channel or avoiding the web pop-up when it appears. You could watch the TV ad via a DVR and fast-forward to skip all the commercials. You could be doing something else at the same time, such as talking to a friend or cooking dinner, and not pay attention to the message. Or you could find the ad boring, irrelevant, or uninteresting, and see or hear it but not really absorb the contents. So when we talk about the reach of a plan, we are really talking about the opportunity-for-exposure (sometimes called opportunity-to-see, or OTS).

And of course we should also emphasize that reach, like all media terms, is merely an estimate. We will never know exactly how many people were reached, or how they reacted. Even with the more precise metrics of the Internet, where we can "know" how many computers clicked on an ad, we still don't know how that message was received. Perhaps they clicked by accident and just ignored the message. But if we are trying to reach women 25 to 54 to persuade them to try our new brand of body wash, then using syndicated data sources, we can find out how many women of that age watch *The View*, or read *Redbook*. To reach a target audience of men 18 to 49 to increase the number of inquiries for Fidelity

Investment's pamphlet on investing wisely, we can learn how many men of that age read a daily newspaper, or watch CNN.

The difference between reach and GRPs is that reach concerns the number of *different* people in the audience you are trying to communicate with through advertising. For media schedules that try to maximize reach, you would place ads in several different media vehicles to reach different people through each one. Complicated formulas are used to calculate the numbers, requiring the speed and power of computers. Here, we look at a simple example.

If the rating for *People* against our target of 18 to 49 year olds is 15 and for *Time* magazine it is 10, then one ad placed in each magazine will deliver a total of 25 GRPs (15 + 10). However, if we know from research that 6 percent of the target audience will see both ads (the duplicated audience) then the reach, or *unduplicated* audience for this schedule is 25 minus 6, or 19 percent. That is, 19 percent of our target of adults 18 to 49 will be exposed to our ad in *People and/or* our ad in *Time*. Even if they see both ads they will only be counted in our audience one time. Exhibit 6.2. depicts this situation. So reach = GRPs minus duplication.

Frequency

It is not enough to know who our media plan is intended to reach. We must also set goals of *how many times* we wish to reach them with our message. As with the concept of reach, the notion of frequency, while it ultimately refers to *message* frequency, in reality is based on the frequency of exposure to the *media vehicle* rather than to the advertisement. A media plan will typically establish the desired number of times that the audience should be exposed to the message, based on past experience,

Exhibit 6.2 Example of Duplication.

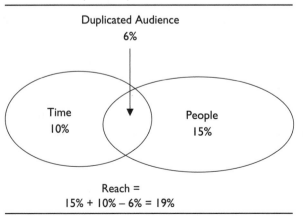

judgment, or previous research into how long it takes for the audience to comprehend and remember the message.

A simple way to back in to the frequency number is from the following equation:

Reach × Frequency = Gross Rating Points

So if you know your reach goal, and you have established the number of GRPs you will be buying, then it only requires simple mathematical division (GRPs/Reach) to figure out how many times, on average, the target will be exposed to the media vehicle(s).

Random Duplication

One of the questions that media specialists are often asked is what the reach will be of a complete media plan. The answer today is typically calculated by computers. But there is a very basic formula that can give you a rough estimate to guide you. It is known as the random duplication formula and makes the assumption that the probability of reaching the audience in one medium (or media vehicle) is independent of the likelihood of reaching them in a different one. In reality, that is not generally the case. For example, if your media plan includes food magazines and cooking shows on The Food Network, the odds are probably greater than average that your target is going to be exposed to both.

The random duplication formula assumes, however, that the reach of two media is the reach of one added to the reach of the other, minus the product of the two. All figures are calculated as decimals. That is:

Combined Reach = Reach A + Reach B − (Reach A × Reach B)

As an example, if your TV schedule has a total reach of 65 percent and your print schedule has a reach of 25 percent, then the combined reach will be:

$0.65 + 0.25 - (0.65 \times 0.25) = 0.90 - 0.1625 = 0.7375$
$= 73.75$ percent

If there are more than two media involved, then you simply take that initial product, and use it as your first medium in the formula to combine with the third medium's reach number.

Beyond Reach and Frequency

If you think about the commercials that you can remember, the ones that are most likely to come to mind are those that you have seen or heard more than once. That is, for a message to be truly *effective* in terms of communicating with the target audience, it generally has to be conveyed more than one time. Now of course this is not a hard-and-fast rule. If your bathroom drain gets blocked up, then you only need one exposure to an ad for Drano drain cleaner at the right moment in time, and that message will be extremely effective. But for the most part, given the limited attention we pay to commercial messages, we need to see or hear them several times before the information is properly absorbed. And even then, it is most likely filed away somewhere in memory for use on a future occasion.

Effective Frequency

The key here is to determine *how many times* an ad has to be received for it to be deemed effective. What we mean by effective is that the target receives the desired communication message. A considerable amount of research was done on this topic during the 1970s and 1980s, following a landmark study by Colin MacDonald, a British researcher. After looking at the relationship between opportunities to see ads for laundry detergent and sales of the product, he concluded that the optimal number of exposure opportunities was three. This was later explained by breaking down what happens with each exposure. The first time someone sees an ad, his reaction is "What is it?" On the second exposure, he asks "What of it?" or "So what?" It is only on the third occasion that the person will start to process the information and decide if the message is relevant and interesting or not.[1]

Since those research studies were first published, there has been much controversy over their accuracy. Many have argued that it is impossible to set an arbitrary number for effective frequency. Some believe that rather than having a single figure, the most effective frequency lies within a range, typically set between three and ten. And others claim that only one exposure is needed, as long as it is placed at the right time (see below). The answer, probably, is "it depends." As with the drain cleaner example above, sometimes a single exposure is sufficient. On the other hand, you might need to see an ad for a breakfast cereal 15 times before it has any real impact. What it ultimately depends on is the relevancy and impact of the message.[2]

The key point to remember here is that when establishing your media objectives and deciding on the strategy to fulfill them, you must keep in mind that your message should probably be heard, read, or viewed several times in order for it to have an effect on the audience.

Exposure Distribution

Most media plans involve placing multiple ads in many different media vehicles so it is important to know how many people are reached how many times (once, twice, three times, and so on). We find this by creating an *exposure distribution*, which shows the percentage of the target exposed to a given schedule at each level of frequency. The method used to calculate it is fairly complex, based on mathematical theories of probability, and today it is done by computer. At a basic level, a media model estimates the likelihood of being exposed to a given number of ads together with the number of different ways you can be exposed to those messages.

For example, if you placed one ad in *Time* and one in *People*, the reader might see anywhere from zero to two ads total—they might not see either ad, or they could see one of the two, or they might see both. Looking at Exhibit 6.2, we already know the percentage of the target exposed two times (the duplication figure) is 6 percent. In addition, we can easily figure out those not exposed at all (the total, or 100 percent, minus those exposed one or more times)—100 − 19 = 81 percent. So to estimate what percentage is reached exactly once you subtract the duplication figure from the number reached one or more times (*reach 1+*)—19 − 6 = 13. You should notice that the final exposure distribution must account for everyone in the target audience and therefore sum to 100 percent. The final exposure distribution is shown in Exhibit 6.3.

Frequency Planning

In the late 1990s, research evidence became available that suggested that reach was a more important determinant of media effectiveness than frequency. Based largely on the work of John Philip Jones and Erwin Ephron, the analysis of sales and TV viewing data from the same households suggested that short-term advertising sales were driven largely by exposure to a TV commercial within seven days prior to purchase. Since we as media specialists never know precisely when that sale might occur, this suggests that it is more important to maintain a lower level of media weight across more weeks than to place sporadic, albeit

Exhibit 6.3 Exposure Distribution

Frequency (f)	Percent reached (%)
0	81
1	13
2	6
Total	100

larger flights of advertising throughout the year.[3] We revisit this in Chapter 8.[4]

Calculating Costs

It is highly unlikely that you will have *carte blanche* to spend however much money you want or need. You will have to provide some kind of financial explanation of how efficiently your plan will spend your client's money. And since there are many different media types and vehicles that could, potentially, be included in the plan, it is up to the media specialist to rationalize and explain the financial reasoning behind selections.

Cost per Thousand (CPM)

Since different media are bought in different ways—a 30-second spot on radio or TV, or a one-page ad in a magazine, or a 30-sheet poster for a billboard—we need some way to compare media in terms of cost. To do so, media specialists turn to the cost per thousand, or CPM. This shows the cost of reaching 1,000 of the target audience either with an individual media vehicle or the complete media schedule. It puts all media on a level playing field and is calculated as follows:

CPM = Total Schedule Cost/Gross Impressions (000)

Let's use an example of 133,000,000 adults 18 to 49, and assume that an ad in *US Weekly* costs $130,000, while one in *People* costs $250,000. A total of 39,900,000 impressions would be generated (30 TRPs/100 × 133 million adults). At a total cost of $380,000, the cost per thousand would be $9.52. This means it costs $9.52 to reach 1,000 adults age 18 to 49 with one ad in *US Weekly* and one in *People* in a given week. By using this formula, you can compare the cost efficiency of one vehicle, media category, or schedule against another.

Cost per Point (CPP)

Another useful media tool is the cost per rating point (CPP), which offers a different way of comparing media schedules. Here, you find the cost of one rating point for each media vehicle against your target by dividing the total schedule cost by gross rating points:

CPP = Total Schedule Cost/Gross Rating Points

With our total cost of $380,000 and total rating points of 30, the cost per point comes out to be $12,667. It therefore costs $12,667 to obtain one rating point against adults 18 to 49 using one ad in *US Weekly* and one in *People*. If you know the cost per point against a particular target group and the approximate number of rating points you wish to buy, you can then calculate an approximate total schedule cost, using the same formula.

Note that the CPM and CPP are interrelated. That is, if you know the size of your target audience, you can calculate a CPP from a CPM, or vice-versa.

CPM = (CPP/1% of target audience) × 1,000
CPP = (CPM/1,000) × 1% of target audience

Gross vs. Net

One of the historical traditions of the media business that remains in place today is the use of gross versus net costs. This was how agencies traditionally made money—they bought the media time or space at one price and charged their advertiser clients a 15% margin (gross up) on the cost. Today, many agencies and clients have different cost structures in place. They may have a flat fee arrangement, so the agency will pay net costs to media companies and charge that same amount to the advertiser, but it is important as a media specialist to understand the relationship between gross and net.

Using the example, above, of a one-page ad in *People* where the gross cost is $250,000, you simply multiply that gross cost by 0.85:

$250,000 × 0.85 = $212,500

This would be the net amount charged to the advertiser.

Category-Specific Criteria

In addition to knowing the general terms that are used in media planning, it is helpful to be familiar with some of the other criteria that are used in selecting each major media category. The rest of this chapter will outline these considerations.

Considerations for Television Advertising

The chief currency for a television plan is the program rating. Historically, there was no measurement of audience exposure to the actual *commercials*, relying instead on the surrogate number of how many people watched the *program* in which it ran. Starting in 2008, we began to look at commercial ratings averaged across a commercial break, or pod. All of the data are available from Nielsen Media Research, for both national and local markets. Both types of ratings are collected on a minute-by-minute basis, but reported for programs based on the audience size at the mid-minute of the quarter hour and for commercials based on the average of all commercial minutes viewed where more than half of the minute was commercial rather than program time. Outside of the U.S., viewing data is usually collected every second, and reported for each minute. The U.S. viewing data is starting to be gathered and reported at this level of detail too, since digital set-top boxes are capturing that anyway.

The U.S. TV marketplace operates based on the laws of supply and demand. The more people who watch a particular show, the more expensive it is to advertise within it. The ranges are enormous. You might pay $500,000 or more for a 30-second commercial on network television during prime time, but only a few hundred dollars to have your ad appear on your local TV station during the night. That cost will correspond to the number of people exposed to your ad—millions, versus a few hundred.

An important measure for television is the *share*. That is, of all those watching television at a given time, what percentage are tuned to the program of interest? The share can be looked at as a percentage of all households using TV (or HUT), or more commonly, as a percent of all of your desired target group (persons using TV, or PUT).

And in today's marketplace, where one-third or more of homes have DVRs, the issue of timeshifted viewing has become critical. As noted earlier in this chapter, Nielsen now provides ratings that include the *Live+3* national ratings and *Live+7* local market ratings, which include the audience (to commercial break for national or to program for local) at the time of airing (live), plus any audience for that same program who viewed it within 72 hours (+3) nationally or within 7 days (+7) locally. The data help account for viewers who recorded a program for later viewing, and therefore watched the commercials after their initial airtime.

In addition to the costs and ratings, it can be helpful to look at the Viewers per Viewing (or Tuning) Household, or VPVH numbers (sometimes called VPTH). This figure provides you with an assessment of the concentration of a given demographic group in a program's audience, showing how many people in every thousand viewers fall into that particular category. If the VPVH among women 25 to 54 for *The Bachelor* is 535, and for the *Masters Golf Championship* it is 155, that indicates you will reach more than three times as many women 25 to 54 with an ad placed in the reality show than you will with the golf tournament.

One way that the VPVH can usefully be applied is in the conversion of household rating points to target audience ratings. This is done by creating a *conversion factor* that is then applied to the household rating. For example, if you know that there are 420 viewers per viewing household for your men 18 to 49 target watching *CSI* and the total population size of that group is 66,000,000, while the total number of households is 110,000,000, then your steps would be as follows:

$(675 \times 110{,}000{,}000) / 66{,}000{,}000 = 0.7 =$ Conversion Factor (CF)
14.3 household rating $\times 0.70$ CF $= 10.01$ M18–49 rating

What you should be most interested in, as a media specialist, is finding which programs are going to best reach your target audience. As we noted in Chapter 3, although you may have a fairly detailed description of your customer, when it comes to getting data on TV audiences you will end up looking primarily at age and gender. Since those have traditionally been believed to be powerful determinants of product purchase and behavior, for many goods and services those numbers will suffice. Newer data that combines household-level set top box data (passively collected) with frequent shopper card data is starting to suggest, however, that looking at viewing behavior based on category or brand consumption may well be a better way to demonstrate how TV advertising works. But until the industry finds an affordable, large-scale, and reliable way of measuring TV viewing according to product usage patterns, it is likely that program ratings among broad demographic groups will remain the primary benchmark.

One other way to analyze TV viewing behavior in a more in-depth manner is by combining the TV ratings data with lifestyle and other media use information from another source. This process, known as *data fusion*, has been successfully used in many countries. It is now being utilized in the U.S. What the process involves is "matching" respondents from two different databases, linking them on a number of common variables (gender, age, geographic location, ethnicity, etc.) known as "hooks," and then "fusing" the data so that the information that is unique to one dataset can be used to describe or explain the behavior of all the respondents in both datasets. It is a complex and intricate process, however, requiring statistical expertise and understanding.

In selecting your TV programs, you should keep in mind that the list may be changed when the commercial time is bought. The plan is just that—a *plan* of which media vehicles are desired. When negotiations take place, it may be that other programs are included, or some of your recommendations rejected, based on other considerations such as cost and availability. What you should emphasize, however, is the *daypart* that you wish your ads to appear in, for although people do tend to watch individual programs rather than time periods, there is more similarity in the kinds of programs watched within time periods than across them. Alternatively, you may wish to specify the *program type*, or genre so that the buy focuses on comedies, for example, or news programming, regardless of when it airs.

The criteria you use to evaluate which programs to use for television do not vary whether you are planning to use network, spot, syndication, or cable. If you are planning on a local level, however, there is additional work to be done. You must select the markets to advertise in (if you have not done so already) and, more particularly, the stations within those markets that you want to use. That will depend in part on the negotiations that are done by the media buyer. That process is explained more fully in Chapter 9.

For cable TV, you may have to rely on broad network information rather than specific programs. Most individual cable shows tend to have much smaller audiences (ratings) than do shows on network or spot TV. But those audiences may be more finely targeted due to the nature of this form of television (see Chapter 4). Often, cable networks are airing programs multiple times, and offering an aggregated rating to advertisers, so that across all showings of an episode of *Biography* on A&E, for example, you will reach 3 percent of the viewing audience even if that audience is spread across three different airings.

Another consideration for cable is the distribution of the network. That is, some of the newer or smaller networks are not available for viewing in all U.S. households, which often leads the networks themselves to try to sell their audiences based on a *coverage-area rating* (a national rating that has been adjusted for the area covered by the distribution). For instance, if Cable Network X is only available in half of the country, its 2.0 nationally reported rating is really a 4.0 since only half of the population is watching it (2.0/50%). Many buyers do not like to adjust for the coverage, since it makes it harder to draw apples-to-apples comparisons.

Considerations for Radio Advertising

Radio uses the same principal term as television for planning and buying purposes. That is, you purchase time based on audience ratings. The main difference here is that the rating is based on a time period, rather than on a program. For the most part, you plan radio by dayparts (listed in Chapter 4), although it is possible, for an additional cost, to specify selected, narrower time periods. For example, if you operate a number of McDonald's franchises and only want to advertise in the hour before lunch (which technically falls in Morning Drive), you could request the noon to 1:00 p.m. hour, and most stations will sell that time to you, though perhaps at a premium.

Radio audiences are measured by the Arbitron Company, and reported on a quarter-hour basis, so you can look at the Average Quarter Hour (AQH) rating for each station in a market. This is the average number of people listening to an individual station for at least five minutes within the quarter-hour period, expressed as a percentage. In many larger advertising agencies, the media planner only specifies the markets to be used, leaving it up to the media buyer to choose the actual stations, based on his or her own knowledge of those markets.

The radio market can be defined (and measured) in several ways. The largest geography is called the Designated Market Area, or DMA. It is defined as the viewing or listening area in which the counties that have the stations of the originating market get the largest share of household viewing or listening. Every county in the U.S. is assigned to just one DMA.

A smaller geography for radio is the Total Survey Area, which consists of the metropolitan area, plus outlying additional counties that listen to the major metro stations. In Chicago, the Total Survey Area would not only include the Chicago metropolitan area, but also the rest of Cook, Lake, and DuPage counties, which can also receive Chicago radio station signals. The most narrowly defined measure is the Metro Survey Area. This is defined by government and includes the city and surrounding counties which are closely linked economically to the central city area.

The total radio listening figure is provided in the Persons Using Radio (PUR) measure, which is equivalent to TV's Persons Using Television, or PUT number. This tells you what percentage of a given audience listens to radio at a particular time.

If you are purchasing radio time yourself, a measure that is worth considering is the Time Spent Listening, or TSL. This gives an indication of how much time people are spending with an individual station in a daypart, day, or week. The calculation is as follows:

$$\text{TSL} = \frac{\text{Number of quarter-hours in daypart} \times \text{AQH}}{\text{Total Listening (Audience)}}$$

The more time people spend listening to that particular station, the greater the chance of reaching them with your message. On the other hand, if your goal is to reach as many *different* people as possible, then the TSL may be of less concern.

The media specialist should also consider the *cume rating*, which is the total number of people listening to a particular daypart, expressed as a percentage. And finally, to find out how quickly a station's audience changes, you can calculate or ask for the audience *turnover* figure, which is the ratio of total number of people listening to a particular station in a daypart to the average number listening to that station in a quarter-hour. If the turnover is high, meaning that people don't listen to the station for very long at any one time, then that would suggest you would need to air your ad fairly frequently in order to reach more people.

An increasingly important area of consideration for radio is merchandising and promotion. Many stations are very willing to organize special contests or announcements or "added value" events if you buy time from them. If you own a Baskin-Robbins ice cream store, for instance, perhaps you could arrange for the station to hold a contest, with the prize being an ice cream party for the winner and his family. For a local Comcast cable operator, a radio station could agree to air additional announcements and public service messages, in return for being mentioned on the local access cable channel. A Toyota car dealership might provide the perfect venue for the radio station to send some of its disk jockeys on the road for an afternoon, airing the program from the actual showroom. All of these "extras" can be negotiated for little or no additional cost, yet they provide valuable "free" advertising for you and your company. Moreover, because they are organized on a local basis, they help to enhance your firm's place in the community, offering you some image-building public relations, too.

For network radio, the terms used are the same, but here you must consider which of the networks to include in the plan. At larger agencies this is often left up to the buyer (where planning and buying are separate functions), based on demographic or format specifications.

Radio audience measurement, which currently relies on samples of people in each market to complete a seven-day listening diary, is moving forward to develop and commercialize a passive means of collecting radio listening activity. Arbitron's Portable People Meter, or PPM was launched in the past few years and is the measurement in more than thirty markets. The PPM is a pager-size device worn by a sample of people wherever they go during the day. The meter passively picks up inaudible codes that have been inserted at the radio station. These codes are used to identify which station was being listened to, by whom, and for how long. In effect, the PPM measures *listening* activity, and does so with far greater accuracy for radio than the listening diary, which requires people to actively remember and write down everything they were tuned to. The technology is able to collect codes from anywhere, including television, sports stadia, or retail stores. Arbitron is using these meters to measure radio listening in 15 different countries outside of the U.S. Arbitron is hoping it will become the new currency measurement for radio and, potentially, for other media too.

Considerations for Magazine Advertising

Some of the criteria to consider when planning for magazines include coverage, composition, circulation, subscription, rate base, readership, positioning, and discounts.

Coverage

Just as for the other media forms, the coverage tells you the proportion of a given target group that saw (were "covered" by) the publication in the past month, or whatever is the relevant publication period. The magazine's coverage is similar to a rating in the electronic media.

Composition

This number will show you how concentrated a magazine's audience is with a particular target group. It can be useful in providing the media specialist with some idea of how well the publication will reach your particular audience. If you are advertising baby formula to new mothers, it would be important to know what proportion of the readers of *Baby Talk* and *Parents* have a newborn. While the one-page cost or the CPM may be cheaper in *Parents* than in *Baby Talk*, you may reach more new mothers in *Baby Talk*, making the cost of reaching one thousand of *those* individuals less expensive.

Circulation

It is important to look at how many copies of the magazine are distributed for each issue. This information is either provided by the magazine itself in an audit report or can be obtained from the Audit Bureau of Circulation, the premier source for circulation data. New or very small magazines may not be audited by this independent organization; if that is the case, be wary of relying on the estimates the publisher provides as they cannot be verified. When looking at circulation, the media specialist should also find out what proportion of that figure is *controlled*—distributed free of charge to potentially interested parties. They are usually not the main target audience for the publication and, therefore, would be less interested in seeing the ads that appear. In addition, you should look at the *net paid* circulation figure, which gives you the number of copies sold at no less than half of the basic newsstand or subscription price. Circulation is usually broken out by geographic area, which can be very helpful, particularly for products that have regional skews.

Subscription or Single Copy

Another valuable number is the percentage of copies that are sold by subscription versus on the newsstand (single copies). If people are getting their copies sent to them every month, that might suggest they are particularly keen to keep receiving and reading the magazine; on the other hand, the argument could be made that the single copy reader renews her commitment to the publication every time she purchases an issue. Whichever side you believe, it is worth finding out how the subscriptions are sold, and at what price. Publishers used to be able to discount subscriptions very heavily (up to 50 percent) and still consider them a full subscription. Beginning in 2002, magazines had to report the net average subscription price paid by consumers, and reveal the proportion of subscriptions sold at 35 percent less than that average. This is to counter the belief that, when the price is very low or there are enticing premiums offered to those who buy a year's worth of the magazine, the subscriber is more interested in receiving the accompanying free gifts than in looking at your ads.

Rate Base

Finally, you should find out how many times in the past six months or one year the publisher has not met his guaranteed audience size, or rate base. This is the number of copies that he promises the advertiser he will sell. Although the advertiser does not get anything back if that number is not reached, a magazine that consistently fails to meet its rate base is probably one you should avoid. This information is provided by companies such as the Audit Bureau of Circulation that measure circulation on a regular basis. The magazine publisher should also release that data upon request.

Readership

For those who have access to syndicated services, there is a wealth of additional information available on reading habits for individual consumer magazines. This includes factors such as the average number of days a title is read, the average number of minutes spent with the publication, where it is read, what actions were taken after reading it, and how many readers saw each copy. These qualitative data are summarized in Exhibit 6.4. They may be provided by the individual publication.

Exhibit 6.4 Qualitative magazine data

Where read
Bought versus obtained
Days spent reading
Time spent reading
Actions taken (e.g., clipped coupon, called toll free number)
Rating of publication
Interest in advertising
Attitudes toward advertising in specific publication
One of my favorites

Armed with all of this information, the media specialist can then compile a list of preferred magazines to use in the plan. Clearly, the cost of the ad page will also be a crucial factor in determining which individual titles are selected.

Positioning

There is conflicting evidence concerning where it is best for your ad to be in a magazine. Some studies have shown a clear advantage for being at the front of the issue or on the cover page, while others suggest there is little difference in terms of likelihood of being seen. Positioning will also depend on the publication. For some magazines, such as *Cosmopolitan* or *Newsweek*, most of the feature articles appear in the first two-thirds of the book. But for more specialized magazines, such as *Network Computing* or *Info World*, readers may also be extremely interested in the smaller ads at the back of the issue which feature products or services for the computer enthusiast.

Discounts

Ten or more years ago, all magazine ads were bought off a rate card that specified exactly how much an ad would cost per issue. While discounts were given for placing ads in several issues, there was little room for any negotiation. In today's highly fragmented media world, magazines have been forced to become more competitive, both between titles and against other media. One positive result of this, for the advertiser, is that magazines are far more willing to negotiate discounts or special deals now than they were previously. An advertiser who places a large *volume* of ads (and, therefore, dollars) in a magazine will get a special deal, as will advertisers who build up frequency or continuity with the publication. There is also a slight discount for cash payments. It is always worth checking with the magazine's representative to find out if there are ways to lower the unit cost.

Considerations for Newspaper Advertising

If newspapers are to be included in the media plan, the first consideration is which markets are to be used. The list of markets can be developed based on population or household size, on sales data of the product, or on CDIs and BDIs. A list created according to population may be a simple ranking of the markets (top 10, top 20, and so on), or it could be a ranking based on the target audience (top 10 markets where the target is located). Market lists that are based on sales data will tend to emphasize those places where current sales are occurring, while one derived from CDI or BDI figures will also factor in potential sales opportunities.

In looking at the individual markets, the media specialist needs to have a clear understanding of the product's distribution within those areas. Is it available primarily within certain parts of the market, or DMA? Is it found more in the metro area or the suburbs? Are there any major ethnic areas of the market that could play a role in product or media usage?

Once you have determined which markets to use, there are three main criteria to consider for newspaper planning: circulation, coverage, and readership.

Circulation

As with magazines, the newspaper circulation figure tells you the number of actual copies that are distributed. This figure is used to compare one paper with another, as well as give some idea of how many coupons might potentially be distributed. Circulation is often broken out into counties or city zones, depending on the size of the market. While one newspaper might have a larger overall circulation, another might deliver more readers in the particular zone where your retail outlet is located and therefore be a more appropriate vehicle to use.

Coverage

The coverage number, also called the newspaper penetration, is the print equivalent of a TV rating. That is, it shows the percentage of households reached by a given newspaper. As with the circulation figure, the numbers might look different depending on how the coverage is defined. Taking Boston as an example, if you only consider the overall market, or DMA household penetration, you might choose the *Boston Globe*, but if you are interested in reaching singles, or African-Americans, the *Boston Herald* has greater coverage.

Readership

Newspaper readership figures provide more detailed information about the paper's readers according to standard demographic breaks or, where available, product usage data. Using these numbers, the media specialist can find out what proportion of the readership is 18 to 49, for example, or how many readers are working women. One newspaper may reach more men than women, or more younger adults than older ones.

The media specialist can use all three criteria to compare different newspapers both within and between markets, as well as help determine which individual papers will do the best job of reaching the given target audience. In markets where there is more than one newspaper available, it is also important to find out how much duplication there is of readers to both vehicles. It could be that one is aimed primarily at the city and the other is read mostly in the suburbs, or that Paper A reaches the northern section and Paper B is preferred in the south. Your selection of individual or multiple newspapers will depend to a large degree on the geographic areas that you wish to cover.

Digital

An increasingly important consideration for newspaper advertisers is to look at what proportion of readership occurs online. For as more and more consumers get their news in digital form, newspapers are adapting to that reality and promoting their online readership in conjunction with their print audiences.

Considerations for Outdoor Advertising

As with newspapers, the main decision to be made when including outdoor boards in a media plan is which markets to select. Once that is known, the media specialist must determine which kind of outdoor board to use— poster panels, or bulletins. In either case, the unit of sale is the *showing*. It is typically sold as a 25, 50, 75, or 100 GRP showing. The number refers to how many panels or boards are required to reach that proportion of the market. A 50 GRP showing, for example, means that your ad will appear on enough boards to reach 50 percent of the total population daily. This is completely market specific. Generally, the outdoor company will provide you with the information on how many boards make up each showing size.

Audience delivery estimates are usually also made available by the company that owns the boards, or can be obtained from the Traffic Audit Bureau, which conducts the independent measurement of traffic past those sites. Outdoor billboard measurement in the U.S. has been greatly enhanced through the development of the "Eyes On" research initiative whereby estimates have been made to calculate the audience of the ads rather than simply traffic counts. The method, discussed in Chapter 4, starts with those counts, but applies "visibility adjustments" based on ongoing research to move from circulation to ad exposure.

Considerations for Internet Advertising

Advertising on the Internet is still being standardized, so the considerations a media specialist needs to be aware of today may well have changed by tomorrow. But several of the basic considerations are comparable to those of other media.

Position

When Internet advertising was first developed, it didn't matter too much where your ad appeared. It was assumed that it would be enticing and involving enough to attract attention anywhere on the site. Soon, however, advertisers realized that position was as important on the Web as in any other medium. Today, advertisers not only have to select the type of ad to use (banners, buttons, pop-ups, etc.) but also when and where those ads will appear. The cheapest form is Run of Site (ROS), but most advertisers prefer to pay for a fixed position on a specific page within the site, to have greater control over who will be exposed to that ad message and, increasingly, differentiation is being made over whether or not the placement is "above the fold" (on the top part of the screen that appears first before the user has to scroll down).

Type of ad

Initially, the most popular kind of ad on the Internet was the banner. This appeared as a rectangle at the top or bottom of the screen or web page. Over time, however, sites introduced a wide variety of alternatives, including the "skyscraper" (going down the left or right hand side of the screen), the button, a small icon or message that links to the advertiser's own site, or an interstitial, a mini-site that appears when the user clicks on the ad. An increasingly powerful form of Internet advertising is search. Here, on websites such as Google or Yahoo Search, consumers type in what they are looking for on the Internet, and a list of possibilities comes up. Advertisers can pay the site to have their product or service appear as a *sponsored link*. Research has shown that, as long as the link is relevant to what the consumer is looking for, he or she will generally not object to the fact that the search result has been paid for.

Metric

Because the Internet is a more "measurable" medium than any other (except direct response), the metric used can vary. Advertisers can pay for their web ads based on a simple cost per thousand (CPM), or can be more specific and agree to a contract that allows them to pay on a cost-per-click or even cost-per-sale basis. Indeed, although the traditional terms of reach and frequency are employed for online campaigns, their meaning differs from other media. Unlike TV or magazines, for example, where the number or percent of the target reached is based on the content in which an ad appears, for online the viewers' exposure to a web page is not necessarily equivalent to their exposure to the ad on that page. The ads are served when the viewer requests a page, so the more frequently he or she does so the more opportunities there are for ad exposure. At the same time, the reach of some online advertising may be more precise and accurate. With search ads on Google or other search engines, people are directly requesting information (including ads) and when they click on the ad, the site knows precisely how many computers (households) were reached, and how many times.

Considerations for Beyond Traditional Communications

For the media forms which were covered in Chapter 5, the considerations for a planner focus on two key areas: traffic and cost relative to value.

Traffic

For sponsorships, sporting events, or other location-based opportunities, the planner should try to estimate, in advance, how many people will be in attendance. Even for skywriting above a popular beach, the vendor is likely to know approximately how many sunbathers typically come there on a weekend, for example. Attendance to sports stadiums is easy to capture, as are the number of people at a rock concert or movie theater, if your product is the concert sponsor or is being given away as samples in the theater lobby. While not a substitute for actual impact, traffic measures at least give an indication of how many people, in theory, will have the opportunity for exposure. For word-of-mouth efforts, the number to determine is how many people could potentially be influenced by the viral efforts.

Cost/Value

Given that it is not enough for marketers to have their name placed in front of hundreds, or thousands of warm, but disinterested bodies, the planner should also try to assess the value of those expected impressions relative to the cost of obtaining them. Here, it is probably good to consider the contextual relevance of the impact. That is, it might make good sense to have Adidas be a featured sponsor at sports stadiums when soccer matches are played, but less so for a prescription drug such as Paxil to be present at those same events. For other less traditional forms, such as mobile marketing or word of mouth, the costs may be relatively low, but the impact may also be small depending on the scope of the campaign.

Summary

In this chapter, we covered some of the basic terms and features of media planning. In order to understand media, it is essential that the media specialist be familiar with the concepts of reach, frequency, gross rating points, and gross impressions. Beyond these, it is also helpful to understand the notion of effective frequency, which assumes that in order for an ad to be effective, the target audience has to be exposed to it more than one time. Frequency planning forces you to think about exposure within the purchase cycle. An exposure distribution lets you know the number of people who are exposed a given number of times to an individual vehicle or a complete media schedule. Media costs are accounted for by calculating the cost per thousand (CPM) and cost per rating point (CPP).

The remainder of the chapter looked at various considerations for each major media category. For television, this includes the program rating, audience composition, viewers per viewing household (VPVH). Radio plans need to examine the time spent listening, cumulative rating, and audience turnover. When magazines or newspapers are included in a media plan, it is important to know the publication's circulation, rate base, and actual readership. The main consideration for outdoor is planning the appropriate showing level to reach a given proportion of the target audience with the correct number of billboards, along with the newer "eyes on" measure of likely ad exposure. For Internet advertising, the specialist should consider position, type of ad, and measurement metric. Finally, for beyond traditional media forms, planners should assess the potential traffic for an event or location, as well as the cost relative to the value of the spending.

Checklist—Terms, Calculations, and Considerations

1. Have you figured out how many gross rating points your schedule will deliver?
2. What is the reach, effective reach, and average frequency of that schedule?
3. If you plan to include television in the schedule, have you looked at both program ratings and viewers per thousand viewing household (VPVH)?
4. If you plan to include radio in the schedule, have you looked at the average quarter-hour (AQH) ratings, cume audience, time spent listening and turnover for each station?
5. If you plan to include magazines in the schedule, have you looked at the coverage, composition, circulation, rate base, ad positions, and discounts?
6. If you plan to include newspapers in the schedule, have you looked at the coverage, circulation, and audience composition figures for each paper?

7. If you plan to include outdoor billboards in the schedule, have you looked at the GRPs available in each market being considered?
8. If you plan to include the Internet in the schedule, have you thought about the ad type, position, and measurement metric you want?
9. If you plan to incorporate beyond traditional communications in the schedule, have you thought about the traffic to be generated, and the cost of the efforts relative to their impact?

Chapter 7

Creating the Plan

Putting together a media plan represents the culmination of all the thinking, planning, and organizing that we have discussed in earlier chapters. That is, with sound advertising and media objectives, a knowledge of who it is we wish to reach with our messages, and a clear idea of what different media can offer us, we are now in a position to start assembling the plan. The key idea to keep in mind when doing this is your *media strategy*. What is it you are hoping to achieve by using media vehicle X as opposed to Y? How will your combination of media categories and vehicles help fulfill your advertising and media objectives? As with any process, there are several steps to the creation of the plan. These are outlined in this chapter.

Target Audience's Use of and Relationship to Media

The first step in building the media plan is finding out which media your target audience uses and what their relationship is with those media. There is not much point in putting your message about Allstate insurance on hundreds of radio stations across the country if the 25 to 54 year olds you are trying to reach tend to be heavy television viewers. Second, you can discover the media habits of your potential customers through syndicated services such as Mediamark Research, Inc. (MRI) or Simmons, or through custom studies that you conduct or solicit on your own. The third alternative, which is the cheapest but may be less accurate, is to do some mini-research on your own. You might want to start asking your clients or customers where they have seen your ads; if you have been advertising in the local newspaper for years but nobody mentions it, then that might indicate the need for a different medium.

By this point, given what you now know about what each media type can offer (and what it can't), you are probably starting to see how the various media will fit in to your particular strategy. So if your goal is to increase awareness of your beauty salon's new manicure and massage treatments, you might turn to the media best suited to that awareness goal—television and the Internet. On the other hand, if you want to increase the frequency of visits to Pizza Hut restaurant, then local radio might be a better bet because you can place a large number of ads at a reasonable cost and keep repeating the message to remind listeners of that establishment.

Once you think you have a handle on which media are used, you should then consider more closely the *relationship* of those people with their media. This notion, as explained in Chapter 2, explores the relationship of consumers to media in order to understand how and why they use the media they select.

For example, the 25 to 54-year-old insurance prospects, mentioned above, might watch more television than average, according to the syndicated audience measurement data. But do they do so as an escape from their routines or because they are constantly looking for new information or because they cannot afford other forms of entertainment? By understanding the target's motivations for media use, the planner will be better able to select the right media types, and vehicles, to communicate the advertiser's message.

As you start to assemble your media categories and vehicles you also need to think about several other considerations—the timing of the plan, its scheduling, and its geographic variations. We consider each of these in turn below.

Timing of the Plan

For many products, the timing of the plan is self-evident. That is, you want to advertise snowblowers in winter and sunscreen in summer. Other items are tied in to specific days or weeks of the year, such as Valentine's Day candies or Thanksgiving turkeys. But for the majority of goods and services, you would ideally want to promote them continually, getting your message out on a very regular and frequent basis to reach as many people as you can as often as possible.

There are two obvious drawbacks here. First, for most advertisers, particularly small businesses, they simply cannot afford to do this. And second, there are good reasons *not* to bombard the media constantly with your message. People are going to tire more quickly of your ads, making them tune out or ignore them sooner. They may even grow so irritated by seeing or hearing them all the time that they actually develop less favorable opinions of your brand or company. Most of all, there is no point advertising something unless you have something worth saying. Remember, an advertising message has got to tell the consumer about something that they will be interested in. If all you did was place a message in the paper or on the Internet 365 days of the year saying "I'm here," you would be unlikely to see much effect, if any, on your sales.

You need to focus your efforts on particular months, weeks, or days. Deciding when to do so is not all that difficult. Most businesses have some seasonality to them, even those that are used or frequented all the time. You probably know, for example, that people stock up on office supplies at the end of the financial period (quarterly or semi-annually); they flock to health clubs at the start of the New Year and when the weather begins turning warmer. Apartment leases tend to be signed in May and October, making the rental business busy just prior to those dates.

You might want to use one of two tactics here. Either you could focus your efforts on promoting your product right before the peak period, reminding people of your existence and trying to take additional share points away from your competitors. Or you could try to build up sales at other times of the year. Or you could try a combination of the two, maintaining a strong presence during the height of your "season," but also keeping a high profile at a couple of other times during the year, too. If you do choose to advertise when people may not be thinking about your product, then it is even more important that you tell them something new and interesting. Perhaps you lower your membership rates to the health club in March or October, and announce that in local newspapers and magazines. You need not be confined to "typical" seasonal patterns either. Maybe you can "create" an event for your business. *Cooking Light* magazine sponsors an annual bus tour across the country, promoting the products of its advertisers while offering healthy recipes to those who visit the tour bus. Or you can find a charitable cause to support that can enhance your image among your target audience. Kraft Foods, for example, supports an initiative in the U.K. called "Health 4 Schools," donating funds to help the program teach elementary school students about a healthy lifestyle that no only covers diet and nutrition, but also cooking and gardening.[1] Since Kraft's key target is women with children, this is an approach that likely makes those moms think more highly of the Kraft brands when they are in the store. These kinds of special activities not only provide excellent opportunities for self-promotion in the media, but they can also generate additional coverage through public relations efforts and publicity.

It is also worthwhile considering the seasonality of the media you are planning to use. Most media categories have seasonal variations—the fourth quarter is often very tight, for example, because of pre-holiday advertising. For media sold on a supply-and-demand basis, such as radio and television, this can affect prices considerably. There are only a fixed number of minutes of commercial time available. Even for those media that have rate cards, such as magazines and newspapers, heavy media demand for space during those months may mean it is especially important to place orders well in advance. Other events happen less frequently but have a predictable impact on media buys. Congressional elections every other year, and presidential elections every four years, mean that the spring primaries and fall elections can have a significant impact on media availability and pricing in those time periods. In the sporting world, the winter and summer Olympics, alternating with each other every two years, affect national media buys around the time of those special events.

Balancing Reach and Frequency

As you develop your media plan, it is important to keep track of how well it will perform. That is, you need to keep calculating your reach and frequency measures to compare one potential plan against another. The goal is to find the right medium, or combination of media, that will realize your media objectives given the amount of money you have to spend. You can do so using the simple calculations shown in earlier chapters, based on the size of your target audience and the ratings of the individual media vehicles.

It may turn out that you will not be able to achieve the specific number you set as your goal for reach and/or frequency. In that event, you need to consider several possibilities. It may be that a 55 percent reach of the target is acceptable, even though you had originally planned to reach 65 percent, or that a frequency of three is all right when four was the ideal. And keep in mind, of course, that we are dealing here with plan *estimates* rather than actual reach figures. You may be restricted in the actions you can take. If your client demands that his message is seen on television, then that medium must remain in the plan. But perhaps you can opt for cable TV instead of broadcast, and, by reducing the cost, be able to place the message more frequently and across more channels, thereby increasing the reach.

Alternatively, you might want to rethink your timing and scheduling strategies. Maybe instead of advertising every two weeks for six months, you could place your message every week for three or four months, concentrating your efforts on the most important period and increasing your reach and frequency within that time-span. Or maybe the addition of a third website will help boost the numbers, by reaching additional target members who are not going to see your ad in the two sites you had first selected.

ROI and Media Models

While media planners should have a good understanding of all the media concepts outlined in Chapter 3, today's advertisers and agencies rely heavily on media models to perform the calculations. A media model is a statistical routine performed by computer software packages that goes through the data and manipulates it to project the effectiveness and efficiency of a plan. Various kinds of models are used, all with the overall goal of providing numbers to support the plan. The models are usually based on original numbers of actual audiences to a media type (magazine readership, TV viewership, etc.). They then rely on statistical techniques such as regression to project out from that data to other demographics, time periods, or markets (depending on the scope of the model).

More recently, marketers have started looking closely at econometric modeling, where statistics are used to try to figure out what marketing (and media) elements are driving actual sales. In so doing, they attempt to measure the media's Return on Investment, or ROI. The key question to be answered is: for every dollar spent on television or radio or the Internet, how much is returned in sales? The goal is to receive at least $1 of net profit for each dollar that they invest. If they obtain much less than that, then some argue the money is being wasted. Conversely, if the ROI is much higher than $1, it can suggest they are not spending enough because if the advertising and media are having such an impact, then they should be spending more to make the most of that effect. While the techniques used are fairly complex, the idea of holding advertising media more accountable for their performance is one that has found favor among high-ranking executives at many corporations. Some find it difficult to believe that any kind of model can truly determine the proportion of sales delivered by any form of indirect and/or brand image advertising (as opposed to truly measurable direct response, promotional, or Internet advertising). But as marketing budgets are increasingly scrutinized, these types of models will only gain in popularity and use.

Much of the interest in ROI has been driven by the growth in digital spending. With Internet advertising, for example, it became possible to look at the behavioral response to an ad. How many clicked on it? And of those, who went through to purchase the product (or take some other action)? Over the past few years, most traditional media have been looking for ways to demonstrate a similar level of accountability. Some, such as radio or magazines, have relied primarily on custom research using the mix models, to show sales driven by ads in their platforms. In television, the development of set top box data collected at the household level has provided new ways to measure the impact of TV spots. One company in particular, TRA, has linked that data to frequent shopper cards in the same household, thereby measuring directly the link between TV ad exposure and product (supermarket) sales.

Indeed, in an increasingly cost-conscious world, marketers want to know precisely what they get back in return for each dollar that they spend in media. Most accountability studies focus on the short-term impact of the advertising. Did it generate immediate sales of the brand? It is much harder to measure precisely the long-term impact. Let's say your ad for Razor Sharp razors appears in a magazine in one month. Your target does not need any razors for the next three months, but in the fourth month, when he is at the store, he sees the product, remembers the ad, and decides he will try it. Many accountability models would not be able to capture that kind of longer-term effect.

Another typically unmeasured effect is what is called the halo effect of advertising. You might see an ad campaign for Fantastik cleaning spray that talks about how SC Johnson, its manufacturer, cares about keeping families healthy by removing germs from their homes. Your favorable impression of the brand may be transferred to other cleaning products made by the same company, such as RAID or Pledge, even if they are in other cleaning product categories. That "halo" is very hard to capture in statistical models, simply because it is hard to measure with any degree of accuracy. How much of the sales results for RAID, for example, can be attributed to consumers' reaction to the Fantastik advertising?

Indeed, advertising's impact is not always reflected solely in terms of sales. Many brands use the media to convey a message that is designed to improve awareness or enhance brand loyalty or increase brand consideration. If every ad was supposed to generate an immediate sale, companies that make cars or computers or other high-ticket items would be wasting the vast majority of their ad dollars! Despite these reservations, more and more advertisers are asking questions about the ROI of their media spending. While you as a media specialist may not have simple answers, you should at least be aware of the discussions going on around the topic.

Scheduling Your Ads

You may have a good idea about when to start running your ads. The next question to think about is how to schedule them. Do you want them running each week for six weeks (continuity), or twice a month all year (bursts), or for alternating six-week periods (flighting)? The answer to this question will depend primarily on two interrelated factors: your media objective and your sales pattern. There should always be a timing component stated in your objective, which will give you some guidance for the scheduling of the plan. If you hope to reach 60 percent of your target during the next six months with the message that your hospital was rated the number one pediatric hospital in the city by a *U.S. News* survey, then you may want to disperse your ads throughout the period to reach as many different people in your audience as possible. For H&R Block that wants to expose people to its message about its electronic tax filing capabilities, there would be good reason to schedule most of the ads in the three months prior to the April 15 tax deadline date, building up the frequency of the message at the time of year when it is most appropriate.

You should also think about the scheduling of different media, and their combination. Perhaps you could advertise your Subway store in the local newspaper every week of the year, and supplement it with local cable, Internet or mobile ads around the time of each special promotion.

Much of what we know about scheduling tactics comes from our general knowledge on reach and frequency. That is, if you wish to reach as many *different* people as possible in your target audience, then you want to disperse your messages across media, vehicles, or days and dayparts, for example. On the other hand, if you want to ensure that your audience hears or sees your ads several times in a given period, you would concentrate them in fewer media, vehicles, days or dayparts.

The pattern of scheduling does not seem to make a difference, however, in terms of total reach. So whether your ads appear in two sequential weeks or alternate weeks (one week on, one week off), or are placed one week a month over four months, the final reach will be approximately the same. One thing to keep in mind, however, is that if you schedule too many ads within a short timeframe, your audience is likely to ignore or tune out those messages, because they are tired of seeing them, a phenomenon known as *wearout*. The timing element could be critical, depending on your product. It would not make much sense to spread ads for a highly seasonal item such as suntan lotion or Christmas decorations across many months; but if you are promoting your Charles Schwab office through newspaper ads and on the Internet, there is something to be said for having a fairly constant presence during the year (perhaps changing the message to tie in to the financial cycle).

Two television scheduling tactics that are sometimes used among major advertisers are *double-spotting* and *roadblocking*. Double-spotting refers to placing two spots within the same program. The effect of this technique is to increase the likelihood of multiple exposure to your ad message (i.e., increased frequency). Often these ads appear at the beginning and end of the commercial break, a tactic known as *bookending*. Part of the expectation is that, even if you have tuned away at the start of the break, you will see the ad at the end of the break when you are returning to watch the program content. *Roadblocking* means placing the same ad across as many channels as possible at the same time, so that when Joe Smith is watching television at 8:06 p.m. on a Friday night, whichever channel he turns to, he'll see the same ad. That has become harder and harder for advertisers to do as the number of available channels grows higher, making it a much more expensive proposition to undertake. The impact, however, is going to be an increase in reach, as your spot will be seen not only by Joe, but by everyone who was watching those other channels at 8:06 p.m.

In the 1990s, considerable research was conducted on how best to schedule ad messages to impact sales. A study done by John Philip Jones examined the purchase records of households who also had their TV viewing captured via TV set meters (to record what channels were viewed). The results clearly showed that to achieve the greatest "short term advertising strength," or STAS, the best scheduling tactic was to place at least one message per week across as many weeks as possible. In this way, the plan could impact more people closer to the time of purchase. While the study had some significant limitations (it only looked at packaged goods, only dealt with television advertising, and only examined households rather than people), its impact was profound. Advertisers began switching their scheduling, moving away from trying to achieve a 3+ reach in a month. Instead, they began looking at a 1+ reach per week, a strategy known as *frequency planning*. Here, the schedule calls for fewer GRPs per week, spread across more weeks of the year. While this doesn't make sense in many categories, especially those that require lengthy or high-involvement decisions by consumers (cars, houses, financial services), for many packaged goods manufacturers, frequency planning has become the norm.

Cost Efficiencies

Costs are obviously very important for the media plan. So, in addition to keeping track of reach and frequency figures as you create the plan, you must also consider the costs involved. Of course, these are closely related. If you need to increase the frequency of your message, it is going to require more media time or space, which means more money. But as we noted above, it might be possible to find a cheaper medium or vehicle to help your funds go further. Cost efficiencies can be calculated in terms of cost per thousand of the audience reached (CPM) and through cost per rating points (CPP). These were explained in Chapter 6. The more "mass" the medium, the cheaper it will be on a CPM basis, but the less targeted it will be for your situation. That is, there will be a lot of "waste" exposures of people who are probably not interested in what you have for sale. For a widely used product or service, such as car tires or a muffler shop, that might not be a bad thing. But if you are trying to reach a narrower group of people, such as Corvette car owners, to offer them a specially designed luggage rack that sits on the roof of the car, then you would be better off with a higher CPM in a more targeted environment, such as car magazines or car enthusiast websites. The introduction of addressable TV advertising, noted in Chapter 4, is designed to reduce, if not eliminate completely, this waste, by only sending ads to the people you really want to talk to.

Tactical Considerations

As you develop your plan, there are probably going to be numerous additional considerations that are specific to your product or service. These might include trade merchandising, consumer merchandising, national–local integration, and testing.

Trade Merchandising

For many goods and services, the trade plays a critical role in the brand's development and sales. Many media plans that are geared primarily to the consumer market also have some side benefits for the trade. When Frito-Lay promotes its Doritos corn chips, it is telling its distributors and retailers that it is pushing the brand and helping to increase their revenues too. A national ad for McDonald's restaurant is also designed to help the local franchisee.

In putting the plan together, therefore, it is important to look at what trade-merchandising elements may be attached to it. Perhaps for a chain of Jiffy Lube oil-lube shops, you can bring all the operators together for a kick-off party when the media campaign begins. Even something as simple as buttons with your new campaign slogan can help give the trade a sense of being part of the program. Sending them copies of the new ads and/or materials lets them know what message is being promoted to customers. The media can help here as well, particularly if you are one of their valued customers. They may be willing to co-sponsor an event for your distributors or retailers, for example.

One particular type of trade merchandising is cooperative (coop) advertising. With this, two groups agree to divide the cost of the advertising space or time. This may be as simple as a tag placed at the end of a retailer's commercial that mentions the address of the local store. Or it can be a joint promotion of a theme park and a soft drinks company, where the latter is helping fund the ads of the former since it makes money on the drinks sold in the park. For local businesses there are significant benefits to this type of merchandising. If you are a small health food store in Madison, Wisconsin, your ability to advertise on cable TV or in the Wisconsin tourism guide is going to be greatly enhanced if you can get supporting (coop) funds from the Clif Bar company, whose products you sell in your store. Not only would it allow you to promote your business in more, or more expensive, media, you will also most likely be able to afford better-looking ads! There are potential disadvantages, however. Sometimes the manufacturer will impose restrictions on the ads, in terms of both their content/appearance and their distribution and scheduling. But even with those limitations, the coop approach works well in many cases.

Consumer Merchandising

Although we focus here almost exclusively on advertising media, it is important to keep in mind many of the other ways in which you can gain additional exposure for and mileage out of your media plan. There are a multitude of communications possibilities available, from coupons or sampling to press releases and exhibitions and displays. If you are promoting a line of gourmet preserves, then perhaps in addition to the magazine ads that you run, you can talk to the local grocery stores to set up sampling booths in their stores, and feature the dates and locations in the ads. For a wireless phone company promoting the latest cell phones, you could go to local community festivals and let consumers see them, letting people know through local cable or radio ads at which events you will be present. The possibilities for these kinds of tie-ins, or integrated marketing, are almost endless. Whatever you do, however, should remain within the overall communications objectives of your plan—increasing awareness, obtaining customer preference, encouraging brand selection, and so on.

To gain as much advantage as possible from consumer promotions, you might also consider increasing other media weight when a coupon is dropped, or placing more newspaper or Internet ads the week that you are holding the promotion.

National–Local Integration

While some products, such as new movies or product launches, are advertised solely on a national level, and others, such as the local coffeehouse, appear only in local ads, the majority of name brands include both national and local advertising in their media plans. If that is the case, you need to ensure not only that the message is consistent (something handled by the creative team), but also that the media placements are aligned. There are different ways of doing this. For some, particularly the bigger spending advertisers, the local media weight is added to make an even greater impact on the national spending, such as buying spot TV on top of network, or local newspapers in addition to national ones. For others, typically with smaller budgets, the addition of local media helps to stretch the media dollars further, creating the illusion (in selected markets) that the advertiser has a constant presence. In either situation, you should ensure that there is not unwanted duplication, and that the messages do not drown out each other to the point of irritating the consumer or be so inconsistent with each other that the consumer is faced with competing messages.

Testing

For smaller advertisers, the notion of testing a plan may seem unnecessary. If you only have a few thousand dollars to spend, then it doesn't seem worthwhile. However, if you are about to change your entire marketing and media strategy, it is a good idea to see first—on a small scale—whether your new approach is likely to increase sales or harm them. For example, Toys R Us, which traditionally advertised primarily in local newspapers to announce whatever was on sale that week or month, changed its strategy to increase awareness of the wide range of items by moving into national television (broadcast and cable). The potential impact of such a media move could be estimated by placing a few of these ads and including some kind of response mechanism, such as a toll-free number or website address. That way, the company could test how effective the TV ads are.

Testing is also a good idea for making changes in media weight (GRPs). If you are trying to persuade your client to increase annual spending from a few hundred dollars to several thousand, and you face resistance to the idea, then you might suggest a test of the proposed strategy in one or more markets, to see what impact those added dollars would have to the bottom line.

Presenting the Plan

Whenever you present your completed plan, whether it is to upper management at your own company or to your client, you need to keep three points in mind. The first is to *be visual*. Most people either hate or fear media because they believe it is a morass of numbers, most of which they don't understand. So the more you can do to present the information in ways that they can *see* what is going on, the better off you will be. That means using charts, graphs, pictures, photos, or video to liven things up and bring the numbers to life. For instance, if you are presenting the demographic statistics on your target, then perhaps you can make a short video that depicts these people in real life, or present charts or photos that demonstrate who they are.

The second point to remember is to be brief. Although you want to have all of the back-up materials and numbers to support what you are doing, when you make a presentation you should focus on the key points. Assuming you have an interested audience, they will look at the details afterwards or ask you questions as you go along. Again, the common perception of media is that it is a mind-numbing experience, filled with mathematical formulas and statistics that are, quite simply, boring.

Third, and perhaps most importantly, remember the consumer. Ultimately, your plan is designed to help your client sell more widgets *to the consumer*. So if your plan simply recites a hundred different statistics and presents all of the numbers in charts, tables, and flowcharts, it may be totally accurate but will seem completely removed from the marketing reality that your client lives in.

Fortunately, there are ways around these problems. The first, keeping it visual, can be accomplished through the use of a flowchart. This can show, at a glance, when the ads will run, in which media and vehicles, at what cost, and to what effect (reach and frequency). It can be done for each target in a given plan, and be broken out by medium, if desired. An example is shown later in this chapter. There are numerous ways of creating a flowchart. You can simply draw one yourself, or use a spreadsheet computer program, or a custom media flowchart package (see Appendix for details).

Being brief is harder to do. It usually comes down to practice. Running through your presentation with a friend or colleague and asking for their advice can be useful. It is particularly helpful to present your work to someone outside of your area—if they can understand your concise explanations of media terms, then you are doing fine! Remember, however, to include all of the pertinent information (including calculations for how you arrived at your conclusions) in the deck of materials you leave behind. In addition, you have to show how your media plan fits in with and enhances the brand's marketing and advertising objectives and strategies.

Learn as much as possible about the end-user of your product, and include some of those findings in your presentation. You might want to spend some of your own money, for example, to survey some of the customers or do a couple of focus groups to find out how they currently use media and advertising in your category. Include a few of the verbatims (what consumers actually said, in their own words), or even some video of your conversations with customers, to remind your client that you know you are, in the end, dealing with people.

Last but not least, it is crucial to remind your audience that you are dealing with estimates. Some of those may be informed by years of experience, but many are based on your best judgment, syndicated data sources, or mathematical reasoning. People tend to believe that because you, as the media specialist, have placed a number on something, that turns it into "reality." If that were so, media planning would be completely automated and done by rote, a pure science, rather than the combination of art and science that it remains today.

A Media Plan Example

Let's go through an example for a fictitious brand of breakfast cereal, BeneFlakes. This is a nationally distributed health-oriented brand that was first introduced in 2009. It competes primarily with Kellogg's and General Mills' healthier cereals.

Situation Analysis

Through the end of calendar year 2011, BeneFlakes sales are up 10 percent versus a year ago. This is the second year of positive sales growth.

Marketing Objectives/Strategies. Increase BeneFlakes penetration among frequent cereal eaters in two ways:

- Year-round focus on health benefits of cereals, with
- Heavy-up during primary cold cereal months (spring/summer).

Advertising Time Period. January through December 2011
Media Budget. $30 million
Promotional Activity. Free-standing inserts (FSIs) in mid-March and late-June.

Marketing Background

Competitive Analysis[2]

- Kelloggs: Total spending: $250 million. 30% network television; 30% cable TV; 15% magazines; 15% syndicated TV; 10% Internet
- General Mills: Total spending: $240 million. 15% network television, 35% spot TV, 40% cable TV, 10% Internet
- Post: Total spending: $90 million. 40% magazines; 20% cable TV; 15% network television; 5% syndicated TV, 5% Sunday magazines; 5% Internet
- Category total: Total spending: $660 million. 25% network television; 30% cable TV; 15% magazines; 15% spot TV; 5% syndicated TV; 3% Spanish-language TV; 4% Internet; 1% Sunday magazines; 1% radio; 0% newspapers; 1% outdoor.

Seasonality

Cereal usage tends to peak in spring/summer months, but the product is used throughout the year.

BeneFlakes					
J/F	M/A	M/J	J/A	S/O	N/D
74	105	126	128	100	63
Cereal Category					
J/F	M/A	M/J	J/A	S/O	N/D
92	96	115	118	102	80

Advertising Objectives

Raise awareness of the health benefits and good taste of BeneFlakes cereal among target from current level of 30% to goal of 36% during calendar year 2011.

Media Objectives

1. Advertise to frequent cereal eaters. The demographics and psychographics of this target are:

    *   Women 18 to 49, Household Income (HHI) $75,000+
    *   Well educated, professional or managerial, nutrition-oriented

    The target consists of 14 million women who can be defined as natural cereal users (1+ individual portions in past seven days). They represent 20 percent of all women.
2. Achieve the following communication goals:
    Average 4-week delivery

Peak period	Rest of year
3+ reach	3+ reach
+ 35%	10%

3. Provide year-round media support to stimulate usage throughout year, with additional weight during the peak summer months.
4. Schedule advertising to run Wednesday–Sunday to complement key grocery shopping days.
5. Provide national advertising support.

Media Strategies

Following the success of the brand during the past two years, the 2011 media plan recommends a continuation of the media strategy, using television as the primary medium with magazines and the Internet as the secondary media. BeneFlakes has multiple presences on the Web, from its own site, to spaces on parenting sites and blogs, where consumers can get diet and nutrition information.

Television

As the primary medium, national TV provides:

- High reach/awareness builder
- Sight, sound, and motion
- Immediacy of message
- Targetability (niche networks)
- Continuity (lower cost cable networks)
- Contextual relevance
- Emotional connection to viewer/consumer.

The following cable networks are more likely to be viewed by the target:

- Bravo
- Food Network
- ABC Family
- Cartoon Network
- The Learning Channel
- Discovery Channel
- Travel Channel
- Lifetime.

One-half of the weight will be in prime time, with the remainder split between weekend daytime and early morning. Prime time offers the greatest reach, while weekend daytime provides suitable context to reach the target when they are relaxing yet likely to be making grocery shopping trips. The early morning weight provides a more news-oriented context to promote the health benefits of the product.

As a smaller brand, BeneFlakes will only include a small amount of broadcast network TV during peak periods.

Magazines

As the secondary medium, magazines provide:

- Long message life
- Repeat exposure
- Targetability—ability to provide contextually relevant and engaging message
- Editorial compatibility
- Inserts
- Website linkage.

All magazine ads will be 1P4C (one-page, four-color). Preferred position will be:

- Health and fitness—Fitness section

- Food—Front of book
- Parenting—News section.

The recommended magazines will include:

	Coverage	Index
Shape	6.7%	140
Self	6.7 %	139
Real Simple	7.6 %	140
Family Fun	5.3%	137
Food & Wine	5.1%	133
Martha Stewart Living	12.0%	132
Cooking Light	11.3%	130

Internet

As the third medium, the Internet provides:

- Response-based advertising
- Contextual relevance
- Behavioral targeting.

A combination of portals, websites, and key word searches will be utilized. The following sites and portals will be included:

Portals	Sites
AOL Health	Myrecipes.com
Yahoo! Health	Fitness.com
	Webmd.com

In addition, Google Adsense will be used to drive Search on natural health-related keywords.

The final plan

The total cost of this plan will be: $30.0 million (including a 6 percent amount as contingency).

The flowchart in Exhibit 7.2 depicts how the plan would be laid out during the year

Although this is a very generalized and simple version of what to include in a plan, it provides the basic information that has been covered earlier in this book. You should note that all of the recommendations need to be backed up by research data, wherever possible, beyond simple tables showing indices or coverage for individual media vehicles or gross expenditures for the year. Here is a brief list of the kinds of analyses that could be included in the "back-up" for this plan:

- Media usage.
- Cable TV network comparisons
- Magazine comparisons
- Website comparisons
- CPM comparisons (e.g., cable versus print versus online)
- Daypart/program rankings by target
- Detailed reach and frequencies by medium
- Media quintiles
- Purchase volume for brand and category
- Demographic/lifestyle analysis of users
- Brand geographic analysis (BDI vs. CDI by DMA)
- Seasonality analysis
- Grocery shopping patterns
- Historical media plans.

Summary

When creating a media plan, it is crucial to consider first the target audience's use of media, in terms of which categories and vehicles they use. You then must determine the plan's timing, if there are seasonal sales or other elements of the marketing mix (pricing, promotion, distribution or product changes) that will affect the plan's timing. For scheduling of your chosen vehicles, financial considerations and reach and frequency goals will help determine when, and how often, your ads appear. Tactical elements are important, too, particularly trade and consumer merchandising, to receive maximum support from dealers, distributors, and retailers, and maximize the impact of the advertising. If funds permit, or major changes to the plan are being contemplated, it is recommended that the plan be tested on a small scale before being launched in its entirety.

Exhibit 7.1 Sample Flowchart: BeneFlakes 2010 Media Plan

		January					February				March			
		3	10	17	24	31	7	14	21	28	7	14	21	28
BeneFlakes														
Television	Cable: Prime time	15	15	15	15						15	15	15	15
	Broadcast: Prime time													
	Total TRPs	15	15	15	15	0	0	0	0	0	15	15	15	15
	Total Cost ($000)							$4,000						
Magazines	All Titles													
	Total TRPs							40 TRPs/month						
	Total Cost ($000)							$950						
Internet	All Sites													
	Total Cost ($000)							$400						

		April				May					June			
		4	11	18	25	2	9	16	23	30	6	13	20	27
BeneFlakes														
Television	Cable: Prime time	15	15	15	15	15	25	25	25	20	25	25	25	25
	Broadcast: Prime time	15	15	15	15	15		50	50	50	60	60	60	60
	Total TRPs	15	15	15	15	15	25	75	75	70	85	85	85	85
	Total Cost ($000)							$8,500						
Magazines	All Titles													
	Total TRPs							120 TRPs/month						
	Total Cost ($000)							$1,500						
Internet	All Sites													
	Total Cost ($000)							$700						

July – September

		July				August					September				Totals
		4	11	18	25	1	8	15	22	29	5	12	19	26	*TRPs/$*
BeneFlakes															
Television	Cable: Prime time	20	20	20	20	25	25	25	20	20	20	20	20	20	*705*
	Broadcast: Prime time	50	50	50	50	25	25	25	20	20	20	20	20	20	*590*
	Total TRPs	70	70	70	70				25	20	20	20	20	20	*1295*
	Total Cost ($000)							$8,500							*$21,400*
Magazines	All Titles														
	Total TRPs							*100 TRPs/Month*							*660*
	Total Cost ($000)							$1,350							*$4,700*
Internet	All Sites														
	Total Cost ($000)							$750							*$2,150*

October – December

		October					November				December				Totals
		3	10	17	24	31	7	14	21	28	5	12	19	26	*TRPs/$*
BeneFlakes															
Television	Cable: Prime time	0	0	0	0	10	10	10	10		0	0	0	0	
	Broadcast: Prime time	0	0	0	0	10	10	10	10		0	0	0	0	
	Total TRPs														
	Total Cost ($000)							$400							
Magazines	All Titles														
	Total TRPs							*50 TRPs/month*							
	Total Cost ($000)							$900							
Internet	All Sites														
	Total Cost ($000)							$300							

TOTAL GRPs	**3,250**
TOTAL $	**$28,250**

Checklist—Creating the Plan

1. Have you found out as much as possible about your target audience, either through syndicated services, or primary research you yourself conduct?
2. Have you determined the appropriate timing for your messages?
3. How will your messages be scheduled—continuously, in flights, or in bursts?
4. Will your reach and frequency goals be met by your timing and scheduling strategies?
5. Are there merchandising possibilities for your brand, with either the trade or with consumers?
6. Do you need to test the plan first in a smaller location before rolling it out?
7. Can you present your plan in a visually interesting and succinct fashion?
8. Do you have a flowchart or schematic that summarizes the distribution, delivery, and cost of your media plan?

Chapter 8

Offering Alternatives

Once you have completed your media plan, you might think your task is over. But like the Energizer bunny in the popular battery commercials created in the early 1990s, and reintroduced periodically thereafter, it keeps going, and going, and going. In fact, even as you are creating the plan, you should be starting to think about various alternatives. For, while you might be convinced that you have created the perfect, biggest sales-generating, best objectives-meeting media plan ever conceived, the chances are fairly good that it will not be accepted at face value. So rather than going into your presentation believing that your job is over and that the client will immediately accept everything you are recommending, you will be in a much stronger position if you prepare some alternatives beforehand. This chapter will consider what some of those options might be.

Spending More Money

The opportunity to gain a larger budget than you were originally expecting does not happen very often, and certainly not as often as a media specialist might like! However, there are several good reasons for being prepared to spend more on advertising media than was originally proposed. The first, from an agency perspective, is that if you are being paid a commission on the media you buy, the more money you spend, the more you will make. But second, and perhaps more importantly today when fewer and fewer advertisers are paying a 15 percent commission rate, it is your job as the media specialist to prove to the client how much more effective the media plan *could* be if there were more dollars available.

To some people this might sound purely wasteful. There is evidence, after all, to indicate that spending more on advertising may actually result in a *decrease* in sales! But for the most part, research supports the notion that placing more dollars in advertising media to reach more people on more occasions (assuming, of course, that they are the right people for your product) will increase sales. That won't occur in a vacuum; the other

"Ps" of the marketing mix have to be working in your favor too. The product must be one that the marketplace needs; there has to be good distribution; and the price must be appropriate. But given those factors, increasing media dollars will tend to increase sales.

So, under those circumstances, how do you best prepare to offer the alternative of spending more? In many situations, the best way is to simultaneously create a second media plan that has a larger budget allocated to it. If your primary plan has an annual media budget of $2,000,000, then you might consider creating an additional one at the $3,000,000 level to see how that would perform. In doing so, you should not simply throw extra media weight around randomly. Instead, you should revisit your advertising and media objectives and consider what you might set as your goals if you had that extra money to spend. If, for instance, your original goal was to boost awareness of the latest Best Buy store to open in Chicago, then perhaps if your budget was to be 20 percent larger, you might think about setting your objectives higher also, proposing that with the additional funds you could increase awareness to 40 percent in that same time period.

Another option with increased funding is to disperse your message across a wider area. If you have coffee stores located primarily in three states, but are starting to expand into five additional states, then perhaps by spending more money on advertising media you could afford to put your messages into those new areas to let people know of your upcoming presence. Having more money might also allow you to branch out into additional media vehicles or forms. If your basic media plan for Tropicana Orange Juice for kids consists of network television and magazine ads, then perhaps the extra dollars you are recommending be spent could permit you to buy radio or Internet ads.

Of course, in suggesting where and how this extra money could be spent, you must always show what will be achieved in return. That is, you need to quantify, wherever possible, the positive impact those dollars will have. This can be done through reach and frequency calculations that show how many additional people in the target will be reached, and how many more times they will have the opportunity to be exposed to the message. Supplementary funds may also end up *lowering* the cost of individual ads, either through volume or frequency discounts, or by reducing the cost per thousand (CPM). So although the bottom-line cost of the plan may go up, the cost efficiency may actually improve.

Another advantage to spending more media dollars is that they may allow you to reach a secondary target more readily. If you are putting a plan together for the Beef Council, where the primary target audience is women who like to cook, then perhaps expanding the plan will allow you to address more clearly a secondary target audience of restaurant chefs. You might also think about using additional dollars to reach people who can influence your primary target. For a media plan aimed at parents offering a college fund, you might spend the extra monies to promote your company to financial planners to whom the parents will turn for advice.

It is also important to think beyond media when considering how additional dollars might be spent. You might want to recommend undertaking some custom research of your proposed target audience, especially if that target has changed in some way from previous plans. Or research could be done to gain a greater understanding of how the target you are trying to reach uses the media in your plan, or where they turn to for information about the product or service that could, in turn, greatly enhance your media plans in the future. The latter could be particularly valuable if there is very little syndicated data currently available, or if you are in a very specialized or new field, such as biotechnology or wireless web devices.

And, of course, the people who actually create the ads would also like to have more money to spend on their work. Production quality could be improved, commercials lengthened, or better talent hired if more dollars were made available. You could make your direct mail piece look far more professional, or enhance the design on your website, or distribute more samples to individuals visiting your exhibit at a trade show. The possibilities are almost endless. But whatever you recommend for your increased-spending scenario, you must justify it in terms of the objectives and strategies that you have stated upfront (even if you propose modifying those objectives if you get additional funds).

Spending Less Money

Unfortunately, for most media specialists, the more common case is that you will end up having to spend less than originally proposed. And while it is generally not a good idea to present to your client or boss a reduced-spending alternative at the same time as you present your main media plan (unless that has been specifically requested), you would be well advised to start thinking about how you would spend less money as you are developing the basic plan.

There are numerous reasons why you might end up having less money than you anticipated available for your plan. It could be that sales of Pepperidge Farm cookies fell more than expected this year, so marketing budgets for the coming year had to be cut (and remember, advertising is usually the first item to be cut when sales go down, despite the fact that those dollars will typically help *increase* sales). New management or ownership will often result in budgetary changes and, again, more often than not these changes are in a negative direction. It could be that the company decides to speed up the introduction of a new brand and so decides to take money away from the established product for which you are preparing a plan. Or the marketer has opted to deliver a corporate message featuring all its brands in one ad, reducing the amount to be spent on the plan.

Whatever the reason, as you are preparing an alternative plan, think carefully about how you can put together a media schedule that will come as close as possible to meeting your original objectives. There may be several ways to cut corners without decimating the plan. Perhaps you can shorten the flight times, running TV ads for two weeks at a time instead of four, or cut the number of websites you are on, or only place ads in magazines every other month instead of monthly.

Many advertisers today are pulling dollars out of regular national television and switching it into product placement deals that have a lower out-of-pocket cost. A total of $4.25 billion was expected to be spent in this non-traditional advertising form in 2005, up 23 percent from the year before. In the 2004–2005 television season, there were about 7,500 product placements captured in primetime in the six broadcast networks. This activity was not undertaken by a handful of advertisers; rather, more than 1,500 of them placed their brands in the programs.[1]

Creating a reduced-spending scenario should not be a case of simply cutting spots or pages arbitrarily. It must be done with strategic reasoning in mind. For instance, let's say you have a media plan to get more parents in your area to consider sending their children to your client's preschool program, but instead of having $300,000 to spend, you end up having only $240,000. You had originally intended to send direct mailings to all parents of young children in the vicinity, inviting them to visit the school, as well as placing newspaper ads in community papers. Now, with less money to spend, you must reconsider how best to allocate your dollars yet still achieve your objective. Perhaps instead of using direct mail, which tends to be very expensive, you could try to get free publicity by sending a video news release to the local TV stations and media kits to other local media. An open house would also be an inexpensive way of offering parents the opportunity to visit the school. And getting your school's website up and running, and linked to local or regional sites that deal with education would also be fairly simple and inexpensive. But in order to reach a broad cross-section of people, sustaining a minimum level of newspaper ads would probably remain an efficient and effective approach.

When considering which ads or insertions to remove, you must also keep in mind that a reduction in frequency may result in the loss of some volume discounts with the media involved. And when you reduce the number of places your message appears in or on, that will also impact your reach. So reductions will likely mean you come up short on your reach and frequency goals.

Sometimes there is no alternative but cutting one or more media forms from the plan. Before doing so, it is important that you consider each one in turn, deciding what would be the result of eliminating that medium on the overall plan's objectives. This should not be limited to reach and frequency considerations, but also thought of in terms of what the medium can do for your ad and how important that medium is in consumers' lives. If you take out all TV from a plan, then remember that you are losing a key medium that offers sight, sound, and motion and the opportunity to deliver the message to a large audience. That might be less important for a Ford dealership, but critical for a Red Lobster restaurant where you want to showcase the food. And it also depends on how consumers relate to their media. For example, if you know from your communications planning research that your working mother target for Welch's juice boxes has a strong relationship with magazines, then removing them from your plan, even if they represent a higher CPM, is likely to be detrimental to the plan's impact and its ability to engage your audience.

Another way to reduce media spending is to use briefer or less expensive ads. Instead of 30-second commercials, maybe you could make do with half that time; instead of a full-page ad, perhaps a half-page will suffice. Once again, however, this must be considered not simply in numerical terms (such as reach, or CPM), but also in terms of the impact on consumers seeing or hearing that commercial message. Although some research evidence suggests that many consumers cannot tell the difference between a 15-second commercial and a 30-second one, there is obviously less time available in the shorter unit to tell the complete story, so you are missing out on the chance to reinforce your message as thoroughly.

It might seem appropriate, given a reduced media budget, to cut the size of your target audience and plan to reach fewer people. In fact, in many situations that can turn out to be *more* costly, for the more narrowly you try to target your media, the more expensive it becomes to try to reach them. If your original plan for a new Pillsbury cake mix is aimed at all women 18 to 49 and uses a mix of magazines and TV, then by trying to narrow it further to reach only those women 18 to 49 who have household incomes of more than $75,000 and have three or more children you will probably end up looking at more expensive media vehicles. Instead of picking a broadly popular woman's service magazine, such as *Good Housekeeping* or *First for Women*, you might end up with magazines that have a smaller circulation and cost more per ad page, such as *Food and Wine* or *Bon Appetit*. Now admittedly, they *will* reach more of your more narrowly defined target, but the cost may be correspondingly higher too.

One way you could consider making cutbacks on your targets is by eliminating any secondary targets you had planned to reach through separate media. A plan that was intended to increase awareness of an environmentally friendly detergent might be aimed at both environmentally aware consumers and opinion leaders. Faced with a cutback in media dollars, you might consider targeting only one of those groups initially, rather than both of them at once.

It is extremely important to outline the implications and results of spending less on advertising media. This should not be done in a gloom-and-doom fashion, portraying a picture of complete failure if $50,000 is removed from the budget, but neither should it be taken lightly and happily accepted without a fuss. If for no other reason, explaining what you believe might happen if those media dollars are removed will show to your client that you have thought through in a strategic way the possible outcomes of alternative plans. Keep in mind that your ultimate goal is to get those media dollars restored as soon as it is feasible to do so.

Changing Targets

Sometimes after you have presented a complete media plan to the client and have apparently won approval for it, a little voice in the back of the room will speak up and say, seemingly casually, "But what would happen if we targeted X instead?" That simple sentence can send the alarm bells flashing and blood pressure soaring for the media specialist. It is important not to panic at that point but, rather, to think carefully about whether there is real merit to the question.

First of all, you must ensure that the media target is in line with the brand's marketing target, otherwise it will be hard for the media plan to fully achieve the overall marketing objectives. Although you may feel indignant that anyone is questioning your plan's target, particularly after all the work you have put into it, you need to step back and take a careful, considered look at the proposition. For as much as you may be reluctant to admit it, it could be that the person making the suggestion has actually hit upon a potentially valuable target which you had simply not considered or realized how important it could be. Sometimes it takes so long for the client and agency to agree on a single target, that once that definition has been pinned down there is a tendency for the media specialist to put on the blinders and work feverishly to deliver a plan with the agreed-upon target. Any considerations of alternatives have been set aside out of gratitude that the client has finally accepted at least one customer group. But as you are increasingly wrapped up in that target audience, the client may have time to sit back and ponder other possibilities, and may come up with one that is more appropriate, or equally so.

In the best scenario, that alternative target *is* in fact one that you had considered and rejected, either because of strategic or financial reasons. You can then explain why the different target would not be appropriate or feasible. If you had not already done so, then it is in everyone's interest to look more carefully at the proposed alternative (unless it seems so outlandish and unreasonable that you are certain there is no merit to it). It could be that a simple discussion then and there will be enough to determine whether this option should be investigated further. Or you may have to go back to syndicated research or whatever sources you were using to define the target and examine the proposed alternative more closely.

There are other situations where it is incumbent upon you, as the media specialist, to consider different targets as you are developing the primary plan. As noted above, this could be because you are creating alternative spending scenarios with more or fewer dollars available. But it might also arise because of disagreement or uncertainty over who the best target for the product is. Perhaps your bank client has always targeted its media plan to promote its mortgages at young couples looking for their first home. You, as the media specialist, might put together a second plan that targets older couples whose children have left home who want to move to a smaller but more elegant home for their retirement, or are perhaps contemplating buying a second weekend home. Clearly, the media that you would use to reach each target group would be very different.

It could also be important to include different targets in a plan, or create a separate plan for those targets, when you think that there are critical secondary audiences who need to be addressed. This is highly dependent on the product category. For medicines or healthcare items, for example, it is often essential to communicate with the medical profession as well as consumers, because they are the ones who influence which brands are selected. With the removal in the late 1990s of restrictions on television advertising of prescription drugs, there has been an enormous increase in the amount pharmaceutical companies are spending on that medium. Even though consumers must still ask their doctors to prescribe these specialized drugs (such as Zoloft, Lipitor, or Abilify), the advertising is aimed at influencing the consumers to ask their physicians for a specific brand-name medication, rather than simply "something to help with my depression" or arthritis or allergies. More recently, there have been calls for such pharmaceutical advertising to be re-regulated, out of concerns that the ads are working too well, encouraging doctors to prescribe more drugs, and more name-brand drugs, than they would otherwise have done.

Another area where critical secondary audiences exist is with children's products. When they are targeted, it is frequently advisable to have a separate target of moms or parents because they are the ones who typically hold the purse-strings. It is estimated that children influence tens of billions of dollars worth of spending each year. In many countries around the world there are strict limits on which products can be advertised directly to children and how, out of concerns that they are more easily misled by advertising.

Whoever the different target is, the media specialist must determine which different media are needed to reach those people. That, in turn, will depend upon the marketing and advertising objectives for that distinct audience—are they identical to the main target's goals, or do they differ in some way? How much do the two targets overlap, both in terms of those objectives and in their media usage patterns? It could be, for example, that if you are trying to encourage both consumers and contractors to select your Grohe faucets, then certain ads placed in home decorating magazines would reach both groups, but more specialized trade publications will do a better job at convincing contractors of the merits of your brand, while TV ads could help enhance your brand's image among consumers.

Changing Media

As the media specialist, your job really entails considering different media from the beginning to the end of media plan development. You are doing so as you assess your media strategy and tactics and as you create the plan. However, it is sometimes worthwhile to make a special effort to consider how the plan would turn out if different media were used. Again, this could be in reaction to a change in the media budget, or a response to a client's question. Or you could take it upon yourself to investigate alternative media options.

In some cases, this could involve looking at different media vehicles within the same media form. If you are recommending magazines, then perhaps you might look at more specialized publications to reach your target. For TV, reconsider whether you should use broadcast, spot, or cable TV to convey your messages, or maybe even switch to product integration. With a radio plan that uses spot markets, perhaps a network buy would be more efficient and appropriate. With Internet buys, you may want to think about whether to buy ads on broad-based portals (Yahoo, MSN, etc.) or pay to be a sponsored link on a search page. If your media plan makes heavy use of newspapers, then think about whether you should move from small-town local newspapers to those that are distributed across broader regions, such as the *Boston Globe* in the New England area, the *Chicago Tribune* in the midwest, and the *Los Angeles Times* in California. The use of different media vehicles will depend primarily on two factors: cost efficiency and targetability. It may be cheaper to use cable rather than spot TV, for instance, but if cable penetration in your area is only at 70 percent, then you are missing out on the 30 percent of the homes who could potentially be exposed to your message. Switching from smaller local papers to bigger, more regional ones may bring you a larger audience, but those people may not be close enough to your chain of Chipotle Grill casual Mexican restaurants to be worth reaching with your message.

The bigger change when thinking about different media is a switch in media forms altogether. Instead of recommending newspapers, what happens if you use local cable TV instead? How about using the Internet instead of magazines? Or what would be the result of switching dollars out of magazines and into television? And how much would that change be affected by the relationship of your target with the media you are considering? The media specialist must think through these scenarios from the point of view of both strategy and cost. How would a move from newspapers to cable TV affect your overall objective of boosting awareness of your health food store? Would the same number of people be reached? Would they be the same people? What is the cost difference? And how would message frequency be impacted? What are the creative implications of such a change? All of these questions need to be answered as you develop a plan using different media.

One of the tools used in helping determine alternatives for a plan is the optimizer. Developed in the U.K. in the 1980s, these computer systems were first designed to select the optimal mix of national TV dayparts or types against a specific target. They use algorithms that balance the reach of a plan against its cost to arrive at a solution that maximizes one or the other (cost or reach). Although they are models based on historical data (ratings), they are now routinely used predictively to help media planners and buyers determine what TV dayparts or specific programs to include. Following their introduction, multimedia optimizers were created that include television, radio, and print, although with varying degrees of success, due to the fact that the ratings data for each medium are collected and reported differently.[2]

The main idea to keep in mind when offering media alternatives is that your original plan is not the only way to schedule media to meet your client's marketing and advertising objectives. Here again we see that media planning is both art and science. There are potentially tens, if not hundreds, of different ways that you could plan your media to obtain the designated goals. Your job as the media specialist is to come up with the one that you believe will do the most effective and efficient job, while fully understanding that there are alternatives available that might achieve the same ends.

Tests and Translations

There are two common ways to conduct tests of a media plan on a local or regional basis. They are known as *As It Falls* and *Little America*. Here, we will consider the basic concepts for each one, rather than going through all of the mathematical calculations needed to prepare such a plan. Although this procedure is really a test, it is also sometimes referred to as a "test translation," to reflect the fact that a national or bigger plan is being recreated in some fashion on a smaller scale. And even though, as media specialists, we are most concerned with testing the media plan itself (increasing GRPs, trying different scheduling strategies, and so forth), tests are also often conducted to determine the impact of new creative, or to see how a new product fares in the marketplace.

As It Falls

This type of test is most often used for brands in existing product categories, where the competitors are well known. The main premise of this method is that the rating points are allowed to occur as they normally would in each market, or *as it falls*. So rather than have the same GRPs across all test markets, the plan's goals would vary somewhat from location to location, depending on how well the individual vehicles perform in each place. That also means that the budgets will vary by market too. It may cost $5,000 to buy 100 radio GRPs in Boise, Idaho, but $10,000 to get the same GRP level in Madison, Wisconsin. The main advantage to this testing system is that it provides a realistic scenario for assessing the impact of the test plan. For if the plan were expanded to a national level, there would still be market-by-market differences similar to those seen in the as-it-falls test situation.

Little America

This test market procedure is used more often with new brands or products where there is no existing competition. What it sets out to do is recreate a national plan in one (or a few) markets, or get as close to that as is feasible. It usually involves more complex planning, first to determine how individual media categories perform in the markets you choose, and then to figure out how to adjust the test plan so that it matches the national delivery.

Summary

While creating a media plan, the true media specialist is already considering various alternatives. One that should always be included is a "what-if" scenario of the effect on the plan's outcome if more dollars were available, looking at the impact on cost efficiency, reach and frequency, and the marketing and advertising objectives. Increased funding could also be allocated to gain additional reach of the brand against its users, or improved production quality of the ads themselves. This chapter also examined a reduced-spending scenario, which must be undertaken with a strategic focus in mind, considering alternative media forms or vehicles, or fewer messages or targets. Indeed, plan alterations will frequently look at different targets or different media and estimate the impact those might have on the plan's effectiveness and its ability to engage consumers with your brands' messages through the right media. All of these potential changes can be tested by translating the plan into a local or regional test market situation, and seeing what happens there first.

Checklist—Offering Alternatives

1. Have you prepared a second media plan at a higher budget level?
2. Have you considered how extra funds would be spent—longer flights, wider geographies, secondary targets—and how those would impact your media (reach and frequency) goals?
3. Are there non-media needs that require additional funds (creative requirements, consumer research, trade allowances)?
4. Do you know the impact of spending fewer media dollars on your plan—(fewer media categories or vehicles, reduced number of targets, reduced schedule, lower reach and frequency results)?
5. Are there other target audiences you should consider?
6. Are there other media categories to be considered?
7. Is it necessary to test your media plan first, either "as it falls" (existing brands) or in a "little America" (new products) test?

Chapter 9

Making the Media Buys

Even the most impressive media plan will not satisfy the client until the time and space have actually been bought. The role of the media specialist may involve none, some, or all of the media buying functions. This chapter provides a brief overview of how print and electronic media are purchased. The subject really requires book-length treatment on its own; the goal here is to show how media buying fits in with the planning process, rather than explain the many details and intricacies of the buys themselves.

Merchandising a Magazine Buy

It is fairly common in many smaller or midsize advertising agencies for media planners to be responsible for magazine buys, although at larger agencies there is usually a specialized staff of print buyers who focus solely on the negotiations. It used to be that all magazines worked off a *rate card*, listing the cost of buying various page sizes, with or without color or other special features. Additional charges were also made for preferred positions, such as the inside front or back covers and the back cover itself, which are believed to be read by more people.

While the extra costs remain, today's magazine buys are far more likely to be made by negotiating. That is, the rate card is usually the starting point, but then it is up to the media specialist and the magazine's representative (or rep) to discuss the final cost for the client. Discounts may be offered for volume buys if, for example, the client purchases ads in multiple issues, or buys several pages in one issue or, increasingly, buys space in several magazines owned by the same publisher. As we learned in Chapter 3, the cost of a magazine ad will depend on the size and nature of the magazine's readership. Obviously, you will pay more to reach more people. It would cost you about $455,000 for one full-page, four-color ad in *Better Homes & Gardens*, which reaches about 18 percent of the population, whereas the same ad placed in *Cooking Light*, which reaches 5 percent, will cost only $110,000.

At the other end of the spectrum, however, you may also have to pay more to reach a highly specialized audience. Although both *Us Weekly* and *Money* have circulations of 1.9 million, the one-page ad will cost $145,000 in the former and $192,000 in the latter because it is assumed that the more focused material of articles about finance is reaching a more interested, involved audience that is more likely to pay attention to the ads in that publication. There have been research studies both supporting and rejecting this hypothesis, with the dissenters claiming that if the reader is more involved in the subject matter, he or she is in fact *less* likely to pay attention to the ads. For the media specialist, the main focus should be on the suitability of each individual magazine to the media objectives, and how efficiently and effectively each vehicle can be used.

When the magazine space is negotiated, the specialist will usually request certain positioning preferences. As noted above, for some of these a premium must be paid. Aside from covers, the specialist may want a Kraft cheese ad, for example, placed near or within the food editorial, or a Cover Girl cosmetics ad to appear in that section of the magazine. Sometimes it is enough to simply request that the ad is in the first third of the issue, under the assumption that those pages are more likely to be seen. The willingness and ability of the magazine to fulfill these requests will vary, depending on who the client is and how many ad pages it needs to fill. One of the important things to remember about magazines is that, unlike electronic media, which have a finite amount of airtime, printed media (including newspapers) can simply add pages if they can attract additional advertisers.

In addition to the practice of magazines negotiating off the rate card, more and more publications are also offering further benefits to their advertisers. These might include special promotions, editorial features, bonus circulation, web pages, or trade deals. While these are usually offered at little or no extra charge, obviously the cost is built into the amount the specialist pays for the ad pages. These extras reflect the extremely competitive media landscape, with an increasingly fragmented marketplace not only within the magazine industry, but also across different media. *Good Housekeeping* does not only compete with the other women's service books (*Better Homes and Gardens, Ladies Home Journal,* and *Woman's Day*), it must also fight for dollars with television, radio, newspapers, outdoor billboards, direct mail, the Internet—the list is almost endless.

Once the magazine space has been agreed on, in terms of price, special features, and positioning, it is time to make the actual buy. At larger agencies this is accomplished through a Magazine Authorization, which sets out the terms of the contract to which both parties must agree. Some clients may like to see this first, to be sure they know what they are getting. If everyone accepts these terms, the media specialist can go ahead and authorize the buy.

Getting News into Newspapers

The purchase process for newspapers is similar to that of magazines. First, the buyer must analyze all possible newspapers available in each designated market, looking at factors such as circulation, coverage, audience composition, color possibilities, and zoning (the ability to customize ads to different areas of the paper's coverage area, or only appear in selected editions). Thanks to technological advances, newspaper ad inserts can be distributed in a more targeted fashion than previously. Today, most newspapers can vary the inserts by zipcode.

Then, the buyer must negotiate with each newspaper to obtain the best rate. Newspapers are purchased in terms of Standard Ad Unit sizes, or SAUs, so that although the size of the newspaper itself may vary, its ad sizes are standardized. Just as with magazines, the newspaper buyer will usually want to specify where in the paper the ad will appear—an ad for Hellman's salad dressing in the food section, an ad for Universal Studio's latest movie in the entertainment section, and an Ethan Allen furniture store ad in the home section. Sometimes, that decision is made based on what the target audience is more likely to read, so an ad for Verizon cellular phone service might appear in the business section, to reach professionals who are more likely to be interested in that item.

Once the deal has been negotiated and agreed upon, an insertion order is placed with the newspaper. At the same time, the agency will issue a Newspaper Authorization that sets out all of the specifications for the ad, such as whether it will be black and white or color, whether it includes a coupon or not, and any special instructions. Then all the print details must be confirmed, including the insertion dates, closing dates, ad size, column inches, inch rate, gross cost, contract rate, and position in the newspaper. This is done for every newspaper in which the ad will appear. After that has received approval, the insertion order goes ahead and the buy is made.

Buying Time on Television

There are three ways that national television is bought, for both broadcast and cable TV and syndication—long-term, short-term ("scatter"), and opportunistic. The first, and most intense, is what is generally known as the "upfront" marketplace. For broadcast TV this usually takes place in late May after the networks present their new programming slate to advertisers, while for cable, it runs from May to July. With either television form, the media specialist negotiates time with the major networks well in advance of the actual air dates. Most typically, these fall during the following TV season that starts in September and runs through to the following May. The time purchased is usually over three to four quarters of the year.

When TV advertising was initiated in the late 1940s, all commercial time was, in effect, bought "upfront." That is because programs were fully sponsored by advertisers, so the negotiations for which companies would put their names in front of new programs' names occurred as those same programs were being developed (e.g., the Philco Theater Hour). After quiz show scandals in the late 1950s, where contestants were secretly fed the right answers in order to maintain viewer suspense, the networks took back control of programming from advertisers (who had sponsored those unfair quiz shows). It was in 1962 that ABC became the first TV network to air all of its new programming in one week, right after Labor Day, and the "new fall season" was created. From then on, the annual schedule was born. The network marketplace is a modified version of supply and demand, with TV ratings (viewers) acting as the supply, and advertiser budgets providing the demand. However, given that the networks have certain profit goals to meet, they will only offer programs at a price that is in line with those goals, therefore diminishing the dynamics of a true supply-and-demand market. In 1967, ABC also became the first network to offer the "guaranteed" program rating, to advertisers who agreed to buy upfront. Although this meant the advertiser had to commit to a buy in advance, the advantage was that "hit" programs might be purchased at a relatively inexpensive cost. Today, upfront buys account for 80–85 percent of all network primetime sales. In 2009, about $8 billion worth of network TV ad time was sold this way.[1]

When you buy *long-term*, you receive a guaranteed rating, along with the opportunity to set up cancellation options. Typically, the options decelerate over the future quarters. For instance, in the first quarter, you might buy all of the spots confirmed; in the second quarter, three-quarters, or 75 percent might be firm, with the option to cancel the remaining 25 percent by an agreed-upon date. Then for the third or subsequent quarters, only half of the spots you negotiate are firm, and half (50 percent) are cancellable by a certain date. One advantage of buying time this way is that more favorable rates may be offered up front, as the networks like to lock in the advertisers to their shows (both new and returning series). Also, advertisers are more likely to get a better mix of programs, and to ensure they get their spots in the time periods and/or shows they want. The disadvantage, from the buyers' standpoint, is that there may be less room for negotiation because everyone is trying to buy from a limited amount of inventory. That is, the networks can choose how much of the available airtime they wish to sell up front, manipulating the demand for that time. The buyers also don't know how well the new programs will perform, basing their judgment on brief promotional excerpts the networks release, along with their historical experience of similar shows from the past.

The commercial minutes the networks hold back or don't sell then form the bulk of the second type of national television time, which is known as the *scatter* market because it is scattered throughout the broadcast day across months. Buyers typically purchase this type of commercial time on a quarterly basis, usually two to three months in advance of the quarter, unless demand is soft. Prices in scatter will vary, depending on the supply and demand, and what happens in scatter tends to impact the long-term, or upfront, marketplace too. In boom years when the economy is thriving, advertiser demand during the upfront period is high, but when a recession hits, advertisers are loathe to commit large funds in advance and so upfront deals tend to decrease while scatter buys rise.

Advertisers who purchase spots in the scatter market may or may not get guaranteed ratings, depending on the supply and demand. Those spots are usually purchased by advertisers who are unable or unwilling to commit to a schedule a year in advance. If demand for scatter time is high, the network can "close" a particular daypart on very short notice, pulling it out of sale and then repricing it for future buyers. Advertisers who do not move quickly enough may find themselves shut out of the daypart completely.

Finally, the third way to buy time in national television is the *opportunistic* buy. Here, the advertiser chooses to purchase at the last minute, picking up whatever remains available. The advantage here is that the rates are usually most favorable to the buyer because the network wants to sell that time. The obvious drawback, however, is that there is less choice and little or no flexibility in the deal. Spots can be purchased as late as the day before airtime. Several sports events are sold this way.

Deciding how to purchase TV time depends on many factors, not the least of which is the size of the advertising budget. The number of quarters in which the commercial is to run also plays a key role here, as does the type of programming mix desired. First and foremost, however, should be strategic considerations regarding the impact of the decision on the marketing, advertising, and media goals.

How Television Time Is Bought

The way the process of buying television time works is as follows. The buyer requests a package of programs from the seller (broadcast, syndication, or cable). The package may be based on costs or on ratings, but is ultimately based on the goals of the plan. The sellers submit their inventory, and the buyer chooses the package that best meets the client's needs and negotiates the price. Instead of purchasing them immediately, however, the buyer "goes to hold," which means the buyer is almost certain he or she will buy that time but has not fully committed to it yet. Both sides agree on how long that "hold" will last; generally, it is three to five days in the scatter market, and four to eight weeks in the long-term market. After that period, the buyer will either purchase the time or drop out. Once the deal is finalized, however, the buyer effectively owns that time. If, later on, the buyer wants to get rid of the commercial time he or she bought, the network may try to sell it to a different advertiser, if the marketplace demand is strong. On the other hand, if for some reason the spot does not run as promised, the buyer is given the option of a comparable spot on the program schedule. This is known as a *make-good*. That might mean moving with a program to another day or time, if the network decides to reschedule it, or staying in the same daypart but switching programs. When programs do not achieve the audience rating that the network had guaranteed to the advertiser, the network will then provide, over the course of a year, *Audience Deficiency Units*, or ADUs. These no-charge units are provided in the same or comparable programs to the advertiser.

All national television time is priced based on a 30-second spot. For advertisers wishing to buy more or less time than that, the rates are adjusted accordingly. Hence, a 60-second spot costs twice as much, and a 15-second spot is half the full rate. Negotiations are conducted based on costs-per-thousand, or CPMs for the target, defined in terms of age and sex. For example, it could be the CPM for reaching women 18 to 49 or adults 25 to 54.

Buying Time on Syndication and Cable

Buying national television time on syndication and cable is not that different from the broadcast network marketplace. There are long-term, scatter, and opportunistic buys available in each television form. Additional considerations need to be given, however, to the individual buys. With syndication, for example, *coverage* is critical. Because syndicated programs are sold to individual stations in each market, they may not be seen in every market across the country. The buyer therefore has to know what percent of stations in the U.S. will air a given program. It may be as low as 60 percent, or as high as 99 percent. The day and/or time of airing will also vary by town or city, and although people do watch programs rather than dayparts, it may make a difference to the effectiveness of a media schedule if you are trying to reach women 25 to 54 with *Oprah* and find that it airs at 9:00 a.m. in Chattanooga, Tennessee, but 3:00 p.m. in Gary, Indiana. The audience delivery and composition could be quite different in those markets because of that airtime variation.

Syndicated programs are guaranteed, but the syndicator almost always overstates the ratings estimate. That means the buyer then has to be given make-goods, either in the form of bonus units or cash back. While this may seem easy to resolve, the syndication marketplace has been like this since its inception, and despite a decline in ratings beginning in the late

1990s, the marketplace still operates this way. Many packaged goods advertisers still rely on syndication to reach their "average" American consumers.

Cable television also sells a good deal of its commercial time in advance, usually with guaranteed ratings. Cable is bought either by individual program or by daypart rotation. A few networks, such as Nick-at-Nite and Headline News, largely sell time this way, because there is strong enough advertiser demand for their units that they do not need to sell individual programs. While this might appear to be a big problem for advertisers, it is less critical on certain cable networks, where the programming is "vertical," and an advertiser knows that his spot will most likely air, for example, between news content on CNN or in classic sitcoms on Nick-at-Nite. Most others have moved to program-based buys, as they have worked to create brand images for themselves based on their well-known personalities or, increasingly, their original programming. Examples here include Comedy Central's *The Daily Show* and ESPN's *Sports Center*.

Local TV and Radio Buys

The purchase of time on spot television and spot radio has both similarities and differences to the network process. Local television buyers usually buy time on shorter notice than for national television. They also have to deal with individual stations in each market, rather than buying a complete network, unless they make a buy across various stations that are linked together into an ad sales network. The planner provides the buyer with the details of the specifications, which include the marketing and media objectives, a demographic and psychographic description of the target, the desired dayparts and flights, the number of ratings points per market and/or time period, the total budget, and the mix of commercial lengths (:15s, :30s, and :60s).

Armed with this information, the buyer can then start negotiating with stations in those markets. Rather than discuss the cost of an individual spot or the cost per thousand used in national television buys, both of which will vary considerably by market, buyers typically negotiate the cost per rating point, or CPP. That way, they ensure that the appropriate number of rating points are purchased, at or below the amount budgeted. The negotiating process is quite subtle. The buyer does not want the seller to know how much money is available (as the station would want to get all of it!), and the seller does not want the buyer to know how much inventory is available (as that would let the buyer know how low a price he or she could get). The buyer will usually talk to all of the stations in the market that have programs or formats appropriate for the target in the desired daypart and ask each of them to submit prices. For some advertisers, price is the most important criterion, so the buyer looks to purchase "tonnage"—lots of media weight at the lowest price available. For others, the program or format is key; they may be willing to pay slightly more to get a closer fit between target and vehicle. It depends on the strategy outlined in the media plan.

Once the buyer has received submissions from each station, he or she can then start negotiating to see if any of the sellers are willing to lower their price any further. While this used to take several days, in today's competitive climate buyers are less likely to give the stations much time to come in with a lower bid, and will usually decide fairly quickly which stations to purchase. Having made that decision, the final prices and terms are agreed to and the buy is made.

In theory, local television and radio buys are fixed; that is, the time is bought on a given daypart and/or program (unless the buyer purchases "run-of-schedule," or ROS, which means that the station can air the spot at any time). In practice, however, stations may pre-empt a spot if another advertiser comes in who is willing to pay more for that time slot. If this happens, the first advertiser will usually request a make-good or compensation if the station airs his spot at a less favorable time.

While buying local radio is similar in many respects to buying television, there are two opportunities for advertisers that are commonly made available in the audio medium. The first is merchandising and promotions. This has become an extremely important consideration for many companies that use spot radio, particularly national advertisers. Local radio stations may be willing, as part of the deal, to run special contests for listeners or set up a remote site broadcast or hold a special event for the trade, for example. The Scion car dealership could offer a new car as the grand prize in an on-air contest; the afternoon music show could be aired from the dealer's showroom, or a cocktail reception for all new Scion owners could be held at the radio station one evening. Such promotions need to be negotiated as part of the buy, but they may add considerably to the efficiency of the purchase.

The second difference that local radio can offer advertisers is the chance for live commercials. In the earliest days of radio, all commercials were spoken live by announcers on-air. Today, that is only possible at the local-market level. Some advertisers believe that having a local radio personality deliver the message adds greater authority and credibility to the product, giving it an implied endorsement. While this is not in fact true (the station never officially endorses any individual brand), it can be beneficial for the advertiser. In addition, because relatively few commercials are presented this way anymore, it offers another way to stand out from the crowd.

The Great Outdoors

Because outdoor billboards are bought on a market-by-market basis, the buying process is, in some ways, akin to local TV and radio buying. Here, instead of dealing with individual TV or radio stations (or rep firms that put stations together into a network), the media buyer must either deal with individual outdoor plant operators, or with networks of plants that are available through large outdoor companies such as Clear Channel or Viacom.

Negotiations for outdoor billboards focus on several key elements: size, location, showing, and cost/CPM. The first criterion to consider is the poster or panel size—from an 8-sheet to a painted bulletin. As explained in Chapter 4, different boards are purchased for different time-frames, with posters typically being sold on a 30-day basis and bulletins sold in a much longer-term deal, such as six months or one year.

Location is really the key as far as outdoor is concerned. For certain products, such as a local restaurant, you might want to be on smaller posters in the city to remind people of your address; for hotels or gas stations, highways would make more sense, to reach drivers as they are passing through your area. And today, many advertisers place their billboards strategically close to their competitors' locations. CVS, for example, looks for boards that are near its key competitor, Walgreen's, reminding consumers as they get close to Walgreen's why they might want to reconsider that decision.

It is important, too, to know which side of the street the board is located (the right side is preferable), and whether there are any potential blockages that could get in the line of sight for the board, such as a tall building or tree. This kind of information can best be gained by actually going to the location to look at the board. The operator can provide you with a complete inventory of addresses for both bulletins and poster panels. In the case of posters, you can also find out if the poster is in an ethnic neighborhood and/or restricted location (no alcohol), and whether it is on a wall or a pole.

The outdoor showing that you buy will tell you what the number of daily exposures are to your message as a percentage of the total market size. A #100 showing, therefore, means that 100 percent of the audience will pass that board in a 30-day period; a #50 means 50 percent will do so, and so on. Poster panels are generally bought at the 25, 50, or 100 showing level, whereas bulletins are purchased at 5, 10, or 15 showing increments. Each showing size in a market will have associated with it the number of poster panels utilized. This is known as the *allotment*. With the introduction of the TAB's newer audience measurement system, information is now available on each board to estimate audience (demographic) and ad exposure (see Chapter 4 for more detail).

Last, but not least, comes the cost of the buy. Outdoor is bought and sold on the basis of the cost of reaching 1,000 of the target audience, or CPM. Unlike TV or radio, though, there are usually only a couple of operators to choose from in a given market, which limits the flexibility that the buyer has to negotiate. With considerable industry consolidation in recent years, many markets are now dominated by a single outdoor company that is part of a multimedia conglomerate. And even where there is more than one company to choose from, one will typically have better locations for a particular size board, while the other will have better offerings in a different size or location.

Once all of the negotiations have taken place, the media specialist will issue an outdoor authorization, laying out all of the details, or specifications, of the buy. These are then confirmed with the client and the seller, and the purchase can proceed.

Implementing an Internet Buy

Given the relative newness of the Internet as an advertising medium, the buying process for it continues to evolve. As with most other media forms, media specialists have the choice of working directly with individual websites, or placing buys with networks of aggregated sites, such as advertising.com. In either case, the media buyer negotiates the ad placement (fixed position or rotation) and cost, along with any special considerations, such as affiliate marketing or opt-in emails. *Affiliate marketing* involves a deal with the website whereby sales that are generated from a user who reached the sales site from your website receives a percentage of the revenue. *Opt-in emails* involve soliciting consumers to sign themselves up for emails from marketers that are based on the individual's declared interests. Another type of buy is based on *behavioral* targeting which targets users based on their prior behavior. For example, if you visit Amazon.com on a regular basis to look at the latest DVDs on sale, then you might be sent an ad from a Hollywood studio or Netflix, because your behavior indicates you have an interest in movies. The benefit for advertisers is that they can find their target audience in places where they might not have expected them to be. Companies such as Revenue Science and Tacoda work heavily in this area. The overall goal of these approaches is to find sites that the target considers *contextually relevant*. This may mean relevance to the campaign, such as an ad for Kellogg's Special K cereal that touts its value in a dieting plan on e-diets.com. Or it can be relevance to the target's mindset, such as ads that include JD Power award rankings appearing when a user is clicking on an automotive website searching for information.

In addition, the buyer has to determine with the seller the basis for the sale—cost per thousand impressions, cost per click, or cost per transaction, for example. Research of those who come to the site is often included as a "value added" bonus, though the drawback here is that it could be biased in favor of the site if they are conducting or hosting the survey. An alternative is to pay for "neutral" third-party research through companies such as Dynamic Logic and Insight Express. In either case, the idea is to sample every n-th person who comes to the site and offer them a survey that can include questions about advertising recognition or brand attitudes and compare those exposed to the ad to the non-exposed "control" group.

Buying Beyond Traditional Media

For advertisers looking to create an integrated marketing plan, the buys may be as varied as the media elements themselves. Sponsorships, for example, are usually sold by the venue (sports stadium, concert stadium). Direct mail is purchased by buying mailing lists and working through a mailing house to execute the campaign. Brand integration into TV shows and movies is currently offered by the producers of the entertainment, though some believe that in the case of television, the networks themselves will want to enter into this highly profitable arena, especially as they lose revenues from traditional commercial sales. And for public relations or viral marketing, there is likely to be no official "buy" made at all. There may be some out-of-pocket costs (creation of a video news release to send to TV stations, for instance, or payment of the people who are "planted" in a social scene to promote your product). Whichever the method used to make the non-traditional buy, it is the media specialist's job to negotiate the price (wherever possible), and determine the metrics against which the cost of the program will be evaluated (traffic, impressions, clicks, etc.). The goal should be to try to make these buys as comparable as possible to the other media in the plan.

Summary

Even the most impressive media plan will not achieve its goals if the buys are not made effectively. That means the time and space need to be purchased in accordance with the plan's specifications, in terms of criteria such as timing, ad size, and placement or position within the media vehicle. For magazines and newspapers, editorial adjacencies may be key, so that the ad message is seen in an appropriate context, such as an ad for Verizon cellular phone service targeting business people in the Business section of *The New York Times* or an Olay anti-wrinkle cream targeting women in the Beauty section of *Marie Claire* magazine. The costs for print media may be negotiable, off the rate card, depending on the competitiveness of the magazine category.

Buying time on electronic media is always done through negotiations, either with a network or individual stations. TV buys may be long-term (purchased upfront) or short-term (in the scatter market). The guarantees and costs of those buys will vary accordingly. For radio, where most time is purchased locally, buyers deal with stations or rep firms that sell them a package of stations across the markets in which the buyer is interested. Deals are usually made based on the cost per rating point. For outdoor billboards, the key buying criterion to consider is the location of the board, whether a poster or a bulletin. Buyers negotiate the cost to reach a given proportion of the market, estimated using showings. The process can be handled with individual plant operators or through networks. For the Internet, the buys are made with individual sites or networks that aggregate those sites. The buys are based on placement, rotation, and metrics. With beyond-traditional media it is the specialist's job to negotiate fair market value and determine the metrics against which to evaluate the media impact.

Checklist—Making the Media Buys

1. Do you have all the necessary specifications regarding the objectives, the target audience, vehicle preferences, GRP needs, and budget limitations to proceed to the buys?
2. Does the client have to approve the buys before they are finalized?
3. For magazines, is a discount available for a volume buy?
4. Do you want a preferred position for your magazine ad?
5. Are you trying to reach a more specialized or generalized audience with magazines (priced accordingly)?
6. Are any special promotions, editorial features, bonus circulation, or trade deals being offered by any of the magazines?
7. Do you want your newspaper ad to appear in a special section?
8. Are there any special instructions needed for your newspaper ad, such as a coupon or inclusion of color?
9. Do you want to buy time on network, cable, or syndicated TV?
10. Is your national television buy going to be made for the long-term (up-front) or short-term (scatter)?
11. Can you get ratings guarantees for your national TV buy?
12. For a syndicated TV buy, what is your clearance?
13. With a cable TV buy, do you want a specific time period or will a rotation suffice?
14. For a local TV buy, is media weight (tonnage) more important than specific program selection?
15. For local radio or local TV, do you want to deal directly with each station, or do you prefer to use a rep firm?
16. Are your outdoor billboards' locations satisfactory?

17. Do you have enough billboards in each market to generate sufficient showings?
18. Have you negotiated ad placement and type with individual websites, search engines, or networks?
19. What are the terms of negotiation for your beyond-traditional media?
20. What are the metrics you are using for the beyond-traditional media against which you will evaluate its cost efficiency and impact?

Chapter 10

Evaluating the Media Plan

One of the most often-repeated quotations about advertising was attributed to John Wanamaker, Philadelphia department store magnate, who said that he knew half of the money he spent on advertising was wasted; he just didn't know which half. Your job, as a media specialist, is to try to ensure that your client's dollars are not wasted. One way to achieve that is by evaluating the media plan before it is executed, and then again once it is up and running.

It is no longer true that an annual plan is left unchanged for a whole year; more and more, advertisers will make changes to at least some part of the marketing plan while the campaign is running. This may be in response to changes in any part of the marketing mix. Consumer response could end up being greater or less than anticipated; product improvements could necessitate additional promotional efforts; new channels of distribution could become important; or competitive pricing strategies may require alterations to the original, approved plan. And beyond that, economic trends can affect almost all marketing efforts. For example, in recessionary times, most "experts" tend to predict that the economic hard times will be over soon, suggesting that consumer spending will improve. What often happens is that consumer confidence in the economy remains low for longer than such optimistic forecasts, leading people to continue their restrained purchasing habits. This has a marked effect on the manufacturers of high-ticket items such as cars and electronics. It also impacts general eating habits, causing people to eat out less and stay home more.

This chapter presents four of the ways that a media plan can be evaluated, before and after it begins running. We have explained the concepts of reach and frequency. With today's sophisticated computer tools, syndicated data on past purchase and media consumption can be analyzed to give a "best guess" estimate of how well a medium, or total plan, will reach the chosen target audience. This can later be compared with actual results on reach and frequency, to see how well the plan actually performed, which is crucial information for preparing next year's plan. The second type of evaluation is to check that your ads actually run as scheduled, a practice known as post-buy analysis. It is up to the media specialist to make sure that if, for some reason, the ad did not run as scheduled or was not positioned in the agreed-upon place, that some form of compensation is given, either monetary or in time or space. Third, it may well be worthwhile spending additional dollars to research the consumer impact of the media (and/or marketing) plan. After you doubled the spending levels in television, are your brand's awareness levels considerably higher? How well is your commercial message being recalled now that you have switched dollars out of magazines and onto the Web? These kinds of questions can best be answered by talking to some of the consumers you were trying to reach. Last but not least, in the weeks and months after your plan is executed, you can hire econometricians to assess the return on investment, or payout, of your plan.

Pre-Plan Analysis

The first time to evaluate the impact of the media plan is before it is presented to the client. That is, in selecting the media vehicles you think will best meet the advertising and marketing objectives, the media specialist needs to figure out which combination of vehicles will do the best job of reaching the target an acceptable number of times. Computer systems and tools are readily available to help make these kinds of analyses simple and fast.

For example, let's say you were considering two alternative combinations for your media plan for Pillsbury cake mix. The first combination would use monthly insertions in *Redbook* magazine, along with periodic commercials in prime time on the Lifetime cable television network. Another possibility would be to place continuous messages on cable, with occasional ads in the magazine. Here is how the two schedules might look for the year:

Schedule One	*Schedule Two*
10 insertions in *Redbook* (50 GRPs)	4 insertions in *Redbook* (20 GRPs)
400 GRPs in Lifetime	1,000 GRPs in Lifetime

And here is how the two schedules would perform against your target of women 25 to 54:

	Schedule One	Schedule Two
Total GRPs	450	1,020
Reach 1+	34.1%	32.6%
Reach 3+	25.2%	22.7%
Frequency	13.2	31.3

So, even though you are using far more cable in Schedule Two, the impact on the overall reach is actually less than if you used more magazine advertising, as in Schedule One.

Post-Buy Analysis

What the media specialist must find out once the plan is running is whether the ads ran as scheduled, and how well the plan actually delivered. For the first part, determining that the ads did in fact run as scheduled, you can turn to various sources, depending on the medium. For newspapers, there are *tear sheets*, which are provided by commercial services, to show you examples of the actual ad in the newspaper. Magazines will usually provide copies of the issues in which your ad appears. For television and radio, you should receive affidavits confirming when your spot aired. And as the buys become wholly electronic, advertising agencies are starting to be able to monitor ad executions within hours or days of their airing (rather than the weeks or months it used to take). With the Internet, you can easily go online to make sure your ad appears, or use a third-party service to verify its location and rotation. In each case, the media specialist must check that the terms of the contract were adhered to. If you requested being in the food section of the paper, or the first third of the magazine, is that where your ad was placed?

For broadcast media, the task is usually more complicated because program schedules are far more prone to being changed. You might have arranged for your radio spot to air between 6:00 p.m. and 8:00 p.m., only to find that it came on at 5:30 p.m. or 8:20 p.m. Or, you could have bought a rotation of spots (ROS, or Run of Schedule), which in theory means that your spots will run equitably in all dayparts. In analyzing the affidavits or electronic reports you might discover that more than half of the messages were aired between midnight and 6:00 a.m., or some other inappropriate time. It is then incumbent upon the station to explain what happened and, in all likelihood, offer some type of make-good, either in the form of free ads or financial compensation for the cost differences between ROS and the overnight period.

In larger agencies or organizations, this post-analysis checking is typically done by the media buyers or business service department. It is more of an accounting than a media function but, ultimately, the media specialist should know what happened, and why.

Later on, additional information becomes available to show how your ad schedule delivered. This is in the form of syndicated data, such as Nielsen for television, Arbitron for radio, Mediamark Research, Inc. (MRI) for print media, and Nielsen Online or comScore for the Web. Each service provides the ratings and audience delivery of media vehicles to help you determine whether, in fact, you met the goals of your plan. Other companies can access this data also, acting as third-party vendors of the information.

The kinds of questions the data can help you answer include what percentage of the target was reached by the media (and vehicles) that you used (reach), and how often, on average, was the target exposed to them? It is worth emphasizing again that these terms refer only to media exposure, and not to actual exposure to the ads themselves. They should therefore be thought of as *opportunities to see* your message. Many advertisers will discount, or "weight" the exposure levels to account for this distinction, assuming, for example, that only half of the people reached by the media vehicle will actually see the ad. Or they may only look at the proportion of the target that is exposed a certain number of times (*effective reach*), assuming here that people will require several opportunities to see your message before they in fact will do so.

Custom Consumer Research

The importance of evaluating the plan's impact on consumers once it has gone into effect cannot be underestimated. For only by doing so will you find out, first, whether you got what you (or your client) paid for and, second, whether the plan worked as you intended. It will provide invaluable help in preparing for next year's plan too. This may be by undertaking surveys of consumers before and after their exposure to your ads, to assess their brand recall and any brand attitude shifts. Or it could be through qualitative research such as focus groups or in-depth interviews, where consumers are asked to explain their feelings about their media exposure in greater detail. Why did they pay attention to the TV ads but ignore the radio ads, for example? How were the Internet ads effective (or not) in influencing their purchase decision? Although, ultimately, the impact of the media plan, and the other elements of the marketing mix, is determined at the cash register, it is helpful to be able to analyze the individual parts to find out what is, or is not, working. Having said that, and acknowledging the truth to this chapter's opening comment by John Wanamaker, you should keep in mind that it is difficult to determine the precise effect of advertising media messages on consumers. We know *when* it is working, though we may not always know *how*.

ROI Impact

For more sophisticated analyses of media's impact, econometric modeling can provide the answer. Here, as noted in Chapter 7, complex statistical models analyze as many of the marketing mix variables as possible (depending on the category), to see what role advertising media play in generating sales (or other goals, such as awareness, consideration, or purchase intent). The models can look at everything from GRPs to distribution to weather patterns, and attempt to isolate the part that each plays in the mix.

Without evaluating how a media plan performs, we are left even more in the dark than when we began. In effect, it means that each time we create a plan, we end up recreating the wheel. This can lead you down two paths. Either the same plan is reproduced because it "seemed to work" (or at least, didn't cause any disasters). Or the plan is completely changed to see if that makes a difference in sales, or awareness, or attitudes. Both of these options are flawed. To continue doing exactly the same thing as before without knowing whether it is working, or if it could possibly be improved upon, is detrimental to your product (and client), keeping them from performing at their best. Similarly, to overturn the plan without analyzing how it worked (or didn't work) means that you run the risk of losing the momentum your ads might have started to build, and jeopardizes your chances for success.

So although there is a strong temptation, once the media plan is completed and the ads are running, to file it away and move on to the next task, the true media specialist will carry on through to the end. He or she is responsible for ensuring not only that the ads run as intended, but also that they delivered what was planned. If these two evaluation tasks are carried out successfully, you will not only have a more satisfied client, but will also have already taken an important step forward in preparing for next year's media plan.

Summary

A completed media plan is really not final until it has been evaluated to see how it has performed. This should be done both before the plan is executed, by calculating estimates of reach and frequency that the plan should achieve, and afterwards, through post-buy analyses to ensure that the ads ran as scheduled. If the messages did not air as intended and specified in the buys, it is up to the media specialist to obtain some type of compensation. Without these checks, there is no way of knowing whether this year's plan should be continued into the following year with or without modifications. And, although it is always difficult to pinpoint precisely the impact of advertising on sales, the process of evaluating the success or failure of the media plan in achieving the media, advertising, and marketing objectives will help the brand and the client know how to do better next year.

Checklist—Evaluating the Media Plan

1. Have you performed reach and frequency analyses of the media plan before presenting it to the client?
2. Have you contacted clipping services or the print media themselves to determine that your ads ran as scheduled?
3. Are the post-buys for electronic media available to ensure that your ads ran as scheduled?
4. Do you have access to syndicated data such as Nielsen, Arbitron, MRI, and Simmons, for future analysis of how your media vehicles performed against your target?
5. Do you have ideas on how your media plan can be improved for next year?
6. Is there need, and budget, to conduct some custom consumer research to assess the impact of your media plan on consumer recall, attitudes, and opinions?
7. Can you bring together sufficient post-buy delivery data to incorporate into an econometric model that shows how each media type performed against your objectives?

Key Research Resources

Advertising Age
711 Third Avenue
New York, NY 10017-4036
(212) 210-0100
www.adage.com
Industry trade journal, published weekly.

Advertising Research Foundation
432 Park Avenue South, 6th Floor,
New York, NY 10022
(212) 751-5656
www.thearf.org
Primary industry research organization.

Adweek
770 Broadway, 7th Floor
New York, NY 10003
(646) 654-5117
www.adweek.com
Industry trade journal, published weekly.

Arbitron
142 West 57th Street
New York, NY 10019-3300
(212) 887-1300
www.arbitron.com
Radio audience measurement company, using weekly listening diaries and personal portable meters (PPM).

Audit Bureau of Circulations
900 N. Meacham Road
Schaumburg, IL 60173

(847) 605-0909
www.accessabc.com
Circulation auditing company for magazine and newspaper industry.

Claritas
9276 Scranton Road, Suite 300
San Diego, CA 92121
(800) 866-6520
www.claritas.com
Company offers computerized mapping system to display consumer, media, and lifestyle traits by geography.

Donovan Data Systems
115 West 18th Street
New York, NY 10011
(212) 633-8100
www.donovandata.com
Third-party processor of Nielsen TV audience data; also, major bill payment system for advertising agencies.

Experian Simmons
600 Third Avenue
New York, NY 10016
(212) 471-2850
www.smrb.com
Collects demographic, media, and lifestyle information on 40,000 adults each year. Also offers special annual studies on children, teens, and Hispanics.

Information Resources Inc.
150 N Clinton Street
Chicago, IL 60661-1416
(312) 726-1221
www.us.infores.com
Collects and reports consumer package goods sales using supermarket checkout data.

Ipsos Mendelsohn
841 Broadway
New York, NY 10003-4704
(212) 677-8100
www.ipsos-na.com
Provides media, demographic, and lifestyle information for upper-income adults.

JD Power & Associates
2625 Townsgate Road, Suite 100
Westlake Village, CA 91361
(805) 418-8000
www.jdpa.com
Provides annual demographic, lifestyle, and media information linked to automotive industry.

Kantar Media Intelligence
100 Park Avenue, 4th Floor
New York, NY 10017
(212) 991-6000
www.tns-mi.com
Measures advertisers' media spending across 20 media types. Owned by WPP.

Kantar Media Research
114 Fifth Avenue, 4th Floor
New York, NY 10011
(212) 303-6700
www.kmr-group.com
Parent company to several audience research companies (TGI), as well as software provider of media optimization systems (X-Pert).

Mediamark Research, Inc.
75 Ninth Avenue
New York, NY 10011
(212) 884-9200
www.mediamark.com
Measures demographic, media, and lifestyle information among 40,000 adults per year. Used for target and audience analysis.

Nielsen
770 Broadway
New York, NY 10003
(646) 654-8300
www.nielsen.com
Main provider of national and local television viewing information. National service based on national panel of 12,000 adults using people meters; local service based on local people meters in top 25 markets; household set meters (top 55 markets), and additional weekly viewing diaries (all remaining non-LPM markets).

Nielsen IMS
770 Broadway, 15th Floor
New York, NY 10003
(646) 654-5900
www.imsms.com
Third-party media software company that provides media planning tools
to assess multimedia audiences.

Scarborough Research
770 Broadway
New York, NY 10003
(646) 654-8400
www.scarborough.com
Measures demographic, media, and lifestyle information in 75 local
markets.

SRDS Media Solutions
1700 Higgins Road
Des Plaines, IL 60018-5605
(847) 375-5000
www.srds.com
Provides databases of media rates and information on all major media
categories.

Telmar Information Services
470 Park Avenue South, 15th Floor
New York, NY 10016
(212) 725-3000
www.telmar.com
Third-party media software company that provides media planning tools
to assess multimedia audiences.

Yankelovich Partners
400 Meadowmont Village Circle, Suite 431
Chapel Hill, NC 27517
(919) 932-8600
www.yankelovich.com
Consumer research company that offers annual trend studies on various
demographic or lifestyle segments.

Appendix B

Key Media Organizations

Advertising Council
815 Second Avenue, 9th Floor
New York, NY 10017
(212) 922-1500
www.adcouncil.org
Organization sponsoring and promoting public service advertising.

Advertising Club of New York
235 Park Avenue South, 6th Floor
New York, NY 10003
(212) 533-8080
www.theadvertisingclub.org
Forum for ad professionals.

Advertising Educational Foundation
220 East 42nd Street, Suite 3300
New York, NY 10017
(212) 986-8060
www.aef.com
Distributes educational content to enrich understanding of advertising.

Advertising Research Foundation
432 Park Avenue South, 6th Floor
New York, NY 10016
(212) 751-5656
Industry organization focused on Advertising and Media Research.

Advertising Women of New York
25 West 45th Street, Suite 403
New York, NY 10036
(212) 221-7969

www.awny.org
Forum to advance women in the field of communications.

American Association of Advertising Agencies (AAAA)
405 Lexington Avenue, 18th Floor
New York, NY 10174
(212) 682-2500 www.aaaa.org
Main trade organization of advertising agencies.

American Advertising Federation (AAF)
1101 Vermont Avenue NW, Suite 500
Washington, DC 20005
1-800-999-2231
www.aaf.org
Protects and promotes advertising. Sponsors annual National Student
Ad Competition (NSAC) and has 226 college chapters with nearly 8,000
undergraduate members. Offers 1,000+ internship opportunities.

American Business Media
675 Third Avenue
New York, NY 10017
(212) 661-6360
www.americanbusinessmedia.com
Association for business-to-business information providers.

American Marketing Association
311 South Wacker Drive, Suite 5800
Chicago, IL 60606
(312) 542-9000
www.marketingpower.com
Professional association for marketers, with strong educational
component.

Art Directors Club
106 West 29th Street
New York, NY 10001
(212) 643-1440
www.adcglobal.org
International group provides forum for creatives in advertising
communication.

Association of Hispanic Advertising Agencies
8400 Westpark Drive, 2nd Floor
Mclean, VA 22102

(703) 610-9014
www.ahaa.org
Trade group for Hispanic advertising agencies

Association of National Advertisers (ANA)
708 Third Avenue, 33rd Floor
New York, NY 10017
(212) 697-5950
www.ana.net
Main trade organization for national advertisers.

Cabletelevision Advertising Bureau (CAB)
830 Third Avenue, 2nd Floor
New York, NY 10022
(212) 508-1200
www.thecab.tv
Trade organization for the cable TV industry.

Direct Marketing Association (DMA)
1120 Avenue of the Americas
New York, NY 10036
(212) 768-7277
www.the-dma.org
Global trade organization for the direct marketing industry.

Interactive Advertising Bureau (IAB)
116 East 27th Street, 7th Floor
New York, NY 10016
(212) 380-4700
www.iab.net
Trade group promoting interactive advertising.

International Advertising Association (IAA)
275 Madison Avenue, Suite 402
New York, NY 10016
(212) 557-1133
www.iaaglobal.org
Professional group focused on advertising as a global industry. Has chapters in 50+ U.S. universities.

Magazine Publishers of America
810 Seventh Avenue, 24th Floor
New York, NY 10019
(212) 872-3700

www.magazine.org
Trade group promoting consumer magazines.

National Advertising Review Council
70 West 36th Street, 13th Floor
New York, NY 10018
(866) 334 NARC (6272)
www.narcpartners.org
Fosters truth and accuracy for national advertisers through voluntary
self-regulation.

National Assocation of Broadcasters (NAB)
1771 N Street NW
Washington, DC 20036
(202) 429-5300
www.nab.org
Trade group promoting the local television and radio industry.

Newspaper Association of America (NAA)
4401 Wilson Boulevard, Suite 900
Arlington, VA 22203
(571) 366-1000
www.naa.org
Trade group promoting newspapers.

The One Club
21 East 26th Street
New York, NY 10010
(212) 979-1900
www.oneclub.org
Organization to promote excellence in advertising through an annual
creative awards show.

Online Publishers Association (OPA)
249 West 17th Street
New York, NY 10011
(212) 204-1491
Trade group for online content providers.

Outdoor Advertising Association of America (OAAA)
1850 M Street NW, Suite 1040
Washington, DC 20036
(202) 833-5566

www.oaaa.org
Trade group promoting the outdoor advertising industry.

Point of Purchase Advertising International (POPAI)
1600 Duke Street, Suite 400
Alexandria, VA 22314
(202) 530-3000
www.popai.com
Trade group promoting the "marketing at-retail" industry.

Promotion Marketing Association (PMA)
257 Park Avenue South, 11th Floor
New York, NY 10010
(212) 420-1100
www.pmalink.org
Trade group for the promotion industry.

Radio Advertising Bureau (RAB)
1320 Greenway Drive, Suite 500
Irving, TX 75038
(800) 232-3131
www.rab.com
Trade group promoting radio advertising.

Syndicated Network Television Association (SNTA)
One Penn Plaza, Suite 5310
New York, NY 10119
(212) 259-3740
www.snta.com
Trade group promoting television syndication.

Television Bureau of Advertising (TVB)
3 East 54th Street
New York, NY 10022
(212) 486-1111
www.tvb.org
Trade group promoting the broadcast television industry, with particular focus on spot TV.

Traffic Bureau of Advertising for Media Measurement (TBA)
271 Madison Avenue, Suite 1504
New York, NY 10018
(212) 972-8075
www.tabonline.com

Audits circulation of out of home media and supports other out of home research initiatives.

Word of Mouth Marketing Association (WOMMA)
65 East Wacker Place, Suite 300
Chicago, IL 60601
(312) 853-4400
www.womma.org
Trade association for the word of mouth marketing industry.

World Federation of Advertisers
120 Avenue Louise
1050 Brussels, Belgium
(011-32) 2-502-5740
www.wfanet.org
Trade group representing the global interests of marketers.

Yellow Pages Association
400 Connell Drive, Suite 1100
Berkeley Heights, NJ 07922
(908) 286-2380
www.ypassociation.org
Trade group promoting yellow pages marketing, both in print and online.

Notes

2 Media in the Marketing Context

1 "Recall and Recognition: A Very Close Relationship," Jan Stapel, *Journal of Advertising Research*, vol. 38, no. 4, July/August 1998, 41–46.
2 See "Consuming Rituals," by Lawrence Osborne, *New York Times* Magazine, January 13, 2002, 28–31; "Visual Attention to Programming and Commercials: The Use of In-Home Observations," Dean M. Krugman, Glen T. Cameron and Candace McKearney White, *Journal of Advertising*, vol. 24, no. 1, Spring 1995, 1–12.
3 "Editorial Environment and Advertising Effectiveness," Valentine Appel, *Journal of Advertising Research*, August/September 1987, vol. 27, No. 4, 11–16; "A Cross-Media Study of Audience Choice: The Influence of Media Attitudes on Individual Selection of 'Media Repertoires'," Elizabeth Gigi Taylor and Wei-Na Lee, Proceedings of the 2004 Conference of the American Academy of Advertising, 39–48; "Magazine Reader Involvement Improves ROI," Britta C. Ware, ESOMAR, Print Audience Measurement, LA, June 2003; "The Medium Is Part of the Message," Maria Christina Moya Schilling, Karin Wood and Alan Branthwaite, ESOMAR, Reinventing Advertising, Rio, November 2000, 207–229.

4 Exploring the Media, Part 1: Traditional

1 "The Winners and Losers of The Digital Transition," Kenneth Hein, *AdweekMedia*, January 5, 2009, 20–21.
2 Nielsen Media Research 2009, as reported in *The New York Times*, July 6, 2009, p. B8.
3 "Why 'Idol' Works for Coke—But Not for Ford," Martin Lindstrom, *Advertising Age*, November 17, 2008, p. 19.
4 "Product Placement: How Brands Appear on Television," Carrie La Ferle and Steven M. Edwards, *Journal of Advertising*, vol. 35, no. 4, Winter 2006, 65–86.
5 "Ad Nauseam," Jennifer Armstrong, *Entertainment Weekly*, July 25, 2008, 39–41.
6 "Product Placement on TV Targeted," Cecilia Kang, Washingtonpost.com, June 27, 2008, p. D01.
7 "Pontiac gets major mileage out of $8 million 'Oprah' deal," Jean Halliday and Claire Atkinson, *Advertising Age*, September 20, 2004, p. 12.
8 "Burger King Cooks Up a Winner: Best Overall," Amy Johannes, Promo Magazine website, May 3, 2005.

9   "Amid cutbacks, ShamWow marches on," Jack Neff, *Advertising Age*, March 23, 2009, 1/14.
10   "What a Spot Costs," *Advertising Age Annual 2009*, December 29, 2008, p. 43.
11   "Predictors of Advertising Avoidance in Print and Broadcast Media," Paul Surgi Speck and Michael T. Elliott, *Journal of Advertising*, vol. 26, no. 2, Summer 1997, 61–76.
12   "Does Advertising Clutter Have Diminishing and Negative Returns?" Louisa Ha and Barry R. Litman, *Journal of Advertising*, vol. 26, no. 1, Spring 1997, 31–42.
13   Nielsen TV Audience Report, 2008.
14   "Consumer Perceptions of Advertising Clutter and Its Impact Across Various Media," Michael T. Elliott and Paul Surgi Speck, *Journal of Advertising Research*, vol. 35, no. 3, May/June 1995, 29–42; "The Antecedents and Consequences of Perceived Advertising Clutter," Paul Surgi Speck and Michael T. Elliott, *Journal of Current Issues and Research in Advertising*, vol. 19, no. 2, 1997, 39–54.
15   "The Role of Consumer Involvement in Determining Cognitive Response to Broadcast Advertising," Laura M. Buchholz and Robert E. Smith, *Journal of Advertising*, vol. 20 no. 1, 1991, 4–17.
16   "Television Commercial Evaluation In the Context of Program Induced Mood: Congruency Versus Consistency Effects," Michael A. Kamins, Lawrence J. Marks, and Deborah Skinner, *Journal of Advertising*, vol. 20, no. 2, June 1991, 1–14.
17   "Multiple Resource Theory and Consumer Processing of Broadcast Advertisements: An Involvement Perspective," Robert E. Smith and Laura M. Buchholz, *Journal of Advertising*, vol. 20, no. 3, September 1991, 1–8.
   "Attention Versus Distraction: The Interactive Effect of Program Involvement and Attentional Devices on Commercial Processing," Kenneth R. Lord and Robert E. Burnkrant, *Journal of Advertising*, vol. 22, no. 1, March 1993, 47–60.
   "How the Digital Video Recorder (DVR) Changes Traditional Television Advertising," Kenneth C. Wilbur, *Journal of Advertising*, vol. 37, no. 1, Spring 2008, 143–149.
   "Television Programming and Its Influence on Viewers' Perceptions of Commercials: The Role of Program Arousal and Pleasantness," V. Carter Broach, Jr., Thomas R. Page, Jr., and R. Dale Wilson, *Journal of Advertising*, vol. 24, no. 4, Winter 1995, 45–54.
   "Context Is Key: The Effect of Program-Induced Mood on Thoughts about the Ad," Andrew B. Aylesworth and Scott B. MacKenzie, *Journal of Advertising*, vol. 27, no. 2, Summer 1998, 17–32.
   "Hearing versus Seeing: A Comparison of Consumer Learning of Spoken and Pictorial Information in Television Advertising," Wendy J. Bryce and Richard F. Yalch, *Journal of Current Issues and Research in Advertising*, vol. 15, no. 1, Spring 1993, 1–20.
   "Program Involvement: Are Moderate Levels Best for Ad Memory and Attitude toward the Ad?" Nader T. Tavassoli, Clifford J. Shultz II, and Gavan J. Fitzsimons, *Journal of Advertising Research*, vol. 35, no. 5, Sept/Oct 1995, 61–72.
18   Radio Advertising Bureau, Arbitron, and Veronis Suhler Stevenson Communications Industry Forecast 2008–2012, all 2009.
19   Arbitron 2009; "Stream It Like You Mean It," Paul Heine, Mediaweek Special Report on Web Radio, July 20, 2009, 1–3.

20 Imagery Transfer Study conducted by Statistical Research, Inc., 1999.

21 Radio Advertising Lab (RAL) studies, as reported in 2009 *Radio Marketing Guide & Fact Book*, produced by the Radio Advertising Bureau, New York.

22 "Information Processing Differences Among Broadcast Media: Review and Suggestions for Research," James H. Leigh, *Journal of Advertising*, vol. 20, no. 2, June 1991, 71–76.

    "Mental Imagery and Sound Effects in Radio Commercials," Darryl W. Miller and Lawrence J. Marks, *Journal of Advertising*, vol, 21, no. 4, December 1992, 83–94.

    "Advertising Clearance Practices of Radio Stations: A Model of Advertising Self-Regulation," Avery M. Abernethy, *Journal of Advertising*, vol. 22, no. 3, September 1993, 15–26.

    "Creating the Contrast: The Influence of Silence and Background Music on Recall and Attribute Importance," G. Douglas Olsen, *Journal of Advertising*, vol. 24, no. 4, Winter 1995, 29–44.

23 Radio Advertising Lab (RAL) studies, as reported on Radio Advertising Bureau website, www.rab.com.

24 Newspaper Association of America, 2009.

25 "Where 1990's Top Papers are Now," Nat Ives, *Advertising Age*, March 9, 2009, p. 4.

26 "Newspaper Web Audience Grows, Revs Decline," Erik Sass, *MediaDailyNews*, January 30, 2009; "The Reality About Newspapers," John F. Sturm, newspaper advertisement in *The New York Times*, May 22, 2009.

27 "Newspapers build digital portfolios," Michael Learmonth, *Advertising Age*, May 4, 2009, p. 4.

28 "A Study of National Advertising's Payout: Image Ads in Newspaper ROP," Stuart Tolley, *Journal of Advertising Research*, vol. 33, no. 5, Sept/Oct 1993, 11–20.

29 "This Season's Must-Have: The Humble Coupon," Stuart Elliott, *The New York Times*, December 4, 2008, p. B7.

30 "Advertiser Registers Its Objection," Stuart Elliott, *The New York Times*, April 11, 2005, p. C5.

31 "McSwindle," Kate MacArthur, *Ad Age*, August 27, 2001, 1/22–3.

32 "How America Shops & Spends," Newspaper Association of America, 2006.

33 "Newspapers Still Send Consumers to the Store," Newspaper Association of America, 2009.

34 "Reenergizing Readership and Revitalizing Newspapers," Kubas Consultants. Presented at Newspaper Association of America conference, November 2003.

35 "The Advertising Exposure Effect of Free Standing Inserts," Srini S. Srinivasan, Robert P. Leone and Francis J. Mulhern, *Journal of Advertising*, vol. 24, no. 1, Spring 1995, 29–40.

    "Ad Size as an Indicator of Perceived Advertising Costs and Effort: The Effects on Memory and Perceptions," Pamela M. Homer, *Journal of Advertising*, vol. 24, no. 4, Winter 1995, 1–12.

    "Predictors of Advertising Avoidance in Print and Broadcast Media," Paul Surgi Speck and Michael T. Elliott, *Journal of Advertising*, vol. 26, no. 2, Summer 1997, 61–76.

    "Communicating in Print: A Comparison of Consumer Responses to Different Promotional Formats," Kenneth R. Lord and Sanjay Putrevu, *Journal of Current Issues and Research in Advertising*, vol. 20, no. 2, Fall 1998, 1–18.

"The Information Content of Newspaper Advertising," Avery M. Abernethy, *Journal of Current Issues and Research in Advertising*, vol. 14, no. 2, Fall 1992, 63–68.

36 The Magazine Handbook 2009–2010.

37 "Digital revenue in 2008 For Leading Magazine Publishing Companies," *Advertising Age*, January 19, 2009, 42.

38 "Digital-Revenue Leaders," in "Digital Climbs as As Pages Slip," Maureen Morrison, *Advertising Age*, Special Report on Magazine 300, October 6, 2008, S-9.

39 "Context Effects on Recall and Recognition of Magazine Advertisements," Claire E. Norris and Andrew M. Colman, *Journal of Advertising*, vol. 21, no. 3, September 1992, 37–46.

40 "Contextual Priming Effects in Print Advertisements: The Moderating Role of Prior Knowledge," Youjae Yi, *Journal of Advertising*, vol. 22, no. 1, March 1993, 1–10.

41 See Magazine Publishers of America (MPA) website at magazine.org for more information on Millward Brown study on ad effectiveness, the AC Nielsen Sales Scan Study, and econometric modeling case analysis, *Measuring the Mix*.

42 "Coming Into Focus," Janet Stilson, *AdWeekMedia*, March 2, 2009, p. 8.

43 "Building a New OOH Currency Through Dialogue," Joe Philport, ANA OAAA TAB Advertiser Forum, October 17, 2007.

44 Buzz Awards 2008, Special Advertising Section to Mediaweek, B10.

45 "Improving the Effectiveness of Outdoor Advertising: Lessons from a Study of 282 Campaigns," Mukesh Bhargava, Naveen Donthu, and Rosanne Caron, *Journal of Advertising Research*, vol. 34, no. 2, Mar/Apr 1994, 46–55. "Split-Second Recognition: What Makes Outdoor Advertising Work?" Lex Van Meurs and Many Aristoff, *Journal of Advertising Research*, vol. 49, no. 1, March 2009, 82–92. "Use and Effectiveness of Billboards," Charles R. Taylor, George R. Franke, and Hae-Kyong Bang, *Journal of Advertising*, vol. 35, no. 4, Winter 2006, 21–34.

46 "Exploring the Effectiveness of Advertising in the ABC.com Full Episode Player," Mark Loughney, Martin Eichholz, and Michelle Haggar, *Journal of Advertising Research*, vol. 48, no. 3, September 2008, 320–328.

47 "Online Video Changes Game For Brand Marketers," Jeff Whatcott, Media-Post's VideoInsider, March 24, 2009.

48 Three Screen Viewing Reaches New Heights," Research Brief, March 3, 2009.

49 "TV Trends: Consumers Demand Control," Ben Macklin, eMarketer Report, June 2008, p. 2.

50 Top Performance Metrics, in Advertising Age Search Marketing Fact Pack 2008, p. 26.

51 "How Kodak Leveraged the Power of Community," Kimberly Smith, MarketingProfs.com, May 20, 2008.

52 "Who Uses Social Networks?", eMarketer, August 5, 2009.

53 Digital Future Report by USC Annenberg School of Communication, cited in *Internet Trends*, a Morgan Stanley report, March 2008.

54 "How the Internet is Reshaping Advertising," Rex Briggs, *Admap*, April 2005, Issue 460, pp. 59–61.

55 "Why Television Still Shines in a World of Screens," Randall Stross, *The New York Times*, Business Section, April 8, 2009, p. 3.

56 Interactive Advertising Bureau Ad Unit Guidelines, at www.iab.net.

57 "Online User Experience Study," Online Publishers Association, 2005.

58 "Internet Uses and Gratifications," Hanjun Ko, Chang-Hoan Cho, and Marilyn S. Roberts, *Journal of Advertising*, vol. 34, no. 2, Summer 2005, 57–70.
59 "Determinants of Perceived Web Site Interactivity," Ji Hee Song and George M. Zinkhan, *Journal of Marketing*, vol. 72, March 2008, 99–113. Other useful research on the Internet includes: "Displacement and Reinforcement Effects of the Internet and Other Media as Sources of Information," Stanley D. Sibley and James C. Tsao, *Journal of Advertising Research*, vol. 44, no. 1, March 2004, 126–142; "Changing Fortunes for Internet Advertising," Chris Dobson, *Admap*, March 2004, no. 448, 32–33; "Determinants of Internet Advertising: an Empirical Study," George Baltas, *International Journal of Market Research*, vol. 45, no. 4, 505–513; "Banner Advertiser-Web Site Context Congruity and Color Effects on Attention and Attitudes," Robert S. Moore, Claire Allison Stammerjohan and Robin A. Coulter, *Journal of Advertising*, vol. 34, no. 2, Summer 2005, 71–84; "Measuring Users' Web Activity to Evaluate and Enhance Advertising Effectiveness," Subodh Bhat, Michael Bevans, and Sanjit Sengupta, *Journal of Advertising*, vol. 31, no. 3, Fall 2002, 97–106; "Advertising Repetition and Placement Issues in On-Line Environments," Idil Yaveroglu and Naveen Donthu, *Journal of Advertising*, vol. 37, no. 2, Summer 2008, 31–44; "Evaluation of Internet Advertising Research," Juran Kim and Sally J. McMillan, *Journal of Advertising*, vol. 37, no. 1, Spring 2008, 99–112.

5 Exploring the Media, Part 2: Beyond Traditional

1 Mediamark Research, Inc., 2009.
2 "Putting a 21st-Century Spin on A Powerful Selling Vehicle," Burt Michaels, *Know magazine*, 51–58.
3 "The Effectiveness of Information and Color in Yellow Pages Advertising," Karen V. Fernandez and Dennis L. Rosen, *Journal of Advertising*, vol. 29, no. 2, Summer 2000, 59–72.
4 "The Customer Pulling Power of Different-Sized Yellow Pages Advertising," Avery M. Abernathy and David N. Laband, *Journal of Advertising Research*, vol. 42, no. 3, May/June 2002, 66–72.
5 *Progressive Grocer* magazine, 2005.
6 "Long Tail Media in the Store," Herb Sorenson, *Journal of Advertising Research*, vol. 48, no. 3, September 2008, 329–338.
7 "Nascar's Sponsors, Hit by Sticker Shock," Susanna Hamner, *The New York Times*, December 14, 2008, Business Section, p 1/7.
8 "Nothing Sells Like Celebrity," Julie Creswell, *The New York Times*, June 22, 2008, Business Section, p. 1/8.
9 "Immediate and Long-Term Effects of Sponsorship on Perceptions of Brand Quality and Corporate Image," Nigel Pope, Kevin E. Voges, and Mark Brown, *Journal of Advertising*, vol. 38, no. 2, Summer 2009, 5–20. "An International Review of Sponsorship Research," T. Bettina Cornwell and Isabelle Maignan, *Journal of Advertising*, vol. 27, no. 1, 1998, 1–21. "The Power of Numbers: Investigating the Impact of Event Roster Size in Consumer Response to Sponsorship," Julie A. Ruth and Bernard L. Simonon, *Journal of Advertising*, vol. 35, no. 4, Winter 2006, 7–20. "State of the Art and Science in Sponsorship-Linked Marketing," T. Bettina Cornwell, *Journal of Advertising*, vol. 37, no. 3, Fall 2008, 41–56.
10 "The Tactical Use of Mobile Marketing: How Adolescents' Social Networking

Can Best Shape Brand Extensions," Shintaro Okazaki, *Journal of Advertising Research*, vol. 49, no. 1, March 2009, 12–26. "Finding the Missing Link: Advertising's Impact on Word of Mouth, Web Searches, and Site Visits," Jeffrey Graham and William Havlena, *Journal of Advertising Research*, vol. 47, no. 4, December 2007, 427–435. "Unleashing the Power of Word of Mouth: Creating Brand Advocacy to Drive Growth," Ed Keller, *Journal of Advertising*, vol. 47, no. 4, December 2007, 448–452. "How Mobile Advertising Works: The Role of Trust in Improving Attitudes and Recall," Shintaro Okazaki, Akihiro Katsukura, and Mamoru Nishiyama, *Journal of Advertising Research*, vol. 47, no. 2, June 2007, 165–178.
11 eMarketer, 2008.
12 "Five Billion Mobiles Worldwide by 2012," Research Brief, January 20, 2009.
13 Mobile Marketing Guide, 2008.
14 ComScore M:Metrics survey, as reported in Advertising Age Search Marketing Fact Pack 2008, p. 32.
15 A useful article on this topic is "The New Unwired World: An IAB Status Report on Mobile Advertising," Joe Laszlo, *Journal of Advertising Research*, vol. 49, no. 1, March 2009, 27–43.
16 "Herd on the Street," Robert Klein, *Mediaweek*, December 8, 2008, pp. 12–13.

6 Terms, Calculations, and Considerations

1 "Memory without Recall, Exposure without Perception," Herbert E. Krugman, *Journal of Advertising Research*, vol. 40, no. 6, Nov/Dec 2000, 49–54.
2 "Effective Frequency—Then and Now," Michael J. Naples, *Journal of Advertising Research*, vol. 37, no. 4, Jul/Aug, 1997, 7–13.
    "If Not Effective Frequency, Then What?" Kenneth A. Longman, *Journal of Advertising Research*, vol. 37, no. 4, Jul/Aug 1997, 44–50.
    "What Can One Exposure Do?" Lawrence D. Gibson, *Journal of Advertising Research*, vol. 36, no. 1, Mar/Apr 1996, 9–18.
    "Effective Frequency: One Exposure or Three Factors," Gerard Tellis, *Journal of Advertising Research*, vol. 37, no. 4, Jul/Aug, 1997, 75–80.
    "Effective Reach and Frequency: Does It Really Make Sense?" Hugh M. Cannon and Edward A. Riordan, *Journal of Advertising Research*, vol. 34, no. 2 Mar/Apr 1994, 19–28.
3 *The Ultimate Secrets of Advertising*, John Philip Jones, Sage Publications, 2002; *When Ads Work*, John Philip Jones, Lexington Books, 1995.
4 "Recency Planning," Erwin Ephron, *Journal of Advertising Research*, vol. 37, no. 4, Jul/Aug 1997, 61–65.
    "Single Source Research Begins to Fulfill Its Promise," John Philip Jones, *Journal of Advertising Research*, vol. 35, no. 3, May/June 1995, 9–17.
    "More Weeks, Less Weight: The Shelf Space Model of Advertising," Erwin Ephron, *Journal of Advertising Research*, vol. 35, no. 3 May/June 1995, 18–24.

7 Creating the Plan

1 Information here found at Kraft's website, www.kraftfoods.com.
2 Competitive spending data provided by TNS-Media Intelligence; all data masked/adapted to protect proprietary information.

8 Offering Alternatives

1   Nielsen Media Research, 2005.
2   "Point of View: Optimizers and Media Planning," Erwin Ephron, *Journal of Advertising Research*, vol. 38, no. 4, July/Aug 1998, 47–56.

9 Making the Media Buys

1   "How the TV nets got the upfront," Erwin Ephron, Ad Age Special Report on TV's "Upfront," May 14, 2001, S2/22; Advertising Age, June 2005.

Index

Addressable advertising 43, 61, 67
Advertising objective 34–5
Affiliate marketing 183
Affiliate stations 54
Aided recall 13
Allotment 182
Ambient media, *see* Guerilla marketing
Ambush marketing, *see* Guerilla marketing
Amplitude Modulation (AM) radio 69
As It Falls test 172
Audience Deficiency Unit (ADU) 179
Average Quarter Hour (AQH) rating 131
Awareness 36

Behavioral targeting 183
Blogs 111
Bookending 149
Brand 12
Brand development index (BDI) 27
Brand integration 64–5, 184
Business-to-business magazines 85

C3 rating 121
Cable television 59–61
Campaign timing 46
Category development index (CDI) 27
Cause-related marketing 108
Circulation 134, 137
Clearance 55
Click through 98–9
Clutter 67, 94, 99, 105
Commercial pod 68
Communication objectives 45

Comparison advertising 13
Composition 134
Consumer context planning 30, 40
Consumer decision process 15, 38–9
Consumer magazines 85
Consumer-brand relationship 12
Context 183
Continuity 148
Conversion factor 129
Cookie 94
Cooperative (coop) advertising 151
Cost per point (CPP) 127
Cost per thousand (CPM) 127, 150
Coverage 134, 137
Coverage-area rating 131
Creative Brief 43
Cume rating 132

Data fusion 130
Designated Market Area (DMA) 132
Development indices 26
Digital video recorder (DVR) 53, 63
Double-spotting 149

Effective frequency 125
Embedded advertising, *see* Brand integration
Ethnography 14
Exposure distribution 126
Eyes on impression 90

Farm magazines 85
Flighting 148
Focus groups 14, 190
Four Ps 10
Free-standing inserts (FSIs) 80
Frequency 123

Frequency Modulation (FM) radio 69
Frequency planning 126, 150

Gross impressions 122
Gross rating points (GRPs) 121
Gross vs. net 128
Guerilla marketing 115–16

Halo effect 148
Households Using Television (HUT) 129

Imagery transfer 74
Independent stations 55
Infomercial 65
In-store, see Retail
Interactive voice response (IVR) 113
Interconnect 61
Internet banner 94
Interstitial 99

Little America test 172
Long issue life 87

Magazine authorization 175
Make-good 179, 189
Market share 28
Marketing objective 33–4
Media 1; Electronic 2; Print 2
Media buyer 8
Media consolidation 4
Media context 30
Media plan example 154–8
Media planner 8
Media researcher 8
Media seller 8
Medium 4
Metro Survey Area (MSA) 132
Mobile marketing 113–14
Multiple System Operator (MSO) 59

Narrowcasting 59
Need 35
Network television 54
Newspaper authorization 176

Online video 95
Opportunity to see (OTS) 122, 190
Optimizer 171
Opt-in emails 183
Outdoor authorization 183

Outdoor showing 138, 182

Painted bulletin 89
Passalong readership 88
Persons Using Radio (PUR) 132
Persons Using Television (PUT) 129
Positioning 136, 175
Poster panel 89
Preference 36
Product category 12
Product category trends 19–22
Product placement 64, 166

Random duplication 124
Rate base 135
Rating, average quarter hour 131
Rating point 120–1
Reach 98, 122
Reach and frequency 47, 122, 146, 167
Rep firm 58
Retail 106–7
Return on investment (ROI) 40–1, 146–7, 191
Rich media 94
Roadblocking 149
Run of schedule 181
Run of site 139

Satellite radio 72–3
Satellite television 61–2
Satisfaction 37
Scheduling 148–50
Search 36; contextual advertising 95; paid inclusion 95; paid placement 95
Search advertising 95–6
Search engine optimization (SEO) 95
Seasonality 145–6
Secondary audience, see Passalong readership
Selection 37
Share 129
Share of market 25
Share of requirements 25
Single copy 134–5
SMS, see Text messaging
Social networking 96–7
Sponsorship 108–9
Spot television 58–9
Standard Ad Unit (SAU) 176
Streaming audio 73

Subscription 134
Syndicated programming 55–8

Target rating points (TRPs) 121
Tear sheets 189
Television daypart 52
Television program format 52
Text messaging 113
Time spent listening (TSL) 132
Timing 144–5
Total Survey Area (TSA) 132
Tracking research 14
Trade merchandising 151
Traditional media 50
Turnover 132
TV opportunistic buy 178
TV scatter 177

TV upfront 176–7

Unaided recall 13
Unduplicated audience, *see* Reach
Unwired network 72
User generated content 63

Video on demand (VOD) 62
Viewers per viewing household
   (VPVH) 129
Viral marketing, *see* Word of Mouth

Wearout 149
Widget 97
Word of Mouth (WOM) 111

Yellow Pages 103–5